D1527453

Gus Van Sant

**Recent Titles in
Modern Filmmakers**
Vincent LoBrutto, Series Editor

Clint Eastwood: Evolution of a Filmmaker
John H. Foote

The Brothers Coen: Unique Characters of Violence
Ryan P. Doom

Roman Polanski: A Life in Exile
Julia Ain-Krupa

Quentin Tarantino: Life at the Extremes
Aaron Barlow

GUS VAN SANT

His Own Private Cinema

VINCENT LOBRUTTO

Modern Filmmakers
Vincent LoBrutto, Series Editor

 PRAEGER

AN IMPRINT OF ABC-CLIO, LLC
Santa Barbara, California • Denver, Colorado • Oxford, England

Copyright 2010 by Vincent LoBrutto

All rights reserved. No part of this publication may be reproduced, stored in a retrieval system, or transmitted, in any form or by any means, electronic, mechanical, photocopying, recording, or otherwise, except for the inclusion of brief quotations in a review, without prior permission in writing from the publisher.

Library of Congress Cataloging-in-Publication Data

LoBrutto, Vincent.
    Gus Van Sant : his own private cinema / Vincent LoBrutto.
       p. cm. — (Modern filmmakers)
    Includes bibliographical references and index.
    ISBN 978-0-313-35776-3 (alk. paper) — ISBN 978-0-313-35777-0
(ebook)
    1. Van Sant, Gus.   2. Motion picture producers and directors—United
States—Biography.   I. Title.
    PN1998.3.V363L63   2010
    791.43'0233'092—dc22
    [B]   2010006574

ISBN: 978-0-313-35776-3
EISBN: 978-0-313-35777-0

14 13 12 11 10   1 2 3 4 5

This book is also available on the World Wide Web as an eBook.
Visit www.abc-clio.com for details.

Praeger
An Imprint of ABC-CLIO, LLC

ABC-CLIO, LLC
130 Cremona Drive, P.O. Box 1911
Santa Barbara, California 93116-1911

This book is printed on acid-free paper ∞™

Manufactured in the United States of America

For Rebecca Ann Roes,
my Sixties child who was born in 1968
and embodies the spirit and soul
of that tumultuous, artistically groundbreaking,
and deeply political decade

Contents

Series Foreword

The Modern Filmmakers series focuses on a diverse group of motion picture directors who collectively demonstrate how the filmmaking process has become *the* definitive art and craft of the 20th century. As we advance into the 21st century we begin to examine the impact these artists have had on this influential medium.

What is a modern filmmaker? The phrase connotes a motion picture maker who is *au courant*—they make movies currently. The choices in this series are also varied to reflect the enormous potential of the cinema. Some of the directors make action movies, some entertain, some are on the cutting edge, others are political, some make us think, some are fantasists. The motion picture directors in this collection will range from highly commercial, mega-budget blockbuster directors to those who toil in the independent low-budget field.

Gus Van Sant, Tim Burton, Charlie Kaufman, and Terry Gilliam are here, and so are Clint Eastwood and Steven Spielberg—all for many and for various reasons, but primarily because their directing skills have transitioned from the 20th century to the first decade of the 21st century. Eastwood and Spielberg worked during the sixties and seventies and have grown and matured as the medium transitioned from mechanical to digital. The younger directors here may not have experienced all of those cinematic epochs themselves, but nonetheless they remained concerned with the limits of filmmaking: Charlie Kaufman disintegrates personal and narrative boundaries in the course of his scripts, for example, while Tim Burton probes the limits of technology to find the most successful way of bringing his intensely visual fantasies and nightmares to life.

The Modern Filmmakers series will celebrate modernity and post-modernism through each creator's vision, style of storytelling, and character presentation. The directors' personal beliefs and worldviews will be revealed through in-depth examinations of the art they have created, but brief biographies will also be provided where they appear especially relevant. These books are intended to open up new ways of thinking about some of our favorite and most important artists and entertainers.

Vincent LoBrutto
Series Editor
Modern Filmmakers

Acknowledgments

Gratitude to my wife, Harriet Morrison. I will say again that she keeps our lives together—and this author functioning on a daily basis. This time, however, she was faced with a seemingly impossible situation that put the completion of this book in jeopardy. Harriet immediately mobilized—in other words, she saved the day, and that's why I love her so. Rebecca Roes, my daughter, to whom this tome is dedicated, has the heart of a lion and the soul of an artist. My son, Alex (aka Slick), sommelier, knows everything about wine and a lot about the cinema.

At Praeger, I thank Dan Harmon for getting this series off the ground and into reality and for choosing me to helm it. Dan is loyal and committed to film literature. I offer my gratitude to everyone at Praeger for their invaluable assistance.

To men who love men and to women and men who love each other, to lesbians and bisexuals—continue to follow your hearts.

To Gus Van Sant for proving film is an art beyond argument and for fighting against being pigeon-holed. He is a filmmaker, not a gay filmmaker or a Hollywood filmmaker or an independent filmmaking filmmaker or an experimental filmmaker. He embraces his love of cinema—openly. Gus Van Sant is not originally from Portland, Oregon, but has adopted the city as his own. The city of Portland captures the spirit of his life's artistic and personal commitment.

I thank Ed Bowes, motion picture creator and film instructor, for discussions concerning Van Sant and avant-garde cinema; John Campbell, for talking to me about his work as a cinematographer on *Mala Noche*, *My Own Private Idaho*, and *Even Cowgirls Get the Blues;* May Kassem, for her constant support and for providing a tape of Orson Welles's *Chimes at Midnight;* Valdis Óskarsdóttir, for talking to me about Portland and the editing of *Finding Forrester;* motion picture editor Pietro Scalia for his insights on collaborating with Van Sant on *Good Will Hunting;* and Peter Tonguette, a Welles scholar, among other things, for discussing the influence of *Chimes at Midnight* on *My Own Private Idaho*.

At the School of Visual Arts I thank my chairman, Reeves Lehmann, for his constant support of me as teacher and author and Sal Petrosino, Director of Operations, for his friendship, support, and kindness. I also must acknowledge Gene Stavis, film historian extraordinaire, and historian Roy Frumkes, who always has an insight to share. My personal good wishes to the 2008–2009 Thesis Committee, Ed Bowes, Joan Brooker, Mary Lee Grisanti, and Elzbieta Litwin, for all the lively debates on film education and the art and craft of the movies—and for being there when the chips were down. I salute all my students past and present for sharing their thoughts on Van Sant and the cinema; they think I'm crazy every year when I tell them I've learned a lot from them.

At American Cinema Editor (ACE) I thank the board for achieving such great work in the promotion of the art of editing.

To my late parents, Rose and Tony LoBrutto, thank you for putting up with a rambunctious kid, letting me use the family movie equipment, and paying my tuition so I could attend the School of Visual Arts Film School which changed my life forever.

Two relatives were key in stimulating and sustaining my interest in the movies very early on. Gene (Gino) Damiani, who photographed all the family movies and projected them in front of my eyes, developed my passion for the American Western as we sat in front of his black-and-white television watching every cowboy movie that was broadcast. When I started film school and studied John Ford, I was thrilled to talk about this great master with my uncle, who replied "Who's John Ford?" Rest in peace, dear uncle.

Joseph Zoine, also departed, was the brother of the late Vince Edwards of *Ben Casey* fame. He went to the movies constantly, and we engaged in many stimulating conversations.

Bless the good people, the cows, and the corn that surround me in Hillsdale, New York, my upstate haven.

My gratitude to Dr. Jean Miller for her expertise and steadfast commitment.

My thanks to James Robert Parish for writing his wonderful *Gus Van Sant: An Unauthorized Biography*, the only book on the director before this one.

As always, my love and respect to all the paisans at Pelham Pizzeria. We lost Luigi Ruffolo this year, the man known as Gino, who fed me well and kept me close to my roots. His friendship will be missed.

I thank master film biographer Patrick McGilligan for his support and advice. Finally, I thank the late great film director Rainer Werner Fassbinder, who, at the New York Film Festival on the occasion of screening his masterpiece *Fox and His Friends* (originally *The Fist-Fight of Freedom*), pronounced "Life is precious, even now."

The Traveling Artist

This book is an intensive examination of the maverick, openly gay, sometimes-Hollywood, sometimes experimental, sometimes true-life, actually born in Louisville, Kentucky, on July 24, 1952, sometimes epic moviemaker Gus Van Sant—the man so indelibly linked to the city of Portland, Oregon.

PARENTS

His dad, Gus Greene Van Sant, a World War II Navy veteran, attended Purdue University on a football scholarship but left school to become a traveling salesman whose territory covered Kentucky to Colorado.

Van Sant Jr.'s mother, Betty, was from Kentucky. Married in 1950, both parents practiced the Episcopalian faith.

In the first year of their marriage, Gus Sr. became a round-the-clock salesman for a men's pants company, Mertit Clothing, while his wife taught second-grade students in an elementary school.

FAMILY AND EARLY LIFE OF GUS VAN SANT

Gus's Dad was constantly on the move, and in 1953 the family relocated to Denver, Colorado. On June 12, 1956, Van Sant Jr.'s sister, Malinda Anne, was born. She was nicknamed Sissy, a coincidental connection to Sissy Henshaw in the Tom Robbins novel *Even Cowgirls Get the Blues* (1976), which the filmmaker would later adapt into a film.

Like Steven Spielberg, David Lynch, and Michael Moore, who reached various levels of the Cub Scouts, Boy Scouts, and even Eagle Scouts (Lynch), Van Sant joined the Scouts (but had attendance problems because of his father's caravan traveling show). The Scouts is a disciplined organization in which boys learn about the world they live in by studying and creating projects in different aspects of the sciences, nature, and environmental studies. Van Sant, who would later become an artist and be associated with the rugged terrain of Portland, embraced the spirit of the Scouts. The all-boy membership of the scouts made him feel comfortable, although this was not the venue of his first homosexual encounter.

Mr. Van Sant took another position with a higher-league firm and quickly became the regional manager. Eventually another move for the nomadic Van Sants occurred—this time to the extreme West Coast. Within half a year, Gus Sr. was promoted to company vice president. To keep Gus Jr. from having to face additional changes of school, his father settled the family in New York City, where the company's corporate offices were located.

Soon after, there was another move that took the family to Darien, Connecticut. For Gus Jr., this was his sixth home in only 10 years, and the transition was taking a toll on his psyche; however, it did teach the boy how to depend on and fend for himself. Eventually these qualities helped him morph into a rebellious young person with a mind of his own, a nonconformist who traveled his own route. Van Sant's sense of rootlessness, a yearning to remain in childhood, crept into the themes of many Van Sant movies.

Gus began to develop an interest in art and even won an award for one of his projects in a high school contest. The multimedia work was disturbing in its dark and, at times, bizarre point of view toward life, although his parents demonstrated their acceptance of his work by buying one of the paintings from the art show and hanging it in the family dining room.

THE ARTIST EMERGES

In 1966, living in Connecticut, Van Sant Sr. saw his career continue to rise, leading to another company move, but this time the family remained in the same state and city. Gus Jr. created a space provided for him into a place to live and paint. Illness struck as Gus Jr. came down with rheumatoid arthritis, but private home schooling kept him up to speed with his classmates.

Art teacher Robert Levine inspired young Gus Van Sant by working in a manner reminiscent of Andy Warhol, which involved artistic interest in the ordinary and a radical approach to tools and surfaces. The teacher was a role model that Van Sant could relate to in myriad ways—as a painter whose lifestyle the youngster understood and as someone who used cutting-edge art materials. He was also gay.

English teacher David Soan encouraged Gus Van Sant to make 8mm movies, which he did using the family Kodak Super 8mm camera.[1] The films were collaborations with two fellow students and resembled the films of Norman McLaren (*Begone Dull Care* [1949], *Neighbours* [1953], *A Chairy Tale* [1958]) and Robert Breer (*Eyewash* [1959], *Breathing* [1963], *What Goes Up* [2003]).

NEW YORK, NEW YORK

Gus was already traveling into New York City to explore its vibrant art and movie scene; from a summer job he earned enough money to buy a Super 8mm camera. He bought *An Introduction to the American Underground Film* by Sheldon Renan, a book that taught him the history and concepts that would influence his lifelong work, especially, *Gerry* (2002), *Elephant* (2003), *Gus Van Sant's Last Days* (2005), and *Paranoid Park* (2007).

At 16, Gus was working on Madison Avenue, but his parents deemed him too young to go to the Woodstock Music and Art Fair. He missed out on the festivities but managed to emulate his boss and ingest LSD 25—better known as acid. The psychedelic experiences expanded his artistic vision and linked him to the hippie subculture.

At this time, Van Sant was aware he was gay—he was attracted to the homoerotic films of Alejandro Jodorowsky (*Fando and Lis* [1968], *El Topo* [1970], and *The Holy Mountain* [1973])—but he was not overtly engaging in sex with men.

At the dawn of the 1970s, the Van Sant family relocated to the place that would forever define the filmmaker and person Gus Van Sant—Portland, Oregon.

In high school, Van Sant met cinematographer Eric Alan Edwards (*Kids* [1995], *Over the Edge* [2001], *Management* [2008]), who would shoot on six Van Sant films, in some cases as additional camera, other times as director of photography. Along with another classmate, Carl Stevens, the young men created a 16mm film[2] about a brother and sister. *The Happy Organ* incorporated time-lapse photography and had a score with songs by Frank Zappa and others.

Van Sant approached an important decision after high school. It was 1971; the Vietnam War was raging in Southeast Asia. The draft was active, but it seemed likely Van Sant would be eligible for a deferment because of his history of rheumatic fever. It is also possible that his homosexuality, though not common knowledge, became evident during the rigorous induction process, during which young men were asked about their sexual orientation.

COLLEGE: THE FILMMAKER EMERGES

So it was to be college for Van Sant for educational and artistic reasons. He had only one school in mind, the Rhode Island School of Design (RISD), because of its cultural and academic reputation. Van Sant was still interested in a life as a painter, and the school had an excellent art department. Eric Alan Edwards and fellow high school classmate Catlin Gabel both were on the RISD track, as well. The school and its environs also had a hippie community filled with those who walked the road less traveled—a perfect atmosphere for the eclectically artistic Van Sant. There were plenty of rock bands and performance artists. Van Sant took courses in painting and filmmaking.

The Van Sant family moved again while Gus was at RISD, this time from Portland, with its rich counterculture, back to the more exclusive Darien, Connecticut.

In his sophomore year, Van Sant decided that he couldn't make a decent living or survive as a painter, and he shifted to filmmaking. The painting background would become instrumental in shaping Van Sant as a motion picture director. He has a painterly approach to cinema composition, texture, and color.

The eclectic artist also played guitar and wrote songs, as well as studying still photography. Van Sant is among a handful of filmmakers, including Martin Scorsese, Quentin Tarantino, and Stanley Kubrick, who understand how to apply music to their films and to use music and lyric as an interpretive tool. The cinematography in every Van Sant film carefully tells the story in light, form, and movement. His personal study of and work in still photography have enhanced Van Sant's abilities to openly and creatively collaborate with his directors of photography.

There was a lot of video work being produced at RISD, not television but a creative, experimental use of the electronic medium, and Van Sant drank in this multimedia mix available to him.

Trains, traveling, and the hobo life play a significant part in Van Sant's films. When he was 20, he rode the rails, and the sights and sounds of those experiences are revealed in visual images and especially in sound design in films throughout his career.

During the RISD years, Van Sant made several films: *Little Johnny* (1972), a 40-second black-and-white short; the two-minute black-and-white 16mm *1/2 of a Telephone Conversation* (1973); and his senior project, *Late Morning Start* (1975), 16mm color, 28 minutes. This last film he describes as being Godardian, although Van Sant continues to state that he knows little about the French maverick. This is a curious fact because his tendency is to rediscover traditional movie genres, color, structure, and content seem markedly influenced by Jean-Luc Godard (*Breathless* [1960], *Perrot le Fou* [1965], *Hail Mary* [1985]).

Van Sant graduated from RISD with a B.F.A. on May 31, 1975. He was 22 years old.

OUT IN THE REAL WORLD

After graduation, Van Sant and a group of film majors from RISD traveled to Italy to observe some of the country's finest filmmakers at work. Van Sant arrived in Rome, where he would return to shoot pivotal scenes of *My Own Private Idaho* (1991). The choices were remarkable. The group watched Federico Fellini (who died on the same day as River Phoenix, star of *My Own Private Idaho*) direct *Fellini's Casanova* (1976). Van Sant would be influenced by another self-named Fellini film, *Fellini's Satyricon* (1969), which in the main was a gay story interpreted by a heterosexual director.

From studying Fellini up close and on the screen, Van Sant learned about cinematic whimsy and saw a kind of surrealism that was in a manner different from that practiced by most experimental filmmakers. Also observed was Lina Wertmüller, Fellini's former assistant director, shooting *Seven Beauties* (1975), which contained a flashback structure important to the lexicon of Van Sant's storytelling style. Pier Paolo Pasolini, arguably the finest gay film director in the history of cinema, was making his difficult and disturbing masterpiece *Salo* (1975). A group of students sat while the great filmmaker sound-mixed a sequence from the gruesome yet somehow brave and beautiful film. Van Sant was able to get a personal invitation to Pasolini's home. They discussed the adaptation of literature to the screen.

Back in the states, Van Sant met a person who would change his life, the Beat writer William S. Burroughs. This led the young filmmaker to adapt a film from the Burroughs short story "The Discipline of D.E." (1973). Burroughs's influence grew out of the writer's experimental approach to his work as part of an early generation of gay men and out of his bohemian life style.

HOLLYWOOD

Van Sant decided to move to the West Coast to see if he could enter the Hollywood film industry. Once there, he decided against living in the gay community of West Hollywood and rented a small apartment not far from Hollywood Boulevard.

Van Sant loved walking up and down the once-illustrious but by-then seedy street of dreams, talking and hanging out with the dregs of society. He found a favorite restaurant, Johnnie's Steak House, where he could get a steak and potato dinner for around three dollars. Gay hustlers, drug dealers, and users abounded on the street. Van Sant considered writing one day about this subject—which ultimately led to *Mala Noche* (1985).

For eight months, Van Sant made the job-hunting rounds, with no success. He was slowly running out of money. He wanted to be on his own, so he didn't write home to his father for reinforcement funds.

His ship came in when he decided, out of the blue, to phone a person he had heard of but never even met—Ken Shapiro. Shapiro was an actor who had become an elementary school teacher in Brooklyn, New York. Shapiro had bought a video tape recorder and begun creating and taping satires of television series and commercials. In East Greenwich Village, he and a partner conceived of and opened the first video theater, where they produced *Channel One*. This was a program of television spoofs that were not ready for prime time. It was a success that led to *The Groove Tube* (1974), a feature film in living color. Produced for $400,000, it grossed more than $30 million.

Shapiro relocated to Tinsel Town and teamed with Paramount Pictures and Lorne Michaels of *Saturday Night Live* fame. Michaels set about forging his future, and Shapiro planned his next movie for Paramount. Ironically,

Van Sant has been quoted as saying that he had been told you could call Hitchcock up for a job, but he skipped over the director of *Psycho* (1960) and moved on to Ken Shapiro, who said "Yes" when Van Sant asked if there was a job available.

Van Sant's job was to take notes and organize materials for Shapiro and his comedy team as they worked on Shapiro's second movie. Van Sant was paid by Paramount, a studio he wandered around while soaking in its hallowed back-in-the-day achievements. He now sums up his job as the guy who rolled the joints to give creative stimulation and inspiration to the writers.

The Shapiro feature project, *Ma Bell,* concerned a teenager who works the telephone system to get free calls and depicts his relationship with "phone freaks," as Parrish calls them in his biography of Van Sant. Occasionally, Van Sant would offer up a sketch idea, and it was summarily shot down by the seasoned pros.

Van Sant moved out of his apartment for better digs on North Argyle Avenue in Hollywood. He shared the apartment with John Howell, an old buddy who was also interested in breaking into show business. Then Shapiro offered Van Sant the pool house at his home, which for a time Gus shared with another childhood pal, Jim Evans.

Paramount was not forthcoming in support of *Ma Bell,* so the team began working on *Groove Tube II* and other movie ideas, eventually arriving at *Modern Problems* (1981), which was given the go-ahead at Twentieth Century Fox. Shapiro moved to Brentwood, and Van Sant had to move out of the pool house.

Shapiro couldn't give Van Sant a position on the project. He gave out jobs to all his friends, and his wife got an assistant spot, so that was it for Van Sant's Shapiro period.

The job had been part-time, so Van Sant had had time to work on his own material, and he received a sobering inside look at how the studios chew up directors and spit them out for breakfast. Shapiro gave his charge excellent advice—stay away from the studios and go indie, which was just what Van Sant now planned on doing.

BECOMING GUS VAN SANT

As the 1970s came to a close, and while Van Sant worked for Ken Shapiro, he continued his private study of the cinema, planning a career in film for the future. At the local library, he read screenplays such as *Citizen Kane* (1941) and *Jaws* (1975). He was most impressed with the screenplay for Stanley Kubrick's production of the Anthony Burgess novel *A Clockwork Orange* (1971). The form was unconventional and read like a poem, with the description down a narrow middle column and the dialogue stretching across the page. The lesson learned was that you could do anything you wanted to make a movie; what counted were content, story, characters, and craft.

Although he hated production assistant work, Van Sant needed cash, so he toiled on *Skateboard* (1977) (he would later make *Paranoid Park* [2007], a skateboard movie like no other), directed by George Gage (*Fleshburn* [1984]).

Next, Van Sant took Ken Shapiro's advice and made a short, *The Discipline of D.E.* (1982), and a feature that didn't become a feature, the notorious *Alice in Hollywood* (1981).

As Van Sant slaved over the editing of *Alice in Hollywood,* he periodically found his finances under a strain, forcing him to take jobs that were available. During any free time, Gus would go to the movies and write screenplays. One of these, called *Mister Popular* (originally titled *The Projectionist,* but not the cult classic directed by Harry Hurwitz), concerns a high school projectionist who puts subliminal messages in audiovisual presentations. He becomes *numero uno* in the school through mind control. It was to be Van Sant's next film after the disastrous *Alice in Hollywood.*

Although Van Sant lived near gay bars and the L.A. gay scene, he did not participate, explaining that he was in a film world writing movies that he hoped to make someday. He continued to watch and "study" the gay hustler lifestyle but lived life through his screenwriting and filmmaking activities. Van Sant told *The Advocate* that he was "a late bloomer" who didn't begin to participate in his now acknowledged sexual mode until he was around 30 years old.

Van Sant was a solid Kubrick admirer, viewing the 9 A.M. show of *The Shining* (1980) for seven days when the film opened at Mann's Chinese Theater, a legendary Hollywood Boulevard theater in its own right. Ironically, just as Kubrick had told actor Vince Edwards that *High Noon* (1952), the classic Oscar winner, "wasn't a very good movie," Van Sant said the same thing about Kubrick's attempt to make the scariest film ever made: that it wasn't "such a good movie." However, because he thought he could learn and be inspired by the master's newest motion picture, he watched it repeatedly.

During 1980, Van Sant was disillusioned. Although he got an editing job here and there, he mostly temped as a secretary. It was during this process that Gus Van Sant discovered his artistic and actual home, in Portland, Oregon. Gus Van Sant senior continued his successful climb to business success. He had left one job at Warnco, then on to Consolidated Foods, Inc., as their Group Vice President. He then made the leap to owning his own business by taking over a woman's sportswear firm and asked his son to relocate to New York City to work for one year in the company's warehouse located in Secaucus, New Jersey. The warehouse was not far from midtown Manhattan, so Gus could get himself together for another try at big-time moviemaking.

While in the factory, Gus continued taking notes for screenplays. One screenplay concerned vampires. Another was *Fizzlem,* concerning an honor student who becomes the town's stumblebum. Other creative ruminations in Van Sant's imagination were about country clubs, commuters, and debutantes, the latter possibly inspired by the classic Bob Dylan line from *Stuck Inside of Mobile with the Memphis Blues Again*—"Your debutante knows what you need, but I know what you want."

On his own, Van Sant Jr. got in touch with the Cadwell Davis advertising agency, where he had worked for a decade back in the day, and procured a job as an assistant production manager for $44,000 a year, although it was basically an organizational position.

Van Sant saved up all the money he could—it wasn't much of a life, but he was heard to say that he was waiting for his cinematic break. He continued to write screenplays, practice still photography, and make short films.

My Friend (1982) was a three-minute 16mm color autobiographical film about a sexual attraction Van Sant Jr. felt for a pal. It sports narration, like many of his features. For decades, many film editors and film teachers have said that when a film isn't working, you put in a narration. On the contrary, narration has existed since the beginning of sound films and is a legitimate storytelling technique.

Where Did She, Go? (1983), also three minutes long and in color 16mm, was about his departed grandmother, who gave him the deathbed advice to "buy IBM."[3] The seven-minute black-and-white *Nightmare Typhoon* (1984), also known as *Hello, It's Me,* is about a caller who continuously phones the director.

Van Sant also worked on his musical interests, writing songs, playing instruments, and adding sound effects like rain and thunder (which is why the sound design in Van Sant's films is so well done and so effective). An album of his called *18 Songs about Golf* was marketed by Pop Secret Records. Van Sant's love of music would lead to great soundtracks and his one music-themed movie, *Gus Van Sant's Last Days* (2005).

This is who the young Gus van Sant was. Who he would become was a blender-mix of his sexual orientation, his artistic talent, and his love for Portland, Oregon, and the movies. He painted, sang, and wrote, but now he was also a film director.

To Feature or Not to Feature: The Beat Gay Mentor and the Openly Gay Opus

ALICE IN HOLLYWOOD (1979)

After returning from Europe and then working in Los Angeles with Ken Shapiro, Van Sant, who had directed and executed several short works, decided to make his first feature.

His original idea would come to fruition later with *Mala Noche* (1985), a film about male hustlers. He shot footage on Sunset Boulevard of the men plying their trade, but only one shot eventually got into *Alice in Hollywood.*

Van Sant scrapped the idea for a film that would satirize the movie business. His initial concept was to do a version of Peter Pan[1] in Hollywood, but that was replaced by a plan to tap into Lewis Carroll's *Alice in Wonderland,*[2] a fable that was beloved by hippies and the drug culture and that spawned the Jefferson Airplane's hit song "White Rabbit" (Carroll as a photographer shot pictures of very young children that got him in trouble with the authorities). Van Sant called the adaptation a combination of Carroll's work and Voltaire's *Candide,* in which an optimistic young man becomes disillusioned when he sees corruption in the world.

Van Sant had always been interested in street youth and underground cultures. He began hanging out on the Sunset Strip, which by the late 1970s no longer had the thriving hippie and music communities it had enjoyed in the 1960s. The famed Whiskey A Go Go had launched Johnny Rivers, the Doors, and other legends of the 1960s, but, by the end of the 1970s, punk music played in the hallowed hall. The Strip in the 1970s was inhabited by bums, druggies, and culture freaks—the lowest of the low. Van Sant, who had a nearby apartment that contained a cot and his film equipment for production of *Alice in Hollywood*, got to know many of the Strip's denizens and began making mental notes for a feature.

As an avid movie-watcher, Van Sant chose the genre of screwball comedy, an offshoot of the comedy film, which utilizes farce, rapid pacing, and machine-gun dialogue. Screwball comedies from Hollywood's studio system include *Bringing up Baby* (1938), *The Lady Eve* (1941), and *To Be or Not to Be* (1942).

The script for *Alice in Hollywood* involves a young naïve actress who tries to break into show business. She is surrounded by the underground characters that populate the once-glamorous boulevard and is given advice and attention. She can't get an audition no matter how hard she tries until finally one day she gets a "job" in a porn film. Later on, she meets a television actor and still later has an opportunity to begin her career on a television show featuring a sleazy actor she had met. After becoming a success, Van Sant's heroine refuses to hobnob with her former friends on the Strip as the film becomes a morality tale.

To raise the majority of the money, Van Sant Jr. went to his major investor, Van Sant Sr. The complete budget came in at $20,000. No one was paid. The investment was for equipment, production, and postproduction. Van Sant installed an editing bench in his tiny flat, which was rapidly filling up with the footage for his feature. Occasionally the director would take his cast and small crew to his fav eatery, Johnnie's Steak House, which doubled as a couple of restaurant sets in the film. Van Sant's hovel was also used for an apartment scene in the picture.

For a dolly, a wheelchair was "procured" from a local hospital, and the cameraman was pushed down Sunset Boulevard to get desired shots. Director of photography Jean de Segonzac moved on to be a prolific television director and as cameraman shot the indie classic *Laws of Gravity* (1992), *Where Are We? Our Trip through America* (1993), and *Normal Life* (1996). Tom Yore, the soundman, did sound and music on another indie classic, the documentary *Hoop Dreams* (1994).

Everyone did his or her own make-up in a car or in the stairwell of a building. To relax, the team smoked pot. The shoot ended just in time for Thanksgiving, as the members of the ensemble waited for the film to come out and launch their careers.

Van Sant had a screening of the footage that lasted for hours and hours. As he slaved over the editing table, it became apparent that the film was not a 90-minute or two-hour feature—it wasn't any kind of feature film. So, editor Van Sant (who would go on to edit or be part of the postproduction team on most his films) kept trimming and altering the timeline as well as adding and subtracting scenes until the film had a running time of 45 minutes—a deadly timeframe. A 45-minute movie is too long to be a short and too short to be a feature. A half-hour film is a recognized film form, and a 10-minute film was legitimate back in the days when short films were programmed with features. Forty-five minutes was, and still is, to the hapless film student who refuses to cut a project or thesis down, box office and film festival dead-on-arrival.

Eventually, Van Sant trimmed the 45-minute version to just under a half hour (29 minutes). He couldn't sell the film even when Ken Shapiro introduced him to industry types at 20th Century-Fox. He tried to enter it in the L.A. and Atlanta film festivals—but it was rejected by both.

Alice in Hollywood was never really completed or shown publicly. Of course, the investors (mainly Gus's dad) lost all their money. The lesson was a painful one, but Van Sant learned that he needed a viable story about a topic that meant something to him. Eventually, this would lead him to *Mala Noche*.

But Gus was becoming Gus Van Sant, film director. He was flexible on location, always ready and willing to shoot what was going on around him. A car crash on the Strip was filmed and incorporated into the film. The cast reported that he understood acting and nurtured the performances. He was easygoing and likeable. Although the film was a mess, it proved he could make a movie and had a vision of the world that would attract future audiences.

THE DISCIPLINE OF D.E. (1982)

Van Sant had long been a hero worshiper of the Beats,[3] especially the junkie who was a writer or the writer who was a junkie, depending how you perceived William S. Burroughs. The iconic and openly gay Beat figure was a mentor to Van Sant, who would later put Burroughs on film in *Drugstore Cowboy.* For years he wanted to adapt the short story "DE," and, after the disaster of *Alice in Hollywood,* he decided now was the time. The nine-minute, 16mm black-and-white sound film featured Tom Sherohman, Michael L. McManus, Frank Birney, and David Worden. Sherohman wrote *Modern Problems* (1981), directed by Van Sant's old boss Ken Shapiro, and played roles in *Vernie* (2004), *To Lie in Green Pastures* (2005), and *Flourtown* (2008). McManus appeared in *The Kentucky Fried Movie* (1977) (a competitor of *Groove Tube*), *Poltergeist* (1982), and *Police Academy 4: Citizens on Patrol* (1987). Frank Birney was also in *Modern Problems* and had roles in *Jennifer 8* (1992) and *Dave* (1993). Worden was living with Sherohman, and his role in the film, in which he played a student, is his only acting credit in a motion picture to date. The narration was spoken by Ken Shapiro.

The story concerns a colonel who creates a calendar that has 10 months with 26 days allotted for each month. DE stands for "doing easy." Throughout the colonel's segment, he demonstrates ways to do everyday tasks in an easy, non-energy-draining manner. *The Discipline of D.E.* ends with the colonel transformed into Wyatt Earp as he schools a gunslinger on how to win in a gun battle.

An offbeat comedy, the film was shot by Van Sant with a handheld camera. He handled the actors with ease and grace and made them feel at home in their parts—a trademark of his work as a director to date. Van Sant's interest in close-ups of objects is in play here and would continue with films to come. On-screen titles are also used, and there is a focus on the male anatomy, with a man zipping and rezipping his fly. Concerned about his lack of experience in filming a shootout, Van Sant storyboarded the 10 necessary shots. Utilizing drawings became a comfortable way for Van Sant (like Scorsese, De Palma, and Hitchcock) to work out sequences.

The Discipline of D.E. was shown at the New York Film Festival in 1978 and was well received.[4] When Burroughs appeared on *Saturday Night Live* in 1981, the short was almost aired, but at nine minutes it was considered too long for the rigors of network television scheduling.

Most, if not all, great directors have a DNA recognizable from their earliest work. Van Sant in these early years was finding his style, based on his artistic instincts and influences.

The film begins with "Gus Van Sant Presents." The "Jr." is absent. The title image is milk from a broken glass dripping off a table; the sound of this action is heard. Fade-to-black—card: "from the story by William S. Burroughs." From the outset, Van Sant is an assured and competent structuralist building the spine or skeleton of his nine-minute film. The narration introduces the colonel. Shots and props deal with the man's organizational skills. Ken Shapiro's narration is spoken in Van Sant's tone of choice—deadpan. The colonel writes precisely in a book about life in a Pullman car. Trains figure predominately in *Mala Noche* (1985), *Paranoid Park* (2007), and other Van Sant films, either in image, sound, or both. Traveling, the road, and the Beat aesthetic are embraced by the young director, born too late to take an active part in the Beat Generation. His relationship with Burroughs and this story cinematically achieve a way of living the lifestyle through art.

The colonel goes back in time and is "jolted back to the now." The actor playing the colonel recalls the face of Udo Kier, the actor often used by Rainer Werner Fassbinder and who appears in Van Sant's *My Own Private Idaho* (1991) and *Even Cowgirls Get the Blues* (1993). The black-and-white cinematography by Van Sant is clean, simple, and conscious of light as a still photographer would see it. The colonel begins to practice DE. An action such as throwing crumpled pieces of paper backward into a trash receptacle is described as replicating a Zen[5] master's use of a bow and arrow. Zen was an interest of the Beats, and the reference here is to the classic Buddhist-inspired text *Zen in the Art of Archery* (1953), by Eugen Herrigel. This and books such as *Zen and the Art of Motorcycle Maintenance* (1974) by Robert M. Pirsig embrace the premise that one must find the simplest path to complete knowledge on a subject. DE is Zen presented with dry humor. The state of relaxation during the procession of life, again a life principle of the Buddhist doctrine, is stated. The structuring of the short continues with a card that states, "The Colonel Issues Beginners DE." A series of examples are given. The funniest is a student taking a large reel-to-reel tape recorder off his desk and placing it out of the way under his bathroom sink. The narration is precise, filled with literary alliterations and metaphors. Repetition, the lifeblood of experimental cinema, presents practice. Picking up a cup of hot tea ends in spilling the steaming liquid on the duchess character. (*Even Cowgirls Get the Blues* also contains a duchess character.) This action/accident is shown in the next cut. A shot of a man zipping up his blue jeans with commentary on how to do this in the simplest way becomes a reference to the album cover of the Rolling Stones' *Sticky Fingers,*[6] which is a black-and-white photograph of a man in blue jeans—the zipper area prominent in the shot. The outward and direct gay image has the viewer staring at the area of a man's "package." The zipping implies that the penis can be taken out and shown to the audience, although it isn't—it teases. A series of shots show a young man tripping and banging into objects. We are told the DE way is to go back and repeat—again the stress on repetition. We are instructed to "Get back on course and do it again." We then see two shots of a man with a space helmet that contain a reflection intercut with a shot of the moon's surface and the earth in the background. These may be an homage to Kubrick's *2001: A Space Odyssey* (1968). We are even told to pretend we are in a movie, a self-referential trope well used by avant-gardists. The concept of doing an action again is compared to doing a retake in a film which makes the viewer wonder how many takes Van Sant made of each shot, another self-referential device. A shot of the young man doing nothing while sitting in a chair provides an opportunity to discuss DE and the art of doing nothing. The shot is a long take to support this mini-Godardian essay on the essence and ease of doing nothing the DE way. A structural cut-to-black changes to a sequence about the Western gunfight and DE. A man who appears to be the actor who played the colonel is now playing Wyatt Earp, saying in what appears to be lip synch, "It's not the first shot that counts, it's the first shot that hits."

The Discipline of D.E. ends with a Western scene. This is Van Sant's early attempt at the Western. He would add elements of the genre to *My Own Private Idaho* (1991) and *Even Cowgirls Get the Blues* (1993). The sequence has Earp counseling a young man on how to win in a gunfight. Van Sant is precise and plays out the scene in just the right number of shots—a step-by-step account of DE at work in a Western bar shootout. The film ends. The cast is listed, and three people are thanked, including Van Sant's former classmates James Evans and John Howell.

MALA NOCHE (1985)

Van Sant created his signature work, *Mala Noche*, in Portland, Oregon. This film, which includes male hustlers and gay sex, preceded *My Own Private Idaho* (1991)—the director's breakout movie. Film history is a careful science, and too many who may have seen a Van Sant movie or two are unaware of *Mala Noche* and its connection to the major body of his work.

This film rises above the first efforts of Coppola's *Dementia 13* (1963) (actually, Coppola directed two nudie feature films before that—*The Bellboy and the Playgirls* [1962] and *Tonight for Sure* [1962], but he doesn't like to acknowledge them); De Palma's feature debut, *Murder à la Mod* (1968); Kubrick's first feature, *Fear and Desire* (1953); and Scorsese's long-form debut, *Who's That Knocking at My Door* (1969).Van Sant had the canny knowledge to direct a film that, while still decidedly amateur, was remarkably free, with some notable exceptions, of film student or novice fingerprints and sand traps. Van Sant got a high percentage of what he wanted on the screen, always an accomplishment for any director, experienced or inexperienced, working with a big, small, or "no" budget. This is an essential film for anyone who wants to study Gus Van Sant and is available in a comprehensive Criterion DVD release.

Mala Noche begins with a black-and-white vista reminiscent of a John Ford Western. The montage that opens *Mala Noche* features a first shot that allows the viewer to experience a self-referential, self-reflective accidental moment, as drops of water kiss the upper left-hand regions of the camera lens while a guitar plays a sleepy but haunting bluesy melody and the sound effect of a moving boxcar train is heard.

From inside the train a point-of-view shot is presented, passing a barn, then revealing a blur of trees. A close-up of Johnny, a young Mexican man (Doug Cooeyate in, up to this point, his only screen performance), is followed by a second Mexican man warming his hands over a Bunsen burner. Then, there is an invisible cut to the next shot, where the camera moves up to him rubbing his hands to keep them from freezing.

The montage continues with the first young man lit in deep chiaroscuro as he reads a comic book, then a medium close-up of his face turning to look out of the open space of the train. Another point-of-view shot reveals the traveling imagery he witnesses. The camera gets close to his face as the traveling shot continues while the sound of the train rumbling over railroad tracks persists. The young gazer's face is repeated.

Cut to black. A profile shot of a lit cigarette jumps on as the titles begin, and the music is still bluesy but quiet—a guitar riff can be heard, along with the gentle tinkling of a soft melodic piano.

Credits. The white squiggly lines give the sequence a handmade quality. Then, borrowing from his beloved experimental filmmaking brethren, a quarter-slice image of down-and-outers appears in the upper-right-hand corner. Walt, a young Caucasian male (named after the author of the novel, Walt Curtis) played by Tim Streeter (who appeared in two 1990 *21 Jump Street* television episodes) appears. Streeter looks like he was separated at birth from River Phoenix (*Stand By Me* [1986], *Running on Empty* [1988], *Dogfight* [1991]), who would appear in Van Sant's masterpiece, *My Own Private Idaho* (1991) before dying of a drug overdose in front of Johnny Depp and partners' Viper Room on L.A.'s Sunset Strip in West Hollywood. The character works in a low-rent convenience store and is the film's protagonist/narrator. Walt has sexual longings for Johnny, the Mexican hustler, and tries to seduce him every chance he gets. The store is a breeding ground for old-school alkies like the one who acknowledges to his partner and the viewer that Walt "likes men."

A time cut[7] finds Johnny crouching in front of a garage or a car dealership. As Johnny talks to Walt, subtitles translate the conversation as the protagonist tries to get "his prey" to stay in his apartment. Streeter's performance and the creation of the character by Van Sant, the screenwriter, embody a sweetness; he is not a vulture but a lonely, hopelessly romantic, failed Romeo. The sequence ends with a cut-to-black.[8] Van Sant uses black to divide his film. Very popular among film students, black dividers provide structure and avoid opticals such as fades-to-black[9] and dissolves.[10] They also allow the creator to go from moment to moment or scene to scene or sequence to sequence freely and without elaborate narrative transitions. The technique can be deliberate or required because the coverage or narrative linking material was not available during the editing process.

Fade from black[11] to the image of Walt sitting at the bar with a Hispanic woman, Betty (Nyla McCarthy in her first and only performance to date) embraces a conversation of Walt's romantic feelings for Johnny. The stark black-and-white cinematography and Hollywood style shot/reverse shot[12] covers a discussion led by Betty, who introduces the possibility of finding Johnny as she blows smoke into the air. Here, the smoke is not used for diffusion, but Van Sant was surely aware of the practice and boldly rejects it for his run and gun guerrilla filmmaking[13] approach and commitment to a realistic and evocative atmosphere.

Time cut. A car pulls up. Walt walks to the door of a video emporium.

Intercut of a more-than-slightly-tipsy man sweet-talking Betty, who is sitting shotgun as this street trash tries to make time with her.

Walt walks through blinding pools of light into the noisy video game emporium, where he finds Johnny playing Pole Position.[14] From a psychoanalytical point of view, the name is highly allusive.

Johnny discusses leaving the club in Spanish with his Mexican pal as white subtitles light up the lower third of the frame. This makes *Mala Noche* a partially foreign-language film. The realism is worth the effort of reading the titles. Too few filmmakers have the courage to go this route and instead have foreigners speaking English with an accent. Some directors choose a British accent (this is often used for Roman soldier characters in religious epics).

Stark intercuts[15] are supported by clacking and whirling sounds transmitted by the now-primitive, then state-of-the-art video games. Walt expresses concern over Johnny—the object of his desire. On the game screen, Johnny's "car" is demolished and graphically indicated as a crash-and-burn symbol. This can represent Walt's efforts to build a successful relationship with the boy, who looks like a Mexican facsimile of Keanu Reeves' character in *My*

Own Private Idaho (1991). The two pairs of men have an eerie connection. Both films are about male hustlers, so Van Sant may have deliberately or subconsciously cast Streeter and Cooeyate to link the films. Stark intercuts are supported by clacking and whirling sounds transmitted by the full-size game boxes. Walla[16] voices play over a two-shot favoring Johnny as Walt expresses concern over the object of his desire.

Walt stomps up to the car. Johnny, his friend, and Walt have a confrontation as a cutback returns to the failed pickup. Betty and the street trash exchange words, and out of nervousness she says to the low-life, "We're going to cook him for dinner." Betty suggests brown rice and vegetables, classic hippie cuisine. Walt finally convinces Johnny to leave with him. Johnny invites his friend, and Walt happily agrees.

Cut to a grocery store shopping expedition. The menu changes.

Hard cut to Betty's apartment. Walt stokes up the fire in a stove contraption outside the kitchen space. The preparation of the meal is in progress. Cinematographer John J. Campbell (*My Own Private Idaho* [1991], *Even Cowgirls Get the Blues* [1993], *The New Age* [1994]) served Van Sant's vision by powerfully utilizing front and backlight to create a stark image in contrast to Walt's tender personality. *Mala Noche* is truly a black-and-white film.

Before dinner is served, Johnny jumps up as he suddenly remembers that he didn't give the key to Roberto.

Cut to "A hard rain is going to fall"-type rain right out of a B movie[17] film noir[18] occurs. Johnny runs up to Roberto, blames Walt (whom he refers to as a "faggot"—a line he repeatedly spews). Walt is excited about Roberto, who is carrying a boom box sitting in the front seat. They drive off.

Time cut to the next scene. The meal begins with the dropping of pasta into a pot of steaming, boiling water. There is a discussion of where the men traveled as they hunch over a map. A train rushes by in a flashback, with sound design that emphasizes their desperate story told in a choker close-up spoken in Spanish and translated by the white subtitles—a fight and the vicious beating of the Mexicans are described. The filling of the screen with the human face is reminiscent of Carl Dreyer's *The Passion of Joan of Arc* (1928).

Walt translates to the pretty Betty, who is decked out in masculine clothing, but Van Sant never reveals whether she is a lesbian or just a stylish young woman. The Mexican men are attracted to her and remark that she is pretty as they check her out.

There is a dramatic emphasis between a two-shot of the listeners and the choker close-up,[19] which holds the enormous face in its gaze.

A time cut finds Walt in a death conversation about experiencing the end of life though a story about McDonald's hamburgers—a hidden metaphor for the harrowing life of the street hustler and the concept of a "meat market." Van Sant would later create what critics call his death trilogy—*Gerry* (2002), *Elephant* (2003), and *Gus Van Sant's Last Days* (2005). His next film, *Paranoid Park* (2007), is about death, as well, as, in a sense, is *Milk*

(2008). There is death in many of his films, and, like many directors, Van Sant has his own view. Death comes swiftly, when you don't expect it. It comes in forms that can't be predicted.

Mexican music segues into a joyous dance; then there is another divisional structural cut to black.

Structural filmmakers take up the concern of structure within the frame. Here Van Sant experiments with editorial structure. Later in his experimental period, especially on *Elephant* (2003), he would bring the influence of structural film[20] into his directorial vision, inspired by a lifetime of watching experimental films.

Van Sant also skillfully integrates Hollywood cinematic grammar with the handheld style seen in documentaries and by using the language of the experimental film. These converge to form his personal style.

Cut out to another rainy street right out of a B movie. Is *Mala Noche* a B movie? It was made inexpensively but was not meant to be shown with another movie. It has a controversial topic, like many Hollywood Bs of the past. It's in black-and-white, like most B movies of the period. Is it a film noir? Who is the femme fatale, and who is the doomed man? Betty and Walt don't fit the format. And who is the victim? Many scenes take place at night. The lighting is reminiscent of the film noir style. As a cineaste, Van Sant has seen much of the canon of American and International cinema. He is also is familiar with film noir and other cinema movements. As an eclectic and complex film director, he borrows from what he has seen to create his style for each film.

Walt's narration comes over black—he is then seen in a chiaroscuro choker close-up pessimistically discussing the unsafe driving habits of Mexicans. Close-up of a speedometer radio dial moving steadily left to right. Johnny is ecstatic about speed. There is a metaphor for speed and the rush of sexual activity. The vehicle is intercut with Johnny smiling as the memory of playing Pole Position is intercut visibly, intended to be a warm thought from a short time ago. The Mexicans enjoy the thrill of Johnny as the "Downhill Racer," not on skis but in an aging boatmobile owned by Walt. At one point, Johnny is so out of control of the vehicle (Walt's car) that he crashes and scrapes along the metal guard rail on the side of the road.

Time cut. The car is stopped, and a feverish deal is in progress for Walt to penetrate Johnny's bum. A spokesman, a manager, better known as a pimp, barters with the desperately-in-love Walt. The storyteller exits the car, enters the rooming house with his eye, and flies up the stairs. The starkness of the photography details and emphasizes the human struggle going on in the out-of-date vehicle. At Johnny's apartment, they are met by a female house martinet. "No visitors!" she shouts at them. Her performance is over the top and yet appropriate; she is just doing her job. A reverse angle is made. She is most unattractive inside and outside compared to the male beauties she confronts.

Time cut. The boys are on the street. Walt, an otherwise sweet and nice guy, expresses his venom, calling the woman a "bitch," a "fat cow," using language to counter the words he used to the supple Mexicans he loves in a romantic and sexual manner. In the adaption process, Van Sant softens Walt's character to suit his own sweet and gentle manner. This outburst is more consistent with the real Walt Curtis.

Walt takes the other Mexican boy home. He tells him to be comfortable and says that he will return after completing an hour's work. The boy looks tentative and nervous, like a victim in a film noir flick. He checks out the apartment, which is alien to his native culture. Church bells from an outside source ring, augmenting the image by imparting a religious aura.

Walt is at work, and he cleans the filthy toilet bowls with an equally grungy mop.

The bells ringing in the background, with echoed heavenly ambiance are in contrast to the graphic sex in the film, which at times makes the point that those engaging in gay sex sing and fly with the angels. To connect Walt with the sex he is thinking about, editor Van Sant intercuts the two actions, giving us a choice of views. Van Sant may not condone male hustling, but he clearly understands and has observed this specific aspect of gay life. To Van Sant, homosexuals are simply a part of the larger human family. "They all say that I'm openly gay," Van Sant explained to Gary Indiana in a *Village Voice* interview published on October 1, 1991, "but they put that in as a little political footnote. . . . They don't say anything about gayness. They just say, 'He's openly gay.' They relate it a little bit to something, but they just get through with that a bit."

Walt glances up toward his apartment periodically while he works in the trashy package store. His sexual drive is building—the broom he sweeps with metaphorically becomes an extension of his sexual organ.

Van Sant, like David Lynch and all good total filmmakers, is a master of sound design. Here the dominant use of a train off in the distance and the church bells make a strong statement about the director's point of view. The train represents the Mexicans' endless ride—with a stop—then it starts again. The bells are also a constant reminder of the public's sense of right and wrong and what behavior will send you to heaven and what will send you to purgatory or the fires of hell. In one scene, a guitar plays on the soundtrack. Crickets make their chirpy, two-syllable sound as accompaniment.

Camera movement in *Mala Noche* is masterfully executed. When Walt enters the apartment, a pan moving in a backward direction picks up the image of Walt and then the refrigerator. Movement is expressive in cinema—this one speaks to desire and physicality. Van Sant brilliantly portrays Walt's nature. This is a true story, but the director never makes value judgments, just pours insight into this multifaceted character.

Bells and trains—the bells repeat endlessly.

The photography ranges from light to dark. Here we are faced with glare that hurts our eyes, as if we had been in a dark bar for hours, then stepped out to a burning street, as in the cinematography that the late great Conrad Hall (*In Cold Blood* [1967], *Butch Cassidy and the Sundance Kid* [1969], *American Beauty* [1999]) accomplished in John Huston's *Fat City* (1972). In *Principal Photography: Interviews with Feature Film Cinematographers,* Hall explains that he wants the viewer to experience reality. If a character is out in a bright sunny day, then spends time in a dark bar, when that person leaves the bar, the sunlight bearing down hurts both the character's and the viewer's eyes. The overall visual impact of the lighting in *Mala Noche* achieves this effect, giving the viewer a sense of time and place along with a Hitchcockian impression of voyeurism into a world most viewers haven't seen in person, only in bad movies.

The cinema has been defined by theorists and critics as based on a voyeuristic act. Alfred Hitchcock was one of the cinema's greatest voyeurs; it drove his dark vision. Van Sant would remake *Psycho,* a Hitchcock masterwork in which the audience watches as a young woman is stabbed to death in the shower.

Water boils in a pot. This image relates to or reminds the viewer of the earlier shot of the pasta pot boiling and can be a metaphor for Walt's anxious state or the physicality of the act of sex. The boy is sleeping; Walt makes coffee. The intercutting between the two characters and their action fuses them. The boiling liquid continues like an orgasm that can't be contained. A long pan connects Van Sant to long-take masters such as Theo Angelopoulos (*Anaparstasi* [1970], *Days of 36* [1972], *Ulysses' Gaze* [1995]), Michelangelo Antonioni (*L'Avventura, La Notte* [1961], *The Passenger* [1975]), Godard (*Breathless* [1960], *Weekend* [1969], *Notre Musique* [2004]), and other international masters who used the uninterrupted take to control pace, create a distinctive mood, and draw the viewer into the film. This works only for those who are willing, but those who are not are missing one of the cinema's most valuable tools—suspending time. Warhol's *Sleep* (1963), *Empire* (1964), and especially *Blow-Job* (1963) have undoubtedly influenced Van Sant, who copied the wizard of pop art and movies, doing everything but creating his version of The Factory, a silver-walled facility where art and movies were created and endless parties we held. Warhol was an inspiration to Van Sant.

The sound design turns on its power once again as the aural wash of a train going by presents the reality of the Mexicans in their hobo lifestyle. A "By" occurs when a moving sound passes by a locked-in recording device such as a microphone, allowing the viewer/audience to feel as if this aural occurrence is happening to them as well as to the characters in the film. Sound is a very powerful medium, and Van Sant utilizes the form in all his movies to get inside the head of the viewer.

Naked actresses, most commonly displaying their breasts, abound in American cinema, sometimes for story and character reasons, other times for exploitation. Less common but also sometimes asked of the actress is full frontal nudity, where the focus is on the triangle of hair covering the female organ, leaving the more gynecological views for the porn industry. Male nudity has different standards. The bare chest and bottom are common, but the penis rarely is seen in commercial or independent movies. When it is, and actor Richard Gere may hold the record, it is flaccid, without the length the porn industry uses as standard. The erect penis has been banned since the inception of the modern censorship (or monitoring) systems. (Two exception are *Shortbus* [2006] and *Bruno* [2009]). In *Mala Noche*, Van Sant respects reality, and when Walt is sexually excited, we see his erect penis. This is an art film, so quick flashes are enough, but the brevity of the shot does little if anything to affect the shock value.

So Walt undresses, his penis erect, and gets in bed with the boy who is the subject of his ardor.

The train sounds continue.

The camera spins around the action; the pictorial contrast is high. Walt gets a jar of Vaseline to aid his rear entry. Flashes of body parts—again the scene is voyeuristic, the camera wildly capturing and reporting the event. The editing is jagged and rapid. A boiling image communicates the obvious.

Some critics and theorists would classify *Mala Noche* as a road movie[21] like *Easy Rider* (1969), *Two Lane, Blacktop* (1971), and the aptly titled film *Road Movie* (1974). There certainly are enough scenes on the road, as well as train scenes and sounds, but in the end *Mala Noche* is neither porn nor blockbuster nor commercial or international—it is a relationship movie about the act of being alive with all the attendant pain, sorrow, and joy.

Mala Noche should be considered a street movie. As Walt struts the streets as if he owns them, a voice-over tells us what he is feeling throughout the film.[22] This literary device is utilized in low-budget films (Stanley Kubrick used it in his first two amateur features, *Fear and Desire* [1953] and *Killer's Kiss* [1955]). He was a supporter of narration throughout his career. Narration has its artistic applications and is used in down-and-dirty moviemaking, as well. The filmmaker does not need synch equipment—sound can be recorded on any machine and transferred (in this case on magnetic film) and adjusted accordingly. The editor, here Van Sant, can cut images to the dialogue, music, and effects without dialogue, and when there is dialogue in this film it is mainly looped. The actors spoke into a tape recorder while watching the screen. Van Sant knows all the tricks, blocking mouths with compositional elements, having a character speak while the camera is on the other's back view. Obscuring the lip movement is the goal, but Van Sant is making a controversial movie, and these strategies are a way of getting the movie made. It's the story and characters that motivated him to create *Mala Noche*, and he used any means necessary to get his ideas on film.

Street movies as a genre include *The Children of Times Square* (1986), *Streetwise* (1984), *Streetwise* (1988), and the cable television series *The Wire* (2002–2008) and *The Shield* (2002–2009).[23] Van Sant knows the streets. Usually, street movies are about drugs or the homeless, but *Mala Noche* is about street people looking for sex, drugs, food—survival.

Either Walt is wearing second-hand clothing or he's worn out his iconic outfit featuring a floor-length coat and a plaid shirt. The wear of the coat is physical texture. *Mala Noche* is filled with human texture of life on the bum. Walt is a young man with pride, although many disdain him. He is above them all, running a store that looks like a warehouse, offering, booze, smokes, candy, any junk a convenience store carries, but this is no 7/11—it is the lowest of the low. What hours does Walt work? Why does he constantly go back to work, seemingly to spend all of his young life among family—the family of man that only God could love? Family is the theme of the majority of Van Sant films. They could be called dysfunctional families, but they are beyond that—a tribe—the unwashed, the ignored, the powerless, the abused and the abusers—this is the heart of many Gus Van Sant movies.

Clouds move across the sky. No matter what the location in a Gus Van Sant film, this director is obsessed with capturing, either at high speed or slow, the image of ominous, sometimes majestic clouds passing over. It is as if God is sending down a directive. Van Sant is also a devotee of experimental filmmaking,[24] especially of the 1960s and 1970s, and this ongoing signature may be his homage to filmmakers such as Stan Brakhage (*Mothlight* [1963], *Lovemaking* [1968], *The Riddle of Lumen* [1972], Bruce Baillie (*Castro Street* [1966], *Quick Billy* [1971], *The P-38 Pilot* [1990], and Ken Jacobs (*Little Stabs at Happiness* [1960], *The Blond Cobra* [1963], *Tom, Tom, The Piper's Son* [1969]).

Landscape shots are also present in Gus Van Sant films. They often capture the scope, terrain, and neighborhoods of Portland, Oregon. They, too, have an avant-garde film connection. Film scholar Scott MacDonald has dedicated an entire book, *The Garden in the Machine: A Field Guide to Independent Films about Place,* to the subject.

A female sings a song in Spanish. The language complements the ethnicity of the characters.

Portland, Oregon, is as synonymous with Van Sant as Saint Petersburg is with Dziga Vertov,[25] Dublin, Ireland, with James Joyce,[26] and New York City with Woody Allen, Martin Scorsese, and Sidney Lumet. Portland embraces each film with its mentality and physicality (at times), but most of all it speaks to the character within the people in the film. This identification is cultural, social, and political. Home is where the heart is, and Portland, Oregon, is Van Sant's spiritual home, as well as a place to live. Oregonians have a live-and-let-live philosophy that permeates Van Sant's soul and manner.

There are many images, signs, and symbols that stamp a Gus Van Sant film. One is the side-part haircut he always sports that goes back to his youth and is still his style in middle age. This represents adolescence—most young men's first hair cut or, more accurately, hair comb when Mommy is no longer allowed to touch it. Van Sant is forever young and stays attracted to young men. This is not deviancy but admiration, love, and a hope that puberty will never end.

Walt is an on-screen surrogate for Van Sant, just as Jean-Pierre Léaud[27] was for François Truffaut in a series of films featuring the character Antoine Doinel. In *Mean Streets* (1973), Harvey Keitel[28] as Charlie Cappa plays the spirit and personality of Martin Scorsese. Keitel, like Walt in *Mala Noche,* shoots home movies. Who is filming the movie? Scorsese remains invisible (except for one frame in the opening home movies), but we see Walt capturing the proceedings before his eyes on camera. By transference, Walt becomes Gus. The filmic results of the home movies are from an amateur. Van Sant, like Scorsese, studied film in college, but Van Sant had other inputs; both had the skill of drawing. Scorsese respected the avant-garde,[29] but Van Sant embraced it.

Both Van Sant and Scorsese understand the language and grammar of the home movie; the shaky cam, jumping from subject to subject, the moment-to-moment action, the anxious and at times distracted "directorial eye," playing with the camera apparatus as if it were a toy.

The life of a young gay man includes negotiation. Dealing with a male prostitute for a man is no different from the endless deal-making that goes on *hondling*[30] with a female prostitute. The services are similar because, as the American youth shouted during the Clinton/Lewinsky mess,[31] "Sex is sex!" Walt, an experienced patron in this area, gets to Johnny through his friend.

Illegals deal with avoiding the law on a daily basis, and here Johnny eludes a cop.

Insert of a clock. Metaphorically, time refers to the running length of the film (78 minutes) or life expectancy or the voyage from youth to death.

The store is so shabby that a bottle on a rope is used to open and close it.

The Mexican faces are carefully photographed in a gritty documentary-like style, with no respect to screen direction.

An abrupt cut to black.

The Mexican cinema has long been strong and has produced many actors, directors, and craftspeople. John Huston (*The Treasure of the Sierra Madre* [1948], *The Misfits* [1961], *Under the Volcano* [1984]) and Sam Peckinpah (*Ride the High Country* [1962], *The Wild Bunch* [1969], *Cross of Iron* [1977]) were two unlikely models; both were macho men who despised gays and found a deep kinship with the land, people, and culture of Mexico. Van Sant displays here a fascination with the people and culture. The Mexican music in this film is right out of Huston or El Jefe (Peckinpah). Mexico is featured in many films, including *Old Gringo* (1989), *The Mexican* (2001), and *Once Upon a Time in Mexico* (2003), as well as in many back-in-the-day Westerns directed by the likes of Budd Boetticher (*The Cimarron Kid* [1952], *The Tall T*

[1957], *Comanche Station* [1960]), Howard Hawks (*Red River* [1948], *Rio Bravo* [1959], *Rio Lobo* [1970]), and Sergio Leone (*A Fistful of Dollars* [1964], *The Good, the Bad, and the Ugly* [1966], *Once Upon a Time in the West* [1968]).

The car owned by Walt sports Oregon plates. A clear view of a license plate also appears in Van Sant's *Psycho* (1998), but in that film the numbers and letters have meaning for the actors, especially Anne Heche (*Donnie Brasco* [1997], *Wag the Dog* [1997], *Birth* [2004]) as the tragic Marion Crane.

A shot of Walt in a landscape takes on the aesthetics of a classical painting.

Walt fancies himself a hipster. He often wears sunglasses, as in skillions of movies, indie and Hollywood, as he walks down the Portland streets like a big shot, again recalling Harvey Keitel in *Mean Streets*. The on-screen representative projects a mind-image the director has of himself that is internal rather than based on reality. Sunglasses have been worn by many hipster actors, including Steve McQueen (*The Magnificent Seven* [1960], *The Great Escape* [1963], *Papillon* [1973]), Tom Cruise (*Risky Business* [1983], *Top Gun* [1986], *Jerry Maguire* [1996]), and, most notably, Marlon Brando (*A Streetcar Named Desire* [1951], *On the Waterfront* [1954], *The Godfather* [1972]). Here they are utilized ironically. To put it in street terms, Walt is the king of shit-town. He waves to everyone like an American president on a visit or out campaigning. The shades make him a star. He swaggers, and the glasses represent his confidence.

Johnny strikes a pose like a muscleman. He is well built but skinny, no meat on the bone, so he looks silly, his six-pack more like one can of brew cut in half.

A scene containing a waterfall reminds us of countless Hollywood movies, especially those featuring nature boy Johnny Weissmuller as Tarzan (who had no confusion about his sexuality, showing his stuff to students and actresses underwater and hoping for a romp in the hay later). Many movies feature waterfalls, such as *Niagara* (1953), *Splendor in the Grass* (1961), and *Dr. No* (1962); there are also many paintings, including "The Waterfall" by Shingei, "Kaaterskill Falls," by Thomas Cole, and "Amazon," by Lysack Gennadiy. Van Sant knows how to use his art and cinema history training to his best advantage. The guitar and whistling lend a haunting splendor to the shot and the scene.

As if he were in a Warner Bros. gangster film such as *The Public Enemy* (1931), *Little Caesar* (1931), or *High Sierra* (1941), Johnny takes to firing the weapon as if it had been born in his hand. He acts like a gangster or a cowboy (both shoot guns—one drives a car, the other rides a horse), blasting off shots of hot lead indiscriminately as he drives too fast.

The boom box plays Tex Mex, a music blending Texas and Mexican music. The street-carried boom box has been extinct since the development of MP3 player and points to *Mala Noche* as a period movie, a moment in time.

The use of Mexican slang and street talk like "gringo" come directly from the Walt Curtis book, pages 18 through 19. Curtis covers "abrazos," which means "embraces," to "watchalo," which means "Look out for me."

Criterion,[32] the high-end DVD distributor that specializes in presenting rare, unusual, and previously unavailable movies, courageously took on Van Sant's controversial *Mala Noche* in 2007. In addition to the movie, the *Mala Noche* DVD contains an interview with Van Sant and a documentary on Walt Curtis that reveals insights into the man and his sexual proclivities. As to the technical specs, Criterion gave *Mala Noche* the careful and delicate technical treatment it deserves. The definition digital transfer of the film in its original 1:33:1 aspect ratio was created on the Spirit 2K Datacine from a 35mm interpositive. Imperfections were removed by the thousands with the MTI Digital Restoration System, and the film was encoded at highest bit rate for maximum quality. The original audio was restored, as well. Van Sant participated in the process and made changes The release was part of Criterion's Director Approved series.

Johnny is very good-looking (like most of the young men in Van Sant's films), but he is desperate. Johnny tortures Walt by scooting away with the car keys, then driving away without the ownership or the registration.

Walt chain-smokes cigarettes. This package store from hell actually sells them individually because of the lack of funds the "patrons" find themselves in.

In his DVD interview, Van Sant (dressed in a delivery jacket bearing the logo of 7-Up, a beverage he seems to have an affinity for; the original slogan, "You like it, it likes you," speaks to Van Sant's gentle demeanor) explains that he had little equipment or plan. He confides that the script was bad and that storyboards drawn for each shot were followed religiously. Van Sant applies long-lens technique, rack focus, and other cinematic grammar he picked up in school and from watching and making movies.

The Mexicans play games with Walt's car, and he begins to join in the tomfoolery. Exhausted, always horny, and addicted to smokes, booze, and pot, Walt is angry and laughing at the same time that he does not understand how he got into this mess but wanting Johnny even more as the illegal becomes the primo game player.

The car is black like a hearse, and the wind continues to howl. Johnny goes through a series of muscleman poses. He is barechested, as is Walt, whose place of work has a No-Credit sign, with some slogan below it like "You have to bring your great grandfather with you, in order to get credit."

Time cut—Walt in store. In front of the Royal Hotel. Sound—rain.

Walt walks down a long hallway (Van Sant repeats this image in his death trilogy *Elephant* [2003], *Gerry* [2002], and *Gus Van Sant's Last Days* [2005], and most famously in *Elephant*, a metaphorical investigation into the Columbine tragedy).

Jump cut on door knock.

Time cut to the steps—Exterior of the hotel.

Now it is really raining as a backlight picks up the pelting downpour on the car.

A window.

The female manager stomps through the hallway.

Van Sant, like his hero Hitchcock, performs a cameo appearance as a resident questioned by Walt regarding the Mexican's whereabouts.

Dissolves are plentiful in *Mala Noche* to link images and ideas.

Electronic music by Creighton Lindsay[33] and guitar play on the soundtrack.

Next, Van Sant crafts a montage of Walt looking for Johnny.

Voice over—Walt speaks over a bar discussion.

Item—Night Train.

This is a cheap wine not recommended by sommeliers but pitched on back-in-the day television commercials by Sammy Davis[34] and Cesar Romero[35]—it was practically wood alcohol. One states "*You'll* love . . .," insinuating that he wouldn't go near the stuff. Before the 1970s, apple wine and other fruit-spiked drinks came into vogue for teenagers; the hardcore winos in the 1950s and 1960s drank Night Train for a devastating high, usually ending in stomach problems. Night Train is a perfect metaphor to address the constant sound of trains going by and the method of transportation the illegals used to get from place to place.

Cigarette packs are everywhere—Pall Mall, Camels, every kind but filter tip. These hard-living men and Walt himself like the taste of the tobacco on their lips and in their mouths.

Coke is sold here, the soft drink that once had a smidgen of cocaine in its formula. The other way to get high with Coca-Cola was to put an aspirin in the bottle.

Van Sant must like the un-cola; he has Walt sell it in the store.

Walt sports a half-beard like a baseball player during a night game or *American Idol*'s Ryan Seacrest. He appears scruffy and not pretty as he has looked throughout most of the film.

Cigarettes are sold separately so one doesn't have to bum one off a buddy or companion. The brand isn't revealed, but they must be cheap, not a premium brand like those described.

The line "My friend Pepper" is spoken.

Bud, the "King of Beers," associated with fine horses and the late Ed McMahon,[36] is the brew of choice among alcoholics who don't drink responsibly.

"Cash only." "No Change."

Old advertising logos are on the glass door, the art of America, Pop Art like that Van Sant created and admired.

A singing saw refrains "Home on the Range."

Campbell and Van Sant backlight cigarette smoke so that it looks like a fog.

In a long take, a Caucasian pimp schools one of the Mexicans in how to make quick and easy money. He is a hustler and is dressed like a punk rocker, which by the film's release was a waning movement and today is still alive but weakened in spirit, more of a fashion statement than a lifestyle choice.

One of the Mexicans becomes sick. He continually coughs and is given medicine. The sickness is represented in constant coughing, sweating; he can't get up.

Mariachi music plays.

The other Mexicans have no respect for the sick. They practice martial arts. A new Mexican character shows the others his slick moves. Shots of them watching him are intercut, and there is a through-the-legs shot, which Van Sant had seen in many movies, such as the famous shot of Mrs. Robinson (the Dustin Hoffman character seen through the legs of Mrs. Robinson [Anne Bancroft]) in *The Graduate* (1967).

Walt nurses Pepper back to health, giving him medicine, wiping his cold, sweaty brow.

Intercut—flashback—Johnny and Pepper have a fake fight in happier and healthier times.

Van Sant employs Iris shots, which go back to cinema's early days. His command of film language for his age and for a first film is impressive and applied correctly for the story he is telling and the characters in the story-telling. He certainly knew his D. W. Griffith (*The Birth of a Nation* [1915], *Intolerance* [1916], *Way Down East* [1920]).

Pepper wants a milk shake. Back in the day it was Coca-Cola syrup; now it's calcium to rebuild a sick body.

Fade to black.

Walt inquires for work for the Mexicans but is told by a farm or industrial manager that it is the wrong season—he should come back another season when there is work.

The distant church bells play "Silent Night." It isn't necessarily Christmas, but it may be.

Pepper is still ill.

Walt smokes a joint. Doctors have proved the medicinal powers of mari-juana, but this doesn't apply; Walt is the kind of retro-hippie who takes a toke at the beginning of the day and whenever he is stressed out, rather than pop an Ativan (Lorazepam) or the tranquilizer of the moment.

Pan down Pepper's body, to see, to want to heal.

Mirror shot. These reflections of a subject in reflection go back to early cinema. Almost every director has employed them; this is a good one, getting into the soul of a character.

The Spanish word *molesto* is used, implying that Walt is a pervert.

Pepper fights Walt and tries to kick his caregiver off the bed.

It is explained that the Mexican likes sex only at night and that is stereotypical—Walt is not. From viewing the documentary *Walt Curtis:*

The Peckerneck Poet, directed by famed animator Bill Plympton (*25 Ways to Stop Smoking* [1989], *I Married a Strange Person* [1997], *The Fan and the Flower* [2005]) on the Criterion DVD, it appears that Walt is very self-confident when it comes to sex, what he knows about it, what he's done, his technique of taking photos, and his use of a towel and other transactional habits. He also recites phrases as poetry or spoken answers to an interviewer. In this light, Streeter is a bad choice; he is a sweet boy, Walt more the "wild man" of Portland. Streeter does not play a poet in *Mala Noche.* The spirit if not the tenor of the real deal is kept, without many of the autobiographical details. Van Sant adapted the story of Walt and Johnny and friends and left the rest of the book for background color when needed in the script.

A classical record is put on.

There is a sequence of Pepper learning how to drive, a long pan, an ugly hair, piece of grass, or some unwanted sliver pops up in the top of the frame. When he approaches a curve, he doesn't listen to Walt and crashes into the side wall.

The car is towed from a pit by a trucker who attaches a line to the car. One flashes forward to a similar image at the end of both Hitchcock's and Van Sant's *Psycho.*

Black.

Filmmakers either buy black film or manufacture it themselves by shooting with the lens cap on.

Pepper watches television.

Friends are around. There is talk that Johnny may have been arrested going through immigration.

In a possible homage to *The Wizard of Oz* (1939) a rainbow appears over Betty's head while she is speaking to Walt.

Pepper is outside talking to a girl. He likes girls better than boys, but having sex with boys earns him his keep, so he tolerates it.

Black.

A woman knocks on their door—she needs the police—she is not let in—sound of police siren accompanied by the singing saw.

Cop.

Slow pan into a Mexican—focus issue may be deliberate or error.

Are the police after him?

Shadows.

Gun.

Again we on are the street. We see a down-market Chinese restaurant, the kind where the food is great and the décor is nonexistent.

A dark man is shot on a rainy street. There is fog; it is cold.

Pappas means French fries in Spanish.

Police capture him.

Drunks.

Van Sant did an excellent job of adapting Walt Curtis's notorious book into a controversial film. Curiously, Curtis has text, drawing, and photos that resemble the art of the "cut up" as practiced by Van Sant hero, collaborator, actor, and fellow openly gay man, William S. Burroughs. Walt is a West Coast Beat poet, and Burroughs plied his trade mainly in New York. The fact that Burroughs helped out a gay kid by selling him a story cheap is heartwarming and part of each man's artistic history and legacy.

Close-up of Johnny in the rain.

It is most like real rain—not Hollywood rain from a garden hose. It has to do with that particular region of the United States that produces hearty independent souls like Curtis and Van Sant. In the guerrilla filmmaking tradition, Gus and his micro-crew shot where and whenever they could. They did not wait months for a storm to come in like David Lean (*Lawrence of Arabia* [1962], *Doctor Zhivago* [1965], *A Passage to India* [1984]). This is immediate filmmaking.

Betty is there—as well as the singing.

Looking for Johnny is as pointless as the waiting in Beckett's *Waiting for Godot*,[37] but he is found. A pair of cowboy boots—there is echo on the track—not Gold Star studios, where Phil Spector[38] worked, but the kind you can get in an expensive or cheap (or homemade) sound studio.

Theme music, piano and guitar.

Johnny runs away.

Lock in key—key in lock.

Bad camera noise. If a camera is not blimped, it makes noise that can be covered up later with music, dialogue, or sound effects, but Van Sant wants reality, and this imperfection of cinema production is perfect for the film and to define its young maker.

Tequila.

The Mexicans mimic a bullfighting routine. Hemingway loved bullfighting. It was actually televised on American television during the 1950s.

The men are doing shots (a dangerous teen habit when they are downed fast and furious). Pack of Pall Mall—bottle of Tequila.

A guitar is played.

The police killed Roberto.

Johnny throws Walt out of the room, Walt leaves without a fight, even though he is called a *puto*, slang for faggot. Johnny notches it into the front of the door of Walt's apartment with his stiletto knife.

Again Walt struts down the street, knowing everyone and everyone knowing him—like Harvey Keitel walking into the red-lit bar in *Mean Streets*. Van Sant shot in Portland, where *Mala Noche* takes place. Scorsese was forced to shoot the New York bar and some street scenes in Los Angeles.

Betty explains that she could easily make $150 a night dancing naked—this is before pole dancing and men's clubs—she's talking about dive bars, where men go to see women dance naked to music, usually from a juke box.

The dancer tells the boss what to play. Women mainly just danced in those days. The girls covered up when their stint was up, when buying drinks for them was allowed. The woman needed money to support themselves and their families. Both now and then, the job attracts college girls with good looks and good bodies.

Wet streets like in a film noir.

Walt keeps looking back at Betty as he drives away into the night. This scene is similar to the end of Scorsese's *Taxi Driver* (1976). Walt is Travis, Betty is Betsy. Van Sant at this point and now and forever is a cineaste—he loves movies and watches them incessantly—by inhaling so many films they reside in his memory bank and are bound to show up in a different form in his work. This is not copying or plagiarism but homage. Van Sant, like Scorsese, incorporates the references (this is also called "quoting") while maintaining his personal vision. Before them, Godard accomplished the same cinematic feat. In a film by Quentin Tarantino or Brian De Palma (*Greetings* [1968], *Carrie* [1976], *The Black Dahlia* [2006]), the references are the content of the film, even as these directors also maintain a personal vision.

The credits roll in color home-movie style, as at the beginning of *Mean Streets* (1973). Van Sant's take on 8mm film is good, but is this film or tape? Scorsese's medium is clearly 8mm film and he has runouts, the dots that run through the end of a side or a roll, flashes, and good stop-and-go motion. Van Sant approaches the film technique of home movies as a fine arts practitioner. In terms of era (the 1980s), he should have used video, but video doesn't have those technical qualities—it's a straight-on image, solid, with no grain but instead pixels.

The end credits are white, executed in painterly style of the opening. Streeter puts a piece of plastic wrap over his face to depict either smothering himself or his becoming a monster. He smiles all through this—he is a fun-loving guy, not in the same way as Walt Curtis, whose idea of fun, according to the Plympton documentary, is having sex with dogs and masturbating to all-boy magazines.

Mexican music plays over the credits.

The actors go through a Beatles/Monkees-type running around, doing silly actions routine to a punk/New Wave song. Van Sant continues to shake the camera like an amateur making his first movie, imitating those two popular pop groups. Ironically, the Monkees copied the Beatles, who copied silent comedies like the Keystone Kops from the cinematic 1910s and 1920s.

Because Doug Cooeyate, who played Johnny, was not a trained professional, Arturo Torres mouthed dialogue attributed to this major character.

Fellini's Satyricon, based on an ancient text, involves sexual frolicking that supposedly led to the fall of Rome. The film is referenced in *Mala Noche* by a scene in Satyricon, a hot night club in Portland. Fellini made his own interpretation, even putting his name in the title. Gus Van Sant would borrow this for *Gus Van Sant's Last Days.* Kubrick claimed authority for the Anthony

Burgess book, naming his film adaptation *Stanley Kubrick's A Clockwork Orange*. These men are not claiming ownership but letting the audience/ viewer know that the film is their interpretation of the established work they are watching.

The credits are written on a plate with white paint like those TCM (Turner Classic Movie) spots, but not with neon, just in pure white paint. They are fluid in style because Van Sant studied Andy Warhol, Robert Rauschenberg,[39] and Jasper Johns.[40]

Sunny Jim (aka Jed Stone), to whom the film is dedicated, is a singer who performs in the Cayman Islands style.

Mala Noche has ended.

$$3$$

The Family Business

DRUGSTORE COWBOY (1989)

Gus Van Sant's second feature film, like *Mala Noche,* is about family—this time junkies. Historically, drug films center on specific drugs, their effects on the body and mind, the drug lifestyle, medical issues experienced by the users, and the punishment if the users are arrested. *Drugstore Cowboy* examines these issues, but they are tangential; the film's focus is junkies as a family unit. Other filmmakers have been successful in putting these matters on screen, but in *Drugstore Cowboy* Van Sant dissects how junkies act with in-depth candor and microscopic intensity, examining their shared personalities as crafted by drugs, especially heroin, and their struggles to live, be free, or die.

The story follows Bob Hughes (Matt Dillon, *Over the Edge* [1979], *The Outsiders* [1983], *Wild Things* [1998]), who also appears in Van Sant's *To Die For* (1995); his wife, Dianne (Kelly Lynch, *Bright Lights, Big City* [1988], *White Man's Burden* [1995], *Charlie's Angels* [2000]); and their drugstore robbing friends Rick (James LeGros, *Guncrazy* [1992], *Mrs. Parker and the Vicious Circle* [1994], *Zodiac* [2007], who worked with Van Sant again on *Psycho* [1998]) and his on-screen girlfriend, Nadine (Heather Graham, *I Love You to Death* [1990], *Boogie Nights* [1997], *Bobby* [2006], and Van Sant's *Even Cowgirls Get the Blues* [1993]).

The characters in *Drugstore Cowboy* are a fully developed family unit: Bob, the father; Dianne, the mother; Rick, the somewhat dutiful son; and Nadine, the wayward daughter. They grapple with issues that all families, especially dysfunctional ones, face. Bob is a strong father figure and leader but is becoming exhausted because his lifestyle has worn him down. He is sexually impotent and constantly on the run. He routinely gets into trouble with the law and eventually reaches a crisis, drops out of "the life," returns home, and enters a methadone program to get clean. Bob is our narrator and begins and ends his journey in an ambulance after he's been shot by a degenerate junkie/dealer.

Dianne is tough as nails, a gun moll and femme fatale who is the getaway driver during the drugstore heists. She is sexually available but can't get Bob interested because of his constant worry and impotence. Dianne still loves Bob but can't handle the straight and narrow. She retains her good looks, but how long will they last? Rick is a loyal soldier and has been committed to Nadine. He can shoot junk with the best of them and has taken on a grunge rock[1] star look before its time. He has an anger problem and an issue with patience. Nadine is a tragic figure, cute as a button, the member of the gang who causes physical commotions in the pharmacy, so Bob can loot the drug bins. Nadine is childlike. She is the youngest and has problems with ego and self-esteem. When Nadine complains she is not getting her fair share of the stash, she takes it for herself and overdoses. To dispose of her body, they hide her in an attic and later bury her in the woods. When Bob leaves to get clean, Dianne becomes Rick's girl; he takes over the family business.

Drugstore Cowboy also features a literary superstar as famous for being a junkie as he was for being the writer of *Naked Lunch, Junky,* and *Queer.* William S. Burroughs, who allowed Van Sant to make *The Discipline of D.E.,* had his own movie career, including roles in *Bloodhounds of Broadway* (1989) and *Twister* (1989); his voice is heard as the preacher on the radio in *The Book of Life* (1998). In *Drugstore Cowboy,* Burroughs plays Tom the Priest, an old junkie.

Van Sant was in his first decade when the Beats roamed San Francisco and New York and traveled the country by car, inspiring Jack Kerouac's masterpiece, *On the Road.* Van Sant has walked through the beatnik, hippie, punk, and grunge movements—a devotee of youth movements and artistic lifestyles, he creates films that reflect their culture and history.

Burroughs was an icon and a hero to the throngs who followed his exploits in literature and life. His most infamous act was shooting his wife with a bow and arrow. Van Sant cherished the anecdotes and sordid exploits that the openly gay Burroughs would recall for hours on end. In *Drugstore Cowboy,* Bob is an on-screen surrogate for Van Sant, listening to the old man for advice and admiring his longevity.

James Remar (*The Cotton Club* [1984], *Boys on the Side* [1995], *Blowback* [2000]), who played the police officer in *Psycho* (1998), plays Gentry, a detective who hounds and stalks Bob everywhere he goes and watches his every move waiting for a misstep.

The drug lifestyle is portrayed as neither glamorous nor squalid. *Drugstore Cowboy* is a realistic film (and at times a black comedy) that chronicles the day-by-day tedium, the boredom, the anxiety-ridden events that are a part of the junkie lifestyle. The characters rarely talk about their lives; the rest of their conversation is about making a score, a big one that will feed their habits for more than a couple of days. Bob is a complex and multifaceted character. He owns a bag full of Ben Hogan golf clubs and is working on his handicap when Detective Gentry and his minions smash up Bob's prize possessions.

Bob is riddled with fear and superstitions he feels doom him. A principal phobia concerns putting a hat on a bed. To him, this can bring nothing but bad luck and in the film causes (in Bob's mind) Nadine's death. In one scene, as a consequence of seeing a hat on a bed, the junkie family leader announces that the family members will be confined to the house for an indefinite period in an effort to ward off a negative outcome.

Drugstore Cowboy is based on the book by James Fogle. The book was not released until 1990, when the author was out of prison, having served time for running drugs. Like Bob, he was a lifelong junkie. It was his first literary attempt and received rave reviews from the *New York Times,* the *Village Voice,* and the *Los Angeles Times.*

Drugstore Cowboy begins in an ambulance, with Bob narrating his story, so the action of the film is in flashback. The opening shot in which the camera looks straight down at Bob is a reference or homage to the notorious Andy Warhol film *Blow Job* (1963), a 35-minute shot of a young man's face as he is given fellatio[2] by an unseen giver rumored by the IMDB Web site to be experimental filmmaker Willard Mass (*Geography of the Body* [1943], *Narcissus* [1956], *Dionysus* [1963]). The young man was Charles Rydell (*The Sand Castle* [1961], *The Queen of Sheba Meets the Atom Man* [1963], and *Union City* [1980]).

Van Sant is skillful at placing the right music for the right moment or scene. *Drugstore Cowboy* begins with a female rendition of "For All We Know," sung by Abbey Lincoln.[3] There is a scratch on the record, a ploy Scorsese used in *Mean Streets* (1973), when he couldn't afford a new copy. The song was written by Fred Carlin,[4] Robb Wilson, and Arthur James, was published in 1970, and won the Academy Award that year for best song sung in a film (*Lovers and Other Strangers* [1970], directed by Sy Howard, *Every Little Crook and Nanny* [1970]). It was sung in the film by Larry Meredith.

Another effective use of music and image occurs in a driving scene as the tribe passes by a bridge, cows, and a dirt field seen from an aerial view. The song is a reggae tune, "The Israelites," written by Desmond Dekker[5] and Leslie Kong[6] and performed by Desmond Dekker and the Aces. The Israelites were ancient tribes who traveled across the desert seeking land they felt God had given them. In *Drugstore Cowboy,* Van Sant portrays Bob and his tribe as the Israelites searching for their homeland while experiencing and fighting the overwhelming toil of modern-day poverty.

As in *Mala Noche,* Van Sant recreates home movies, this time using rapid camera movement, the lens swinging right to left, up and down, displaying grain, pixels,[7] and scratches. He includes slow-motion, high-speed photography to alter the timeline of the movie.

Drugstore Cowboy concludes with one of Van Sant's most successful excursions into home movie art scored to "The Israelites." The dead Nadine comes to life; everyone is friendly and most likely more silly than stoned. Back in the 1940s, 1950s, and 1960s, most families had regular and Super 8mm cameras to document their lives. In the 1980s, 1990s, and into the 21st century, video and digital video cameras have taken on the job. Always on the cutting edge of technology (in a funky but experimental manner), Van Sant employs what is available in the marketplace.

The special effects in *Drugstore Cowboy* consist of layering images of hats and other floating objects to explore Bob's mind-space. Syd Dutton (*Glory* [1989], *Cape Fear* [1991], *The Bourne Identity* [2002]) and his associates at Illusion Arts[8] have worked on many such sequences for Van Sant, who looks to the films of Stan Brakhage (*Interim* [1952], *Dog Star Man* [1962–1964], *A Child's Garden and the Serious Sea* [1991]), Bruce Baillie (*Castro Street* [1966], *Quick Billy* [1971], *The Cardinal's Visit* [1980]), and Kenneth Anger (*Fireworks* [1947], *Scorpio Rising* [1964], *The Man We Want to Hang* [2002]) for inspiration and tutelage. Among many other things, Van Sant is a psychedelic[9] filmmaker, growing up on experimentalism and films like *Chappaqua* (1966), *Easy Rider* (1969), *Fando and Lis* (1968), and *Koyaanisqatsi* (1982). A drug-like aura pervades *Mala Noche* (1985) and *Even Cowgirls Get the Blues* (1993).

The overwhelming majority of Van Sant's films (*Finding Forrester* [2000] is one exception) take place in Portland, Oregon. *Drugstore Cowboy* unfolds in the Pacific Northwest. The man from Portland prefers to film in his own backyard because of its beauty, roughness, and endlessly moving skies, which he uses as a backdrop for the myriad stories Van Sant tells. Nontravelers who watch Van Sant's oeuvre can say they've been to Portland countless times. The people, the terrain, the city, the country all are part of cinematic lore.

Van Sant favors several colors in his films: blue, green, and yellow. In *Drugstore Cowboy,* his color of choice is green. There has long been a correlation between junkies and the color green, in this case signifying death. Production designer David Brisbin (*The Chamber* [1996], *The Exorcism of Emily Rose* [2005], *The Day the Earth Stood Still* [2008]), who worked with Van Sant on *Drugstore Cowboy* and *My Own Private Idaho* (1991), understands this color/content connection. Here from the author's article in *American Cinematographer,* Lisa Rinzler (*Guncrazy* [1992], *Trees Lounge* [1996], *Pollack* [2000]) talks about collaborating with Brisbin and the junkie/green/death connection on *Dead Presidents* (1995).

> There is a character called Skip who dies of an overdose. . . . As soon as I read
> that scene I thought "Green is a good color for death by overdose," and I asked
> the production designer David Brisbin, "Could you give me a green lamp?" It

had an oval, light-green shade, so we spent a lot of time gelling it darker. That lamp motivated the use of green light.[10]

Green may not always signify death as it does here; it will be analyzed in context as it appears in the films that follow. Blue is the color of water and the sky and eyes, but for Van Sant it often represents majesty and the force of nature.

Yellow or gold can be a warning sign. Production designer Patrizia von Brandenstein (*Amadeus* [1984], *State of Grace* [1990], *All the King's Men* [2006]) utilized yellow in *Silkwood* (1983). It can be used to symbolize an exalted state, as employed by Vittorio Storaro (*The Conformist* [1970], *Last Tango in Paris* [1972], *1900* [1976]) in many Bernardo Bertolucci (*Before the Revolution* [1964], *Luna* [1979], *The Dreamers* [2003]) movies.

The directing credit for *Drugstore Cowboy* reads "Directed by Gus Van Sant Jr." Van Sant Sr. wasn't a film director, so why did this director feel compelled to distinguish himself from his father? It was at the beginning of his career, so he was a junior (novice) director. His father was in the business world and helped his son throughout the years with money matters. The only logical reason must have been that the son liked the way "Directed by Gus Van Sant Jr." sounded and looked. He was proud of his father, even though the man moved the family far too much; he also wanted audiences to know he was not his father.

Drugstore Cowboy, both book and movie, takes place in Portland, Oregon, in 1971. Portland is situated in the Northwest of the United States. It is near the Willamette and Columbia Rivers. Known for the brewing of beer and for hearty souls who can brave fierce weather, it has been called the City of Roses politely and Rip City not so politely. The flag is white, green, blue, and maize, colors often featured in Van Sant films. Portland is a city of youth culture and home to radical feminist and lesbian activity. Punk, hardcore, and anarchist lifestyles prosper in Portland. Other filmmakers who have made Portland their home include Todd Field (*In the Bedroom* [2001], *Little Children* [2006], *Blood Meridian* [2009]) and Todd Haynes (*Poison* [1991], *Safe* [1995], *Velvet Goldmine* [1998]). Haynes is an openly gay director who is a friend of Van Sant's.

Van Sant can go to the movies whenever he wants in Portland and can even drink a beer while watching one of his or another filmmaker's movies. Most of the theaters are second-run or revival houses, so one can get a free film history education there. The theaters include the Academy Theater, the Bagdad Theater, the Clinton Street Theater, and the Mission Theater. To satisfy Van Sant's love of art, he can visit one of Portland's many museums and galleries, including the Portland Art Museum. If he wants to read, he can go to Powell's City of Books, the largest indie bookstore in the United States. It's not that easy to get a good steak, as many restaurants serve vegetarian cuisine.

It is not surprising there are so many trains and train sounds in a Van Sant movie; the city has light rails, a commuter line, and a transit mall. Urban bicycling is encouraged, as featured in a few of the films.

In terms of sex entertainment, Portland has more strip clubs per capita than Vegas or San Francisco thanks to the city's strong free-speech protections. In Portland, full nudity in clubs is considered protected speech, and a nude bicyclist was not charged because the judge said the "World Naked Bike Ride," with up to 1,200 riders, "was a well-established tradition in Portland."

Art schools include the Art Institute of Portland, the Pacific Northwest College of Art, the Oregon College of Art and Craft, and the Northwest Film Center.

In an interview by Bart Blasengame for the February 2009 issue of *Portland Magazine*, Van Sant reminisced about the artistic community and cultural figures. In Portland, the Storefront Theater, led by Ric Young, produced rad-theatrical events. Holland-born painter Henk Pander, who worked with thick textured paint on large canvases and portrayed the passage of time and inevitable change, was in Portland in the 1960s and continues to work there. Also, Van Sant's experiences at RISD were life-changing. One of the artists he met there was David Byrne. Van Sant attended Byrne's first performance at a school's Valentine's Day dance before he formed the Talking Heads in New York City. Van Sant explained that he lived briefly in the United Kingdom in 1975 and bunked in a factory near the notorious punk band the Sex Pistols. He also lived on Hollywood Boulevard in Los Angeles, a block from where the West Coast punk scene was evolving. In the Northwest, Van Sant explained that the Nike shoe company and Microsoft were creating future cultural changes. "I remember in like '71 or '72 I saw this guy named Mike Slade wearing a pair of Nikes. I said, 'Cool, you have your name on your shoe.' He was like, 'No, these say Nike. Not Mike.' He became an early Microsoft employee and went on to run things for Paul Allen. He knew early on that something like that was worthwhile."

Van Sant's re-creation of the 1970s in *Drugstore Cowboy* is flawless. He not only got the details right; he captured the zeitgeist of the times. Although *Drugstore Cowboy* is primarily an interior film, Van Sant, his art department, and his camera crew managed to translate the exterior world of the 1970s in all its down-market glory. The houses, the drugstores, and the street scenes are correct in feel and atmosphere. Anyone who came of age or was alive during this "Me Decade" (a phrase coined by journalist Tom Wolfe) will feel transported by a cinematic time machine. For the young, it is an educational lesson on the decade many artists still talk about. Young people yearn to go back to those times, which they find romantic and exciting. Through Van Sant's film, they are taken there.

There will probably always be a drug culture within American society. Those "into" drugs and the lifestyle can see both the similarities and the extreme differences between the milieu of the 20th century and that of the 21st. In today's world, drugs are either accepted or scorned; in the 1970s they were a way of life. Heroin, which Bob's "family" thrived on, made a comeback in the 1990s and even became a fashion chic event. Bob's world in the 1970s was grimy and paranoid, living for the fix, similar to its depiction in Jerry Schatzberg's *The Panic in Needle Park* (1971).

Marilyn Quayle[11] may still believe that not everyone was part of the 1960s and 1970s counterculture, but it was the culture of the times, and *Drugstore Cowboy* delineates how the drug world fit into the larger society. Both sides struggled and Van Sant keeps his eye on the underground here.

MY OWN PRIVATE IDAHO (1991)

My Own Private Idaho, a queer cinema[12] landmark, put Gus Van Sant in the forefront of motion picture creators. It is cinematic work that hovers somewhere between independent and commercial cinema. Van Sant took the duo of Tim Streeter, who played Walt, and Doug Cooeyate, who played Johnny in *Mala Noche* (1985) and transposed them into River Phoenix (Mike Waters) and Keanu Reeves (Scott Favor).

My Own Private Idaho is about many things: hustlers, gay sex, loneliness, the road, family blood, inherited mentors, and, above all, the disease of narcolepsy and the Orson Welles Shakespearean masterwork *Falstaff* or *Chimes at Midnight* (1965).

The NHS Direct Web site describes narcolepsy as a chronic disorder that disrupts the normal sleeping pattern.[13] It can cause the patient to fall asleep suddenly, without warning (known as "sleep attacks"), and also tends to make those with the illness feel excessively drowsy during the day. Other symptoms of narcolepsy can include sudden loss of muscle control (cataplexy), hallucinations, disturbed night time sleep, and difficulty concentrating.

In *My Own Private Idaho,* Mike Waters suffers from narcolepsy. Van Sant's interpretation of this malady is that it occurs whenever Mike is under stress—which is often. The young displaced man is searching for his mother, for his identity, for friendship, and for love. Throughout the picture, there are many occasions where Mike is under the influence: when he's having gay sex for money; when he is with Scott, a man he thinks he loves; when he meets with his father; and during the countless daymares and nightmares he experiences concerning the mother who left him.

The Fine Line Pictures[14] release begins with a pedal steel guitar, also known as a Hawaiian guitar. This music is also used in Van Sant's disastrous film adaptation of the Tom Robbins lit-masterpiece *Even Cowgirls Get the Blues*. The instrument utilizes a metal slide run up and down on the strings rather than fingers as used on a standard six-string guitar. It is fashioned into a table-like stand and has a pedal that manipulates the sound. It has been used extensively in country music over the past several decades.

Bill Stafford (*Tarzan the Ape Man* [1981], directed by John Derek and Bo Derek), composer and arranger of the *My Own Private Idaho* music, performs the pedal steel guitar on the soundtrack, for which he won the Independent Spirit Award for Best Film Music in 1991. Stafford was a legend in the field who used two 10-string necks and a tuning system all his own. Before he died, at a young 63, Stafford played with many country, rock, and pop performers.

In *My Own Private Idaho*, Stafford plays "America the Beautiful." Musicians and others have over the decades and years petitioned politicians to make "America the Beautiful" the national anthem, replacing "The Star Spangled Banner."

The lyrics have a direct connection to the films of Gus Van Sant. "O beautiful for spacious skies" speaks to the spectacular sky shots in the majority of his films. "Purple mountain's majesty" refers to the cosmic beauty of northwestern mountain ranges. "And crown thy good with brotherhood, from seas to shining sea" was originally intended to embrace unity and mutual responsibility among the diverse people of the United States, including the gay, lesbian, and transgender communities during the modern era, of which Van Sant is a part.

The other unusual instrument utilized in the film is the saw, played by Richard Meyers (*Syncopation* [1929], *I Dood It* [1943], *Susan Slept Here* [1954]). This unique application of a carpentry tool to make music is achieved by sitting with the handle of the saw between the legs, bending the top part of the tool, and stroking the nontooth side with a bow. The result is a singing quality that brings an ethereal atmosphere to the soundtrack.

The last unconventional musical element is yodeling, defined in Wikipedia as "a form of singing that involves singing an extended note which rapidly and repeatedly changes in pitch from the vocal or chest register or 'chest voice' to the falsetto voice making a high-low-high-low sound." Yodeling is believed to come out of Swiss culture as a communication tool. It is practiced in many cultures and has a firm place in old-school country music.

The title card for the film has *My Own Private Idaho* in white letters on a blue background. Van Sant (along with so many of his contemporaries) has been heavily influenced by the aesthetic vision of Stanley Kubrick, especially *A Clockwork Orange* (1971). In *A Clockwork Orange,* Kubrick uses blue and orange cards for titles and credits. Pablo Ferro (*Harold and Maude* [1971], *No Way Out* [1987], *The Manchurian Candidate* [2004], directed by another Hitchcock enthusiast, Jonathan Demme, *Melvin and Howard* [1980], *The Silence of the Lambs* [1991]), is uncredited as the title designer of *A Clockwork Orange,* but he worked on several films for both directors. Van Sant, who hero-worships directors he admires, may have made a specific effort to work with people who have collaborated with his idols. Kubrick Ferro, who designed *Dr. Strangelove* (1964), designed *To Die For* (1995), *Good Will Hunting* (1997), and *Psycho* (1998) for Van Sant.

In *My Own Private Idaho*, Van Sant applies and heightens the intensity of the color blue for the overarching sky under which the open road lies ahead. When the film is finished and the end titles are running, Van Sant will have used maize, purple, green, and red. Each color has classical significance, the purple almost but not quite pink, the color used by the Nazis to identify homosexuals, green to represent the earth, and red for sex, hell, and anger.

At the beginning of the film, Mike is out on the open road, wearing a sock hat and a mechanic's shirt with the name tag "Bob" (another character named Bob will later become a major individual in the film).

The road is a key location in *My Own Private Idaho*, which also figures in *Drugstore Cowboy, Good Will Hunting* (1997), *Psycho* (1998), *Finding Forrester* (2000), and *Gerry* (2002). In the DVD special "Kings of the Road," the late film critic Paul Arthur talks about the connection between *My Own Private Idaho* and the road movie genre. In speaking about the old and the new, Arthur makes comparisons that illuminate Van Sant's entry into the genre as a way of expressing the gay lifestyle, as does Gregg Araki in *The Living End* (1992) and *Smiley Face* (2007).

The road movie is a tradition in film history. Good examples of Hollywood entries are the Hope/Crosby road movies, *The Wild One* (1953), *The Grapes of Wrath* (1940), and *It Happened One Night* (1934). The most infamous is Monte Hellman's American New Wave masterpiece, *Two Lane Blacktop* (1971), featuring rock stars Dennis Wilson and James Taylor, elaborate 360-degree coverage even though Hellman often plays only one camera position, a high-take ratio, and concludes with the film catching fire. The road movie is about traveling to find the soul of a person or a country, as in *Easy Rider* (1969), a film that Van Sant has referenced throughout his career. The road movie is about speed, time, and space.

There is a close-up of a stop watch. Time is fleeting for Mike. He never knows when another attack will be upon him. He is surrounded by American iconography. The sculpture of a cowboy appears in close-up. David Lynch, an American movie director, created in *Blue Velvet* (1986) an image of "anywhere USA"—suburbia with a white picket fence and blue skies. However, in postproduction Lynch oversaturated the white of the fence and the blue of the sky, which creates a surreal and unsettling emotional state in the viewers mind.

Van Sant learned this Lynch lesson but *My Own Private Idaho* takes places in the Midwest, not "anywhere USA," so Van Sant adds a blue mountain range and his signature moving clouds, here moving tumultuously through the sky as Mike is hit with a narcoleptic attack and a shooting star streaks to the sky.

The Wizard of Oz (1939)[15] is another seminal film that Van Sant has referenced at several points in his career. Here a barn comes falling out of the sky and crashes into the ground as a pile of worthless wood. It is the symbol of an orgasm, as well as a sign of the nomadic adventures of the Van Sant family.

Van Sant talks about repeatedly painting this image and the emotional toll it took on the boy who was forced to reestablish himself with each move to a new community.

My Own Private Idaho opens a window for the straight world to look into the life of the male hustler. The uninformed would think that the customer is paying to have the hustler perform fellatio on him, but here Mike is serviced by the customer. Mike Waters looks surprisingly like James Dean (*East of Eden* [1955], *Rebel without a Cause* [1955], *Giant* [1956]) in this moment. Mike's hair is combed back and up in a pompadour style similar to that worn by the iconic actor, who died at age 24 in a head-on collision with another vehicle. (River Phoenix was 23 at the time of his fatal drug overdose.) Dean was hounded by rumors that he was gay or bisexual,[16] a fact pretty well proved by numerous Dean biographers, friends, and director Nicholas Ray, whose *Rebel without a Cause* (1955) put James Dean on the map. The passing of River Phoenix was comparable to the passing of James Dean for an earlier generation, as was the plane crash that killed Buddy Holly,[17] Richie Valens,[18] and the Big Bopper[19] (Jiles Perry Robinson Jr.), whose deaths became known as "the day the music died," according to Don McLean's song "American Pie."

Mike is shown in the middle of a trick with a John. The camera holds on the young man as the older man, below frame, performs fellatio on Mike.

There is a shot of fish jumping out of the water. Its meaning is described in the following passage from the unclesirbooby Web site:

> Water symbolizes your feelings as it constantly moves and flows. Deep water can represent your subconscious feelings. The fish then represent issues over which your views are shaping and forming. Think about changes in your feelings taking place and subconscious feelings forming in your mind. Fish tend to link to new moods and motivations. They symbolize the deep emotional connections that underpin our relationships. They also link to strong urges and motivations that are pushing us in new directions.[20]

This startling image of the fish leaping out of the water is also a symbol of the beauty and bounty of the land, of hunting, and of escaping the big city. Van Sant decided to present the fish image in sepia tone, a brown monochromatic effect that reminds the viewer of old still photographs or particular scenes in a silent movie. Also used toward the beginning of *My Own Private Idaho* is an iris shot made famous by the father of American film grammar, D. W. Griffith and his longtime cameraman Billy Blitzer (1872–1944). An iris shot is related to the camera iris or eye and the human eye. A black circle appears on the screen and either widens or shrinks, depending on the effect wanted by the moviemaker. The iris is directed at a particular spot on the screen and is often used to begin or end a sequence or scene.

A red "don't walk" sign flashes. Mike is in a city now and thinks he sees his mother. There is a *Vertigo* shot[21] of Mike as he tries to process the face of the woman who is not his mother. Van Sant's respect and admiration for Alfred Hitchcock shows up well before he took on a so-called shot-by-shot copy of *Psycho* in 1998. Thunder is heard over a moving-cloud sky.

River Phoenix, who plays Mike, was born in Oregon. In 1969, the Bottom family (the father's surname at birth) was part of the infamous Children of God cult. Of River Phoenix's four siblings, brother Joaquin and sister Rain became actors, and both appeared in other Van Sant films.

River Phoenix met *My Own Private Idaho* co-star Keanu Reeves in *I Love You to Death* (1990), which was a film about a wife wanting her husband dead, the premise of Van Sant's *To Die For* (1995). A further association is with William Richert, who plays Bob in *My Own Private Idaho* and who directed *A Night in the Life of Jimmy Reardon* (1988), in which Phoenix appears. Casting Richert as Bob, the Shakespearean figure who is a mentor to a group of gay hustlers and misfits, was a stroke of directorial genius. Van Sant took a risk in hiring another director to be on his set, one who had directed his lead actor in a starring role in his own film. The iconoclastic Richert, an actor in films of his own and others, and director at the time of two other films, *Winter Kills* (1979) and the *American Success Company* (1980), had the girth for the part and looked like a hippie[22] version of Orson Welles in *Chimes at Midnight*. Van Sant reports in interviews that he had no reason to be concerned and found Richert a great collaborator.

The unique idea that transforms *My Own Private Idaho* into something more than just a gay movie is the integration of the Orson Welles film, which combines Van Sant's hero worship for Welles with the language and characters of William Shakespeare.[23] Many aspects of filmmaking are central to a successful result, but none is more critical than the ideas within a motion picture. "Here is a film not only influenced by but practically modeled after a film that is not particularly well-known, certainly compared to *Citizen Kane* (1941). So that in itself endears me to the idea. And it's a very good idea," states Welles historian and film scholar Peter Tonguette.[24] Welles had directed *Five Kings*, a stage presentation in 1939 that embraced the Henry V and Falstaff stories. Welles returned to the play in the early 1960s, casting Keith Baxter[25] as Prince Hal; Baxter plays the role in the film. The cast of the stage production became the cast of the film version. "Welles said famously," Tonguette continues, "that if there was one film that he wanted to get into Heaven on the basis of—it would be *Chimes of Midnight*." Tonguette believes that Welles identified with Falstaff, so this endows *My Own Private Idaho* with another layer of identification.

"The roles of Bob and Falstaff are handled in similar ways," Tonguette continues. "When we first see Bob, we hear medieval music on the soundtrack, which seems inspired by the score of *Chimes at Midnight*. And Van Sant very often shoots Bob in these low angle quasi-Wellesian shots. Usually Van Sant's visual style is nothing like Welles' at all. But when Bob is on the screen Van Sant's staging and selection of shots is very directly influenced by

Welles. The character of Bob played by William Richert is very, very close to Falstaff."

"I actually find Prince Hal more sympathetic than Scott," Tonguette explains.

> The staging of the rejection scene in the restaurant is very exactingly recreated from Welles because Scott almost processes through the space as though it was a coronation. One of the best realized updates of the Shakespearian language of *Chimes at Midnight* occurs when 'I know thee not, old man' becomes 'I don't know you, old man.' It is a ruthless rejection. The most moving and impressive paraphrase of Welles is indeed the rejection scene and the way it's transposed in a very clear way and yet not in a too obvious way; in fact a very witty and smart way. He's taking this relationship from Shakespeare but via Orson Welles.

Chimes at Midnight contains one of the most spectacular battle scenes in all of film history. It would seem unlikely to have a battle scene in *My Own Private Idaho*, but Van Sant actually pulls it off in a sequence in which Bob and his tribe attack a drunken rock group for their goods. The scene is comical, clumsy, and silly at times. Bob and his crew wear hooded outfits that simulate the soldiers gear in *Chimes at Midnight*.

The environment in which Bob and the boys live and hang out in also mirrors (in a modern way) that of Falstaff. "They are very, very close. Bob's temple very much feels like the Boar's Head Tavern in *Chimes at Midnight*," Tonguette contends. "At Bob's temple there's even a stand-in for the Margaret Rutherford character. The actress even looks like Margaret Rutherford.[26] Perhaps the most direct paraphrase in *My Own Private Idaho* of *Chimes of Midnight* is in part of Bob's opening scene. It's a take-off of Falstaff and Master Shallow at the very beginning of *Chimes at Midnight* where they sit before the fire and say, 'We have heard the Chimes at Midnight. . . .' And Bob and the stand-in for Master Shallow in *My Own Private Idaho* have nearly the same dialogue—and they are saying it in front of a fireplace."

In another scene with a client, Mike dresses up as a little Dutch boy and cleans the client's house, scrubbing furiously as the man does a strange dance scene, takes off his shirt, and writhes around the room. This fantasy role-playing is not much different from the kind employed by female prostitutes and married heterosexual couples.

Throughout *My Own Private Idaho* are home movies. Here the technique visually identifies Mike's pain and his longing to see his mother again. A woman who may remind him of his mother is Alena, a customer who hires three men to separately have sex with her because she takes some time to warm up. She is played by Grace Zabriskie (*The Big Easy* [1987], *Fried Green Tomatoes* [1981], *Inland Empire* [2006]), who worked with Van Sant in *Drugstore Cowboy*.

An attractive older woman known in the porn underworld as MILF (Mother's I'd Love to F—), Alena chooses Mike as the lead-off man. He becomes so stressed when he sees her, in a white terry-cloth robe, approaching him for sex that he has a narcoleptic attack and collapses in the room.

Several real hustlers were hired to act in the film. In a montage of stories about their exploits, mostly horrific, we get a roundtable discussion of the subject similar to the scene in Spike Lee's *Jungle Fever* (1991) in which a group of women discusses the bad qualities of men for the audience of a wife who was cheated on by her husband.

A visually inventive sequence takes place in an X-rated shop when the male explicit magazines come to life and talk to the audience and one another. The discussion includes the merits of modeling over hustling; Scott is one of the orators.

Van Sant delivers a tribute to the late openly gay mad wunderkind of the cinema, Rainer Werner Fassbinder (1944–1982) (*The Bitter Tears of Petra von Kant* [1972], *Ali: Fear Eats the Soul* [1974], *Fox and His Friends* [original title *The Fist-Right of Freedom*, 1975]) who died of an overdose at age 37. Van Sant casts a favored Fassbinder performer, Udo Kier (*Lili Marlene* [1981], *Lola* [1981], *Breaking the Waves* [1996], directed by another cinema madman, Lars Von Trier) as the flamboyant Hans from Germany. A second bizarre dance number occurs when Hans demonstrates his performance art piece for Scott and Mike. It consists of a cassette tape and a lamp, with him jumping around the room with bizarre facial expressions and movements. This scene is reminiscent of the scene in David Lynch's *Blue Velvet* (1986) in which Dean Stockwell (*Compulsion* [1959], *Tracks* [1976], *Married to the Mob* [1988]) lip-syncs Roy Orbison's "In Dreams" while his face is illuminated by the light bulb of a work lamp on a cord.

There are more stories from the hustlers and prostitute kids. One hustler tells about having a wine bottle shoved up his rear; a girl cries.

Bob wears a blue robe and snorts cocaine. He talks about his true son. The family theme is never more apparent in a Van Sant movie than here: a family of hustlers, led by a down-on-his-luck fat father who is a stand-in for Falstaff and who is slowly and steadily losing power and influence over his flock of the unwanted and the homeless who have looked up to him as their one true father.

The influence of the Western[27] is visualized in a startling shot of a young blond gay hustler facing the camera while swinging two pistols laying down lead. The image can be read as a tribute to the first acknowledged Western—Edwin S. Porter's (*The Cavalier's Dream* [1898], *Life of an American Fireman* [1903], *The White Pearl* [1915]) *The Great Train Robbery* (1903), in which a grizzled cowboy fires his pistol directly at the camera/audience. This is also referenced at the conclusion of Scorsese's *GoodFellas* (1990), when Tommy DeVito (Joe Pesci) fires his guns at the camera.

My Own Private Idaho also celebrates the psychedelic through the craft of production design, paying tribute to movies like *The Trip* (1967), *Psych-Out* (1968), *Chappaqua* (1966), *Fando and Lis* (1968), and the granddaddy of acid trip films, *Something Weird* (1967). The term "psychedelic" relates to the colorful visions that result from the use of LSD, strobe lights,[28] and swirling Op Art,[29] an artifact of the 1960s that was both art and lifestyle.

A slide down a roof during the "battle scene" looks like a skateboarding[30] image, which will become vital imagery in *Paranoid Park* (2007). Another campfire scene appears in *My Own Private Idaho,* again celebrating *Easy Rider.*

Scott's father is in a wheelchair, which looks like something out of David Lynch's landmark television series *Twin Peaks* (1990–1991). There is a photo of Jack Favor (Tom Troupe) with his son Scott in which the boy resembles Gus Van Sant.

The family of outcasts humiliates Bob by saying he is so fat he can't see his own penis. There is a reference to *Compulsion* (1959), in which Welles plays Jonathan Wilk, a lawyer based on Clarence Darrow, who defended the homosexual murderers Leopold and Loeb.

There is a fire in a barrel inside Bob's temple, an image that relates to street scenes in *Mala Noche* (1985). The police in yellow garb break down the door and catch Scott having sex. A suit from the company delivers a message to Scott from his dad.

The top shot[31] has been around since the days of Busby Berkeley (*Dames* [1934], *Babes in Arms* [1939], *The Gang's All Here* [1943]) and is brilliantly and often employed by Martin Scorsese in many of his pictures. Here Van Sant executes one of a restaurant.

Blue card—Idaho.

A return to the road via the iris shot. Another campfire scene. Indian drumming. An orange sky recalls *Gone with the Wind* and *The Wizard of Oz* (1939), the first Golden Age of film, the second the 1970s, and the third a golden age of gay films in the 1990s.

Is Keanu Reeves (*Bill & Ted's Excellent Adventure* [1989], *Little Buddha* [1993], *The Matrix* [1999]) gay? Rumors abound, but there is no proof (or lawsuits). He is just one celebrity that the public and the tabloids love to dish about. The list also includes Ryan Seacrest,[32] Tom Cruise,[33] the Jonas Brothers,[34] and Kenny Chesney.[35]

The Van Sant signature image of a slow-motion sky appears throughout Van Sant's body of work. This image imparts varied meanings and artistic purposes. It speaks to the landscape of Portland, Oregon and reminds us of our place in the universe. Avant-garde filmmakers often repeat an image to ramp up its visual and psychological power with each appearance, and here Van Sant displays the influence of these directors. Then there is the mysterious artistic aspect of how a creator becomes attracted to a sign, a symbol, and draws it into his work.

Mike goes to visit his father, Richard Waters, played by James Russo (*Extremities* [1986], *No Way Home* [1996], *Donnie Brasco* [1997]). The scene has a different emotional heat from those before it. We are now in the psychodramatic world of Elia Kazan (*On the Waterfront* [1954], *A Face in the Crowd* [1957], *The Arrangement* [1969]), and Sidney Lumet (*Twelve Angry Men* [1957], *Serpico* [1973], *The Verdict* [1982]). Russo is from the New York school and is known for playing gangsters and psychopaths. Here he portrays Mike's father as a broken but angry man in a film about the search for family. Mike cannot accept his mother's leaving him, so his search leads him to his real father after Bob's father figure fails to center the young man.

Again, Van Sant is a unique film director who channels myriad influences with autobiographical strains and personal interests. Van Sant's search for home ended when he settled on his own in Portland, Oregon. Home is where you feel you belong. This grueling scene, with his father spewing bile about Mike's mother, grounds the film, which uses many modalities. *My Own Private Idaho* may be the most personal gay movie yet made. It is not a polemic like *Longtime Companion* (1990) or *Poison* (1991) but a film made by a director with many artistic agendas.

Richard Waters is a painter. He does odd portraits of everyday people who give him a photograph. When they are not happy with the results, he puts them on his wall. In an offhanded cameo, one of the pictures looks like Gus Van Sant. Van Sant personalizes his films by doing cameos à la Hitchcock and by giving characters his distinctive haircut. Van Sant wants to be young and vital—not aging and brittle like Bob, who has lost the allure of his past.

In his angst, Richard tries to convince Mike that his mother was a *putana*, a whore who went with other men. The home movies of her as an idealized mom represent the son's stuck-in-time memory of her and the pain he is in without her. The stress continues to trigger his narcolepsy and multiplies his sexual confusion concerning hustling and love.

Scorsese's *Who's That Knocking at My Door* (1969) pays homage to Howard Hawks's *Rio Bravo* (1959) with a breakdown montage of a gun fight accomplished with stills from a poster. Van Sant pays his own homage either to Hawks's film or to Scorsese's by working *Rio Bravo* into the storyline as Richard continues to belittle Mike's mother. He tells the boy that she killed a man during a screening of *Rio Bravo*, the story of a sheriff who hunts down a bad guy with a crew of misfits. Then Richard drops a bombshell, telling the boy that the man his mother murdered is Mike's real father, adding to the boy's confusion about his past.

Gus Van Sant's cameo in *My Own Private Idaho* is as a bellhop. He has uncharacteristically long hair worn in a ponytail and plays the scene in a deadpan manner. This style comes from Buster Keaton (*The General* [1926], *Steamboat Bill Jr.* [1928], *The Cameraman* [1928]), the theater of the absurd, and the persona of Lou Reed[36] (whose song in *Gus Van Sant's Last Days* [2005] drones on repeatedly and whom Gus Van Sant emulates on his own record, as well as in the narration on the short film *My Friend* [1982]).

A card with a red background identifies that the film is switching to Rome. This is also an autobiographical strain, relating to Van Sant's tour of the Italian film industry after college. Here the film switches narratives again. Scott and Mike are in a piazza filled with angry Italian gay hustlers who don't want the visitors horning in on their turf. Another shift in the plot takes them on a search for Mike's mother, to a country house where she had lived. There, Scott, in his quest to become legitimate in order to take over his father's empire when he reaches 21, expresses a heterosexual side when he meets a beautiful young Italian girl, Camella, played by Chiara Caselli, who appeared in four Italian feature films and has enjoyed a long career since her lovely and delicate performance in *My Own Private Idaho*.

The film contains two sex scenes that are more artful than erotic. The first is a three-way involving Scott, Mike, and Hans. The second is the coupling of Camella and Scott. Both are shot in a static montage,[37] where the participants are posed in various positions. These are not freeze frames but show the actors posing as if they were artist's models. This technique is also used in the television series *Heroes* (2006–) when the character of Hiro Naksmura (Masi Oka) is able to freeze time and all the people, vehicles and action in a scene. The result in *My Own Private Idaho* is not highly sexual but quietly beautiful. Van Sant's painting background lends a Cubist approach to deconstructing the sex act into moments, not action. This becomes a signature for real sex in the movie, as opposed to the more graphic but simulated hustler sex.

Camella is also a conduit for Mike because she knew his mother and can give yet another point of view to the mixed-up boy.

Mike is jealous of the couple. He blows smoke at them and is kept up many nights by their loud lovemaking. They are both in love with Scott.

Mike returns to hustling, but a date with a handsome middle-aged Italian man turns bad when Mike has a narcolepsy attack probably triggered by his inner turmoil over Scott and Carmella. The image of clouds moving here represents Mike's emotional state.

The landscape of the farm area is in direct contrast to the city sequences. There are sheep, a dog, and bright green grass.

A blue card signals a return to Portland.

Scott's father dies, as does Bob, his surrogate father. The two funerals commence together. Scott's father's is in the traditional manner. Everyone wears black, and a priest presides. Bob's is raucous, with the crew dressed in wild colorful clothing and dancing on his coffin to accordion music. Scott's father's segment is similar to the graveyard sequence in *The Godfather* (1972), which signifies a changing of the guard from the rule of Don Corleone to that of his son Michael.

To the seasoned moviegoer, watching a Gus Van Sant film is a feast of cinema. Images and scenes recall other movies. In a Van Sant film, the director's autobiography and personality are on the surface, not hidden.

Mike is back on the same road at the end. He is rolled by two men. "America the Beautiful" plays. A car drives up, Mike is put in the car, and it drives off. The barn images repeats, as do the clouds.

A blue card states "Have a Nice Day," an ironic nod to the smiley-face philosophy of positive thinking in the face of reality. The remaining credit cards feature blue, green, purple, yellow/maize, and green in a rainbow coalition version of *A Clockwork Orange*.

In *My Own Private Idaho,* Van Sant has realized one of his great achievements—a gay film that is layered in meaning and nuance and is visually challenging and artful. By working in the Falstaff theme, Van Sant simultaneously enriches his film with Shakespeare and Welles. Those two men are firmly linked in Welles's lifetime love of the Bard, so the invisible relationships within the film are rich. Films are about ideas. And this one, concerning Bob as Falstaff and Scott as Prince Hal, is as brilliant as the best of them.

4

A Miss and Two Hits

EVEN COWGIRLS GET THE BLUES (1993)

The first acknowledged feature film in America was D. W. Griffith's *The Birth of a Nation,* released in 1915. It was with *Intolerance,* in 1916, that Griffith experimented with openly gay subject matter in the ancient-world segments showing half-naked women seducing each other.

The Birth of a Nation was based on the novel *The Clansman: A Historical Romance of the Ku Klux Klan,* by Thomas Dixon (*The Foolish Virgin, The One Woman, Comrades*). The film's newly discovered and invented cinematic grammar influenced motion pictures from the beginning of the 20th century up to the present. Some of the properties of the medium Van Sant inherited from Griffith and early cinema include the match cut,[1] intercutting, and the iris.[2] *The Birth of a Nation*'s racist content inspired moviemakers to attempt to stamp out hurtful, discriminatory, and unjust social blight by telling their own stories about the human condition. Gus Van Sant has certainly tackled a number of societal issues and themes, especially gay culture and lifestyle.

Over the decades, American filmmakers have adapted novels for the screen. *The Age of Innocence,* by Edith Wharton, written in the 1920s, has been adapted three times, including a 1990s version by Martin Scorsese. In the 1930s, Dashiell Hammett wrote *The Maltese Falcon,* which was adapted for the screen twice, including the John Huston[3] classic filmed in 1941. During the 1940s, Margaret Landon penned *Anna and the King of Siam,* which was made into two movies, *The King and I* (1956) and *Anna and the King* (1999). The 1950s William March novel *The Bad Seed* has been adapted twice for the movies and once for television. The 1960s novel *Hotel,* by Arthur Hailey, was adapted as a film and as a television movie. All these have had relative success. Literary classics such as *Moby Dick*[4] and *Ulysses*[5] do not adapt well to the screen. They are long books that need the space to develop, and the density and meaning of their prose are lost when adapted to visual images and sound. Both of these legendary books were brought to the screen—*Moby Dick* (1956) by John Huston and *Ulysses* (1967) by Joseph Strick—and failed at the box office, not living up to studio expectations. Not all adaptations succeed because, inevitably, audiences compare the book to the movie. In Van Sant's case, this never got much of a chance to happen; *Even Cowgirls Get the Blues* barely played out in theaters.

Tom Robbins published *Even Cowgirls Get the Blues* in 1976. Rumors had it that Robert Altman (*M*A*S*H* [1970], *Fool for Love* [1985], *A Prairie Home Companion* [2006]) was interested in adapting the book for a movie. In 1980, Warner Brothers signed Shelley Duvall (*Brewster McCloud* [1970], *The Shining* [1980], and *Changing Habits* [1997]) to adapt the book and to star in the project as Sissy Hankshaw, Robbins's heroine. The project never materialized. In 1994, 18 years after Robbins wrote his counterculture classic, Gus Van Sant adapted the book into a motion picture.

Even Cowgirls Get the Blues is one of the only major critical and box office failures of Gus Van Sant's career to date.

Paradoxically, in 1977, at a Portland, Oregon, book signing, a 25-year-old Van Sant asked Tom Robbins to autograph his book. Van Sant vowed to make it into a movie and at some point convinced the whimsical Zen master Robbins to narrate the film, as well.

Shot in "poppy" colors (tones that pop off the screen), *Even Cowgirls Get the Blues* is an early example of this au courant style. The film, photographed by Eric Alan Edwards and John Campbell, has a lesbian theme. There is a lovely song score by k.d. lang, an openly gay singer, recording artist, and soundtrack performer, but even these elements could not help the film.

Even Cowgirls Get the Blues centers in on Sissy Hankshaw (Uma Thurman) and her hugely oversized thumbs. (Ironically, Van Sant's sister, Malinda, was nicknamed Sissy.) If ever there was another commercial film that features the thumb as a symbol for the penis, the film historians haven't found it yet.

Even Cowgirls Get the Blues concerns the large-thumbed hitchhiker's exploits on the road and with a group of lesbian cowgirls at the Rubber Rose Ranch. The child with the large thumbs is told she can either be a butcher (bringing up the weight and price of a selection with a heavy thumb) or a hitchhiker.

The hitchhiker has a long tradition in television and the movies. In the 1960 episode of *The Twilight Zone* titled "The Hitch-Hiker," a man symbolizing death tries to silently communicate to a young woman driving on a road that she is already dead. The IMDB Web site has 10 titles for movies and television named "The Hitchhiker," released between the 1930s and 2007, and 3 under "The Hitch-Hiker," released between the 1930s and 2004, including one directed by Ida Lupino (*Never Fear* [1949], *Outrage* [1950], *On Dangerous Ground* [1952]). Other films about hitchhiking include *It*

Happened One Night (1934), *Detour* (1945), *The Hitcher* (1986), *The Hitch-Hiker's Guide to the Galaxy* (2005), and *Into the Wild* (2007), directed by Sean Penn, who would star in Van Sant's movie about Harvey Milk, released just one year later, in 2008.

Hitchhiking, the art of thumbing a ride, has a link to the Beat Generation, with famous practitioners including Jack Kerouac,[6] Neal Cassady,[7] and Hunter S. Thompson, creator of gonzo journalism.[8] Thompson claimed the most miles clocked for hitching in Bermuda shorts and featured a hitchhiker in his masterpiece *Fear and Loathing in Las Vegas,* adapted by Terry Gilliam (*Brazil* [1985], *The Fisher King* [1991], *Twelve Monkeys* [1995]) as a drug/road movie.

If dolphins had thumbs, they would rule the world. For human beings, the thumb is essential for picking up items, gesturing—as in thumbs up or down—or for hitchhiking, which is illegal in some countries and encouraged in others. Sissy Hankshaw was born with extra-large thumbs and was teased and bullied as a child but came upon the revelation that she could become the greatest hitchhiker the world had ever known. It is considered dangerous for women to hitchhike, but our heroine is brave and adventurous.

Despite its obvious shortcomings, the film features some fine monologues. As a director who receives consistently measured and complex results from his actors, like Ingmar Bergman (*The Seventh Seal* [1957], *Persona* [1966], *Fanny and Alexander* [1982]), Sidney Lumet, and Elia Kazan, Van Sant nurtures each performance in every one of his films. His respect for the monologue may have its genesis in his voracious reading, filmgoing, and theatergoing. The monologue develops characters by allowing them to speak out, speechify, and reveal their inner psychological workings. According to the Victorian Web Web site, the monologue was invented by the Victorians, most notably Alfred, Lord Tennyson[9] and Dante Gabriel Rossetti.[10] The rules are:

1. The reader takes the part of the silent listener.
2. The speaker uses a case-making, argumentative tone.
3. We complete the dramatic scene from within, by means of inference and imagination.

Put in viewer or audience in 1 and the actor in 2 and the viewer or audience again in 3, and you have a good working definition of the movie monologue.

In *Even Cowgirls Get the Blues,* the point of the monologue is to express pride in loving women and in being a lesbian, which categorizes this film as gay, like Van Sant's masterworks *Mala Noche* (1985) and *My Own Private Idaho* (1991).

Even Cowgirls Get the Blues is also a road movie. The road movie is a genre in which the characters ride or drive in a vehicle and either know where they are going and gather life lessons on the way or don't know where they are headed and look to the road for answers and to explore their psyches—the destination can remain unknown. Here in *Even Cowgirls Get the Blues,* the road is for getting from here to there while searching for sexual and personal nirvana.

There is a countess character in *Even Cowgirls Get the Blues,* who is played by John Hurt (*The Elephant Man* [1980], *Love and Death on Long Island* [1997]) in drag. She is a major character who lends a very gay aspect to Van Sant's cinematic adaptation of *Even Cowgirls Get the Blues.* (There is also a countess in *The Discipline of D.E.* [1982].) The countess in *Even Cowgirls Get the Blues* has an Asian boy by her side. At a party, the countess serves "fruit punch with a hard on."

Keanu Reeves, sporting a Van Sant side part, makes his second appearance in a Van Sant film, here playing Julian Gitche, a young rich man with a loaded name symbolizing "got ya," a reference to a gay man grabbing another before a sexual encounter. The Tom Robbins novel is a work of metafiction—a style of fiction that is long in length and complex in character and plot. Metafiction has many story lines and lots of information on subjects, such as the banana section in Thomas Pynchon's masterpiece *Gravity's Rainbow* (Pynchon is one inspiration for the reclusive writer in *Finding Forrester* [2000]). *Even Cowgirls Get the Blues,* at 95 minutes (there are rumors the studio tinkered with the editing), is too slight to do justice to Robbins's 365-page book. Van Sant needed at least from two to two and a half hours to properly put this masterful book on the screen, but, because of budget constraints, that was not going to happen.

Buck Henry (*Catch 22* [1970]; *The Man Who Fell to Earth* [1976], in which he played a gay man; *Gloria* [1980]) plays Dr. Dreyfus, named either after the actor Richard Dreyfuss, who played a gay Hamlet in *The Goodbye Girl* (1977), or Albert Dreyfus, the French officer convicted of treason in 1894.

Buck Henry, a longtime screenwriter and actor, is known in the industry and in the public eye for his offbeat humor. He often portrays himself as a sexual deviant who will try anything. Henry is a highly skilled scriptwriter and performer who hides behind that persona. He adapted the Joyce Maynard[11] novel *To Die For* (1995) into a screenplay for the Van Sant film and also played Mr. H. Finlaysson in the picture. Maynard had a long relationship with J. D. Salinger, another one of the influences for the lead character in *Finding Forrester* (2000). Finlaysson may be a reference to the Laurel and Hardy[12] film stalwart James Finlayson, who always played the duped foil for the boys' shenanigans.

Dr. Dreyfus in *Even Cowgirls Get the Blues* is a strange and perverse member of the medical profession and gives the satiric comedy just the edge it needs. Henry and Van Sant share the same offbeat humor that Ken Shapiro nurtured in Van Sant.

The film is dedicated "For River." His sister, Rain, is in the film; possibly Van Sant would have cast River Phoenix in *Even Cowgirls Get the Blues* had he lived.

There is a landscape montage in *Even Cowgirls Get the Blues*, a staple in Van Sant films that roots the viewer in the terrain of the movie's location and of the story and how the characters relate to their environment.

Uma Thurman (*Henry and June* [1990], *Pulp Fiction* [1994], *Kill Bill* Volumes 1 and 2 [2003, 2004]) is effective as Sissy. Her movements on the road while hitchhiking are exciting and visceral, but she fails miserably with her cowgirl accent, sounding more like a drone than producing the proper lilt.

In a spoof on road kill, Sissy talks about perfect road food, American cheese sandwiches, which she packs for the ride—they come from the kitchen, not the asphalt.

Much of the clever dialogue from Robbins's novel falls flat in Van Sant's movie adaptation. It is as if Van Sant had temporarily lost his ability to direct actors. Much of the acting is wooden and stilted. With the exception of the monologues, lines sound like they were written and delivered as practice line readings.

William S. Burroughs makes his second appearance in a Van Sant film, this time playing himself. He is shown walking and babbling through the Gramercy Park area of New York City. His commentary may seem useless and excessive, but Van Sant mines the information to layer the narrative with metafictional detail.

The theme of family appears once again. The countess has a family of hangers-on. The lesbian cowgirls at the ranch are a family, as are the workers at the spa facility that is part of the Rubber Rose ranch complex.

The humor in this film comes from Robbins, who adapts Zen culture to his novels. This fits in with Van Sant's dry sense of deadpan humor, but it's not enough to help this film. The humor here is compressed into one-liners, whereas in the novel the development structures their impact.

The design of the film and the costumes embrace a gay sensibility.

One theme is the preservation of whooping cranes, which the cowgirls nurture. They make this movie a radical feminist tract by protesting the concept of women smelling good, which the spa promotes. At one point the cowgirls storm the spa with their pants down in protest, announcing that they haven't showered in weeks. There is whimsy in this segment for those who grew up seeing 1950s and 1960s movie magazine advertisements for "feminine odor" products.

Lorraine Bracco (*GoodFellas* [1990], *Medicine Man* [1992], *The Basketball Diaries* [1995]), as Delores Del Ruby, gives one of her least successful performances. Her thick New York accent goes against the cadence of the dialogue and the image of the cowgirl.

Fassbinder performer Udo Kier makes another appearance in a Van Sant film, this time as a TV commercial director shooting a spot at the ranch. There is a long tradition in film history of directors having a cache of actors or repertory company who appear repeatedly in their films. Frank Capra (*It Happened One Night* [1934], *Mr. Smith Goes to Washington* [1938], *Pocket Full of Miracles* [1961]) and John Ford did this often with character actors who appeared in many of their films. Capra and Ford would search or find for a role for them; if there wasn't one, they ordered the screenwriter to create one. Udo Kier is not perfect for his role in *Even Cowgirls Get the Blues,* but his flamboyant and ultra-extroverted personality provides the right ingredients for a juicy cameo role. Actress Roseanne Arnold (*She-Devil* [1989], *Blue in the Face* [1995], *Home on the Range* [2004]) is not a member of the Van Sant repertory company. She is as infamous for her work as an actress as she is for her bizarre personal behavior, but she doesn't fare as well as Madame Zoe, the gypsy fortuneteller; her celebrity personality unbalances the rest of the cast.

To capture the spirit of the times as presented in Robbins's novel, Van Sant gives roles to Merry Pranksters Ken Kesey and Ken Babbs. Kesey was the author of *One Flew over the Cuckoo's Nest* and was the subject of the Tom Wolfe nonfiction classic *The Electric Kool-Aid Acid Test,* which Van Sant would later make into a film. Ken Babbs was a friend of Kesey's and participated in the legendary bus and acid trips.

Even Cowgirls Get the Blues will go down in film history as a failed experiment. Maybe, one day, a new maverick director will take it on and succeed. This is not to imply that the porn director Alan Lickman and his star Elektra Luxx (*My Perfect 10s* [2002], *Best Deep Throat on the Planet* [2005]) will accomplish it with their production *Even Reverse Cowgirls Get the Blues,* which is not based on the Tom Robbins book, anyway.

TO DIE FOR (1995)

Gus Van Sant matured as a motion picture director on *To Die For.* He finally dropped the "Directed by Gus Van Jr." credit for "Directed by Gus Van Sant."

To Die For is one of Van Sant's most popular and successful films. It stars Nicole Kidman (*Dead Calm* [1989], *Eyes Wide Shut* [1999], *Australia* [2008]) as Suzanne Stone, a wannabe television journalist who entices three high school students, Jimmy Emmett (Joaquin Phoenix),[13] Russell Hines (Casey Affleck),[14] and Lydia Mertz (Alison Folland)[15] to murder her husband, Larry Maretto, portrayed by Matt Dillon, so that she can be free of any encumbrance that would get in the way of her goals.

Buck Henry adapted the book of the same name by Joyce Maynard (*At Home in the World: A Memoir* [1999], *The Usual Rules* [2004], *Labor Day* [2009]). Active and open filmmakers like Van Sant gather a lot of connections in their lives and career; Maynard even delivers a cameo as Suzanne's high-powered lawyer. The novel was based on a true incident of murder.

To Die For was shot in Canada, but the story takes place in Little Hope, New Hampshire. Production design was overseen by Jane Musky (*Blood Simple* [1984], *Glengarry Glen Ross* [1992], *Notorious* [2009]), who did an excellent job of re-creation.

Danny Elfman's distinctive music begins while the Columbia Pictures logo is shown. This practice has been used by other filmmakers. Here, it sets the mood and atmosphere through the signature musical style of Elfman, who can go from a playful macabre theme, as for a Tim Burton picture (*Beetle Juice* [1988], *Ed Wood* [1994], *Alice in Wonderland* [2010]), to a rural-home theme reminiscent of a classical Hollywood score or the music of Aaron Copland[16] in *To Die For,* played during a montage of the quiet snowy town. Pablo Ferro, known for his title design for *Dr. Strangelove* and for his collaborations with Van Sant and others, created a montage of tabloid headlines and photos of the murder case as it unfolded in the media. Most startling is a zoom into a picture of Suzanne until she is nothing but dots—a metaphor for the artificiality and control of news that consumer her and for the classic theme of fame and its potential for deadly consequences.

To Die For has a complex narrative structure that unfolds with ease thanks to Buck Henry's clever screenplay and Van Sant's direction and editing structure, on which he collaborated with Curtiss Clayton, who also cut *My Own Private Idaho* (1991).

Over the newspaper collage, which is filled with movement and texture, Suzanne delivers a voice-over. There is a video eye here also, which not only refers to the theme of the dangers of an omnipresent electronic video media but is another example of Van Sant in a self-referential[17] conceit, reminding us that we're watching a movie.

What empowers *To Die For* with such energy and imagination is that Van Sant allows viewers to feel they are watching a commercial film, even though he fills it with many tropes that reflect his personal vision.

Present time in the screen story of *To Die For* is after the murder. Suzanne addresses the camera—a technique often applied in films by Jean-Luc Godard. This view appears throughout the film, as does a scene of the parents of Suzanne and Larry discussing the murder case on a daytime talk show called *The Laura Show,* a reference to Sally Jesse Raphael (actress [1996] in the television series *Touched by an Angel* [1994–2003], celebrity contestant [2003] in the television series *Hollywood Squares* [1998–2004], celebrity participant [2005] in the reality television show *The Surreal Life* [2003–], and the host of her own self-named daytime talk show), who is mentioned during the film by Suzanne, as are other hosts, news anchors, and reporters whose name she drops to sound "professional," even though she is only the weather girl on a local cable station. All of the narrative lines in *To Die For* are utilized to tell the story in a nonlinear manner, a structure that is used in many of Van Sant's films.

Flashbacks[18] connect the wedding of Suzanne and Larry to his murder, signifying the cycle of life that has been interfered with by Stone's lust for power. She uses sex to seduce viewers and anyone who can advance her career, including her station manager and his techie—but intimacy is a tool. She has sex with Jimmy to get him to murder Larry. Suzanne Stone is one of the most manipulative female characters in recent film history, a throwback to the femmes fatales, the mysterious and attractive women who contributed to the demise of the protagonist in Hollywood's film noir pictures of the 1940s and 1950s.

Throughout the course of film history, non-Italian Americans have played Italian Americans in films. Jewish actor James Caan and Dutch/Irish/German/English actor Marlon Brando in *The Godfather* (1972) and Jewish actor Harvey Keitel in *Mean Streets* and *Taxi Driver* delivered masterful performances. A notable exception was the landmark HBO (Home Box Office) television series *The Sopranos* (1999–2007), which cast mostly Italian American actors, thereby enhancing the reality of the semicomedic classic. In *To Die For*, the methodology of casting without regard to ethnic type worked, but in the case of African Americans, Asians, Latinos, and Native Americans, it can fail miserably and often does. Among the most outrageous cases are the black-faced Caucasian actors in *The Birth of a Nation* (1915) and the Caucasian actress Katherine Ross (*The Graduate* [1967], *Butch Cassidy and the Sundance Kid* [1969], *The Stepford Wives* [1975]), playing, with too much dark tan makeup, a Native American in *Tell Them Willie Boy Is Here* (1969), directed by Abraham Polonsky (*Force of Evil* [1948], *Romance of a Horse Thief* [1971]), who as a politically astute individual should have known better.

In *To Die For*, Dan Hedaya (*The Hunger* [1983], *Blood Simple* [1984], *Nixon* [1995]), playing Joe Maretto; Illeana Douglas (*GoodFellas* [1990], *Household Saints* [1993], *Ghost World* [2001], granddaughter of actor Melvin Douglas), as Janice, his daughter; and Matt Dillon, as his son, are not of Italian American descent. Only Maria Tucci (*Me and My Brother* [1969], *Sweet Nothing* [1996], *Once More with Feeling* [2009]), who portrays Angela Maretto, the wife and mother, is an actual Italian, having been born in Italy. Through casting, acting, and context, all the players are authentic within the black comedy style. So Van Sant got the actors he wanted, without restricting himself to ethnic authenticity, and they give wonderful, nuanced performances. Van Sant understands that, given solid cinematic logic within the framework of a picture, the audience will believe almost anything within reason.

The nonlinear structure of the film keeps the audience curious and guessing, wanting to know more. At the end of *To Die For* we learn that Suzanne's monologue, presented as a talking head statement throughout the film, was actually self-recorded by her in her home with a video camera. This is revealed by a full shot from another angle that reveals that Suzanne is indeed in her home and has used her own video camera to create this "dialogue" with the audience. To achieve this Van Sant and his frequent collaborator, cinematographer Eric Alan Edwards, filmed Kidman against a stark white background most likely a role of paper similar to that used as a background by still photographers. In the actual shot Suzanne did not use such a background and behind her are windows, but this setting would not achieve the same effect. This cheat by the filmmakers is not noticed by the viewers because the surprise of the reveal controls their reaction and awareness of the relationship of the monologue to the actual location of this filming.[19]

Van Sant understood that the traditional linear storytelling mode was not been exhausted but was well worn during the 20th century. Films such as Stanley Kubrick's *The Killing* (1956) and Quentin Tarantino's *Pulp Fiction* (1994), influenced by the former, led progressive filmmakers like Van Sant to explore new storytelling possibilities.

To Die For sets up a time continuum that belies the original point of view. While the parents are on the daytime talk show, they at times address the camera in a manner that goes beyond the format of that genre. They are talking to the viewer, giving their inner feelings about Suzanne and Larry. Janice is a semiprofessional ice skater (there's an ice skating sequence in *Paranoid Park* [2007], as well), and she addresses the camera, talking about her hatred of Suzanne, which began the moment she laid eyes on her. Janice is one of the only characters who wasn't fooled and seduced by the media star-in-training with a vengeance. Janice is on the ice at a rink and skates up to the camera to start her talk. The recurring question that tantalizes the viewer is whether these scenes are shot by someone in news or by a documentarian making a movie about Suzanne or gathering material for a TV news story on her and the case. It can be either, because during the film Suzanne is shooting and editing a seemingly never-ending documentary on high school kids—which is who they really are. This leads right into the plot to kill her husband when Larry makes it clear that he feels Suzanne is not going to succeed in journalism and that he wants her to help him run his father's restaurant, instead.

There is also an interview or self-referential addressing-the-camera-segment with Lydia, the one girl in the teen "gang" trio. The film offers two perspectives on this character's story. She gives the homogenized version to the camera. Her relationship with Suzanne also plays out from other backstory[20] modalities. When the murder is accomplished, Suzanne wants nothing to do with the three teens. Earlier, Suzanne was using Lydia to get a gun and acted like her mentor. After the murder, she tells the confused and not very bright adolescent that she has "lesbian tendencies" and makes awful remarks about her being a slob and a drip.

One of the film's themes is intelligence. Suzanne is highly intelligent in a shallow, one-way-street manner. She tries to appear bright about world affairs and the careers of famous television journalists, especially Jane Pauley,[21] whom Suzanne feels she resembles in looks and personal style. The teens are dumb. James has a low IQ and is guided by lust for the teasing Suzanne. Russell is a Cro Magnon with only silly, dirty ideas on his mind. The Marettos are middle-class Americans. Mr. Maretto has a controlled bad temper but loses it when he sees Suzanne on TV after the murder; he smashes the large screen in the restaurant "to death" with a baseball bat, with Suzanne's voice, coming out of the television speaker, still taunting him. The Stones are of a higher class, bright but aghast at the situation they find themselves in, coping with the Marettos and having their daughter accused of murder. Larry Maretto is a poor dumb sap—not very bright but with a good heart. He has *Leave It to Beaver*[22] values and just wants to live a "normal" life away from media frenzy.

To Die For is also concerned with the media's effect on society. The news is no longer controlled by Edward R. Murrow[23] and Walter Cronkite.[24] The tube is filled with lies, deceptions, and facades. The pretty young things have taken over television, and money and fame rule the waves. Suzanne gets her Warholian 15 minutes of fame thanks to her good looks. Her attitude is that no one will ever say no to her, but eventually her luck runs out.

The black comedy genre[25] is perfect for this story. The true story is tragic, but the comic eye sees the absurdity in the situation presented in the book and in the resulting film.

Van Sant gets away with stereotyping. There is talk about the Marettos being "connected," which turns out to be true when Joe Maretto hires a hit man to kill Suzanne after Larry's murder. In an inspired piece of cameo casting, the hit man talks in Italian on the phone to Maretto to confirm that the hit has been accomplished. This bit is played by Canadian filmmaker David Cronenberg (*Scanners* [1981], *Crash* [1996], *A History of Violence* [2005]). Cronenberg, like Van Sant, has a distinctive and personal vision. Both men embrace the major theme of sexuality, but Cronenberg has a cold eye, while Van Sant's is hot. Cronenberg is especially interested in the mysteries of the human body. Van Sant pursues this theme in *Mala Noche* (1985), with probing shots of the characters' naked bodies. In *Drugstore Cowboy* (1989), Van Sant examines the effect of heroin on the human body. In *My Own Private Idaho* (1991), (simulated) sex acts are photographed. In *Even Cowgirls Get the Blues* (1993), consider Sissy's enormous thumbs; in *Psycho,* there are the violent effects of a knife repeatedly stabbing a female body. Van Sant is interested also in wholesale slaughter in *Elephant* (2003), the effect of distance and lack of food and water on the walkers in *Gerry* (2002), and the spirit and soul leaving the body upon death in *Gus Van Sant's Last Days* (2005).

Van Sant performs not an on-screen cameo in *To Die For* but a vocal one. During an interview with Janice, he can be heard asking questions that lead the viewer to believe that this is footage for a documentary or the local or nightly news. The director is clever in putting this in one spot, while most of the talking heads appear to be offering self-referential musings into the camera, as in *Citizen Kane* (1941), with a narrative of multiple viewpoints on the same story. This trope was also applied by Todd Haynes, director of *Poison* (1991), *Safe* (1995), and *Far from Heaven* (2002). Haynes is a friend and admirer of Gus Van Sant and a fellow openly gay resident of Portland, Oregon, whose *Velvet Goldmine* (1998) is a multiple-point-of-view narrative of the life of a glitter/glam rock music star as a *Citizen Kane*-like reporter investigates his life through the people who knew him.

Movies often mirror other movies. In Oliver Stone's *The Doors* (1991), Matt's brother Kevin Dillon (*Platoon* [1986], *A Midnight Clear* [1992], *Poseidon* [2006]), plays Doors drummer John Densmore. In *To Die For* (1995), Larry Maretto plays drums in a garage band that performs at the family restaurant. The point of this scene is to demonstrate that many young women are infatuated with him, including Suzanne. A subtle gay innuendo comes when the camera moves to one young man jumping up and down with lustful glee as he watches Larry pound the drums. There is a one shot cameo of Rain Phoenix,[26] sister of Joaquin and River, who had earlier played Bonanza Jellybean in *Even Cowgirls Get the Blues* (1993).

Like Brian De Palma's *Carlito's Way* (1993) and John Boorman's[27] *The General* (1998), which both reveal the death of the main characters in the opening scenes, Van Sant's *To Die For* discloses that Larry will be murdered by showing an interview with Jimmy in prison in which he talks about his motive for killing Maretto. He claims that he believed Suzanne's lies about spousal abuse and that these convinced him to carry out the dirty deed.

Suzanne is portrayed as a child prodigy; home video images show her enjoying her time in front of the camera. Her parents also tell stories about the precious little girl who talked about committing her life to an electronic media career.

The story structure can be attributed to Joyce Maynard, who restructured her novel in a *Citizen Kane/Velvet Goldmine*[28] style into the film's narrative as described. Maynard chose to create a separate chapter for each voice, with the name of each character as the title of a given chapter. In many respects, the novel resembles the form of the nonfiction oral history made famous by George Plimpton (who plays the part of a psychiatrist in *Good Will Hunting* [1997]) and by Jean Stein in *Edie: An American Biography* (1982), about Edie Sedgwick, who was a motion picture superstar in the ensemble company of Van Sant's idol, Andy Warhol. As is usually the case, the book contains more background details than the film adaptation. In the book, Larry begins as a hippie rock drummer with long hair. He cuts his hair and grows up when he courts Suzanne and gets married. The adaptation, like all good ones, is faithful to the novel and close to the narrative and character composition. Van Sant's vision of the film and the personal themes and concerns connect with the book. Van Sant, except in *Even Cowgirls Get the Blues* (1993), has so far been highly successful in finding books that speak to his sensibility, and his artistic goals maintain a practical and creative balance between being loyal to the literary source and respecting to his own directorial vision.

Van Sant employs the infrequently applied and undervalued method of the double flashback[29] (using shots either identical or similar to ones previous used). *Paranoid Park* (2007) raises this technique to a sublime art. During *To Die For*, moments like Suzanne and Larry's wedding are recurring, as is his funeral.

A later funeral sequence goes beyond the obvious narrative purpose to reveal the inner conceit of the devious and transparent Suzanne. To present the public impression that she is emotionally distraught over the loss of her husband, she takes out a boom box and plays "All by Myself" by rock crooner Eric Carmen.[30]

The double flashback was effectively utilized in Stanley Kubrick's second feature, *Killer's Kiss* (1955), and a triple flashback is discernable during the trial scene in *JFK* (1991), by Oliver Stone (who would later try to hire Van Sant for a film about Harvey Milk).

Van Sant likes to go to slow-motion photography at times in his movies. Here a revisiting of the wedding scene (not inspired by *The Godfather* [1972]) is photographed in slow motion.

Slow-motion photography was invented by an Austrian, August Musger (1868–1929), a priest and physicist who in 1907 patented an invention that utilized a mirrored drum as a synching device. In the earlier days of filmmaking, an established frame rate was in the neighborhood of 60 frames per second for slow-motion shots. This became clichéd and is best exemplified by a back-in-the day television commercial for Clairol hair coloring. In it a boy- and a girl-next-door type run in a field with their hair bouncing. This was aesthetically exploded by Arthur Penn (*The Left Handed Gun* [1958], *Little Big Man* [1970], *Dead of Winter* [1987]) in *Bonnie and Clyde* (1967) during the slow-motion murder of the infamous duo in which Bonnie's blond hair is bouncing but she is also being riddled with bullets; the cutting is rhythmic, as opposed to the original presentation of letting slow motion play out until the sophisticated viewer is "taken out" of the movie.

In *The Wild Bunch* (1969), various frame rates of slow motion are intercut during scenes of intense violence. Here, in *To Die For*, Van Sant applies his sensibilities as a fine artist, painter, and admirer of experimental film to manipulate the image in slow motion to suit the story and situation. Throughout his career, he uses slow motion as a complex piece of cinematic grammar.

Kidman's costumes are designed to show maximum character development. Created by Van Sant's longtime costume designer Beatrix Aruna Pasztor, the wardrobe reflects the professional and personal prism of Suzanne Stone. She has a taste for polka dots, brightly colored business suits that suit her professional image, and a skin-tight tiger print number that reveals the "animal" in her when she wants to be a seductress.

Janice, Larry's sister, also is an aspiring professional with some talent. One scene integrated with the murder plot reveals Janice trying out for the Ice Follies—her equivalent of Suzanne auditioning for an up-market city 6:00 P.M.

co-anchor spot. The last shot of *To Die For* shows Janice triumphantly skating on a pond in a winter setting after her nemesis, Suzanne, has been buried by the results of seeking family revenge. Janice's skating is average, but she works the ice as if she were Dorothy Hamill. Her glee in skating for the viewer as the end credits roll shows Van Sant's charm and his gentle sardonic side as a director.

Cold is a metaphor in *To Die For*. The weather is cold, snow is on the ground, and Suzanne has ice water in her veins. Her emotional temperature is set on frigid when it comes to the feelings of others. She is calculating and focused only on her career in television. She becomes a cartoon of what a journalist, person, and wife should be. She would fit in with *The Stepford Wives* (1975)[31] and the *Desperate Housewives*[32] (2004–), among other tabloid fictional television characters. Suzanne is selectively influenced by what she sees on TV and communicates Van Sant's and Buck Henry's dim view of the influence of the media. This is McLuhanism[33] on steroids.

Another self-referential moment in *To Die For* occurs when Suzanne says "Cut" after she's finished being videoed. The line works in two ways: it speaks to her obsession with being on TV, and it refers to the director Van Sant, calling cut at the end of each take during filming.

The dénouement comes when Larry wants the couple to have children. Suzanne becomes angry, dropping her façade, and demeans motherhood by talking about having a fat stomach while interviewing someone on television. Suzanne tells us that you are nobody until you've been on TV—that the medium makes you into "something." Obsession is another major theme in *To Die For,* one that Van Sant shares with a number of film directors, including Abel Ferrara, Nagisa Oshima, Stanley Kubrick, and Alfred Hitchcock.

Suzanne is willing to do almost anything to be famous on TV, but only on her own tricky and mercurial terms. During her honeymoon, she walks into a broadcasting convention and meets the keynote speaker, devilishly played by George Segal (*Who's Afraid of Virginia Woolf?* [1966], *Born to Win* [1971], *The Mirror Has Two Faces* [1996]). This lech is very interested in the sexy Suzanne. He invites her to his table and tells a story about a woman who pretended she was someone else and wrote a letter stating that a particular job applicant gave good oral sex, implying that you have to go the casting couch route to succeed in the television business.

When he wants to take her up to his room, she wiggles out of it. Later, when Suzanne goes for a job interview, she gets the position and is shown throwing out her own version of the letter, revealing how complicated and manipulative she really is. One could see Suzanne as a borderline psychotic, but Kidman's light-as-air approach and her ability to turn on the dramatic heat when necessary keeps the film on its black comedy track. Everything is arranged by Suzanne to be a piece of her success puzzle. She knows that the convention will be at a particular hotel on a specific date, so that's where she books her honeymoon. When Larry goes fishing, Suzanne goes hunting for big fish and is unable to come to grips with the fact that she is in over her head and deluded about the real TV world.

Suzanne is interested in all the fairytale aspects of electronic journalism. When she and Larry get a dog, Suzanne names him Walter, after Walter Cronkite.

When Suzanne goes to the local high school to recruit teens for her documentary on their real lives, there are several shots that depict the three culprits walking down the hall. The shots show hallways eerily similar to those in *Elephant* (2003). It is as if Van Sant took the cinematography to high school hallways in *To Die For* and later, while creating *Elephant,* applied those images as part of the content of the movie. As testimony to Van Sant's commitment to youth culture, he remains in touch with his feelings about high school. This and the scene where Suzanne talks to the class about her idea are time-machine accurate.

Suzanne favors pink[34] for her lipstick and eye shadow shade and some of her outfits. Pink is a girly color that suits her character; she is a woman who uses her wiles to get what she wants. It is also the color associated with the gay liberation movement. Red, signifying bleeding or death, is represented in Suzanne's fingernail color.

According to speculative-fiction writer Harlan Ellison, Tom Snyder, the host of the late, late television program the *Tomorrow* show (1973–1982), received a letter from a viewer stating that his show had been unable to air the previous night because she was not home to watch it, implying that if she didn't watch, there was no show. Buck Henry and Van Sant take advantage of the audience's fantasies concerning television. In *To Die For,* Jimmy has quickly become infatuated with Suzanne. While at home watching her do the weather on television, he imagines she is coming on to him sexually and begins to masturbate

Van Sant returns to D. W. Griffith's beloved iris shot when the camera is on Suzanne as she reacts to Larry telling her she won't get any network offers.

An example of Suzanne using her sexuality appears in a montage in which she is rapidly trying on a series of bras and panties in front of Lydia. Stone knows the girl is vulnerable and would like to be like her, rather than in her frumpy and disheveled adolescent state. Suzanne can turn her sexual powers on and off, using them as a tool for control over others.

Suzanne also seduces the teenage trio by putting them on tape so often. In a scene where she urges them to get up and dance, Stone dances with her video camera, titillating Jimmy, who has also bought into the concept that TV makes an individual "someone."

Movies are made up of moments. Although there is an overall arc of a narrative, key images capture the viewer's attention. Most films have a seminal shot; one of the most famous is the opening image of Robert De Niro as Jake La Motta in the ring alone, moving, bobbing, and throwing punches in the air in *Raging Bull* (1980). We associate this moment with the entire film because it sums up his character as a man like Don Quixote, battling windmills.

In *To Die For*, the signature image is of Suzanne dancing at night in front of a car while "Sweet Home Alabama" by Lynyrd Skynyrd plays on the radio. Jimmy stares at her in sexual heat. The automobile headlights function as stage illumination, another allusion to being on television. Suzanne unabashedly plays to the helpless boy, swishing her dress and even flashing her panties. This is Suzanne the party girl, Suzanne the sexual terrorist.

Other memorable scenes of this nature include Harrison Ford and Kelly McGillis[35] in *Witness* (1985) dancing to "Don't Know Much about History," performed by Sam Cooke, and Robert De Niro's quirky bravado character dance to "Mickey's Monkey," by the Miracles, in *Mean Streets* (1973). In these scenes, too, the source music plays on a radio and there is a car with the headlights on. The car, a potent American iconic symbol, becomes the manifestation of the means of expression.

Suzanne and Jimmy have sex in cheap motels as Lydia hangs around outside. One is reminded of the Bates motel, recreated in Van Sant's *Psycho* (1998), and transient lodging as an American icon for the legitimate traveler and for those looking to use the rented space for illicit sexual encounters.

The male gaze or, in the case of a gay filmmaker, a homosexual gaze is also applied to images of Jimmy. During one of the sex scenes, the camera lovingly captures the boy's six-pack abdominal muscles. Suzanne uses the promise of fellatio to a-begging-for it Jimmy to get her way with the murder plan. Finally, when he agrees to what she asks, Suzanne moves down to do the deed. The framing now is reminiscent of Warhol's *Blow Job* (1963). Flashes of River Phoenix as Mike the male hustler in *My Own Private Idaho* (1991) receiving fellatio from a male client pass though the consciousness of the informed viewer. Jimmy's face is in ecstasy, like Deveren Bookwalter[36] (*The Omega Man* [1971], *The Enforcer* [1976], *Manholed* [1978]) in the Warhol opus.

The staircase plays a significant role in American film. There's the grand staircase of *Gone with the Wind* (1939), signifying elegance and sexuality. There's the mystery of steps in *Spellbound* (1945), and there are comic approaches that exploit the staircase for sight gags. In television, the stairway in the living room off the front door implies a second story in a middle-class home, and that's how it is rendered in *To Die For*. Nicole Kidman's participation in the film reminds the movie-literate viewer of *Risky Business* (1983), a black comedy starring Kidman's former husband, Tom Cruise. Van Sant returns to the staircase so often in *To Die For* that one can't help make the connection.

In a sequence as brilliant as the baptism/mob slaughter montage in *The Godfather* (1972), the murder scene in *To Die For* is deftly intercut with Suzanne's weather broadcast. When she says "Good night, honey" to Larry over the air, the intercutting emphasizes the connection between reality and media, as if she were actually saying goodbye to her husband at the moment of his death.

Van Sant employs a top shot to show Jimmy and Suzanne on the floor having sex. This distancing effect reminds the viewer that he or she is watching a movie, and it also allows a unique opportunity for us to see from above and out of the range of other shots taken at ground level that pull the audience into the story and characters.

As Larry dies, one of his eyes turns color. The image reminds one of a television picture tube that has been extracted from the set and put on a table while an image still emanates until it is abruptly turned off. The curve of the tube's surface can be compared to a human eye and the color comes on or off at the will of the watcher. The principal difference between Maynard's book and the film is this attention to television. It seems that Van Sant, a man obsessed with the cinema and video, made it his raison d'être.

At the moment of Larry's passing, one of the mélange of shots shows Suzanne in the studio finishing her broadcast. The lights go out on her as Larry's "lights" go out and he lies dead in his living room.

The cable station Suzanne works for has the traditional back-in-the-day sign-off, showing a patriotic image of the American flag while "The Star-Spangled Banner" plays over it. This is a subliminal message to the viewer, whose perception of Suzanne that TV is reality at the station literally goes off the air. Is she still special now or more mysterious? There was a time when television broadcasting had viewing hours. As television viewing became more popular the networks and later the cable stations made the decision to broadcast around the clock with no down time. Current 24-hour programming has its value, but it is responsible for increasing the psychological power of the medium over the viewer.

Like many Gus Van Sant movies, *To Die For* is a multigenre film. Besides being a black comedy, it also is a film noir. Suzanne Stone falls easily into the femme fatale prototype, and Larry is the doomed hapless male who is overcome by the woman. When Larry gets in her way, she eliminates him as the noir tradition dictates. This is supported visually with, at times, classic noir lighting, which includes striking contrasts between black and white, stripes of light, and low-angle lighting instruments placed to make the evil more evil.

Van Sant returns to a montage of the quiet and tranquil-looking town for dramatic distinction. In American suburbia, it appears as if all is normal on the outside, with pretty houses and manicured lawns. In the case of *To Die For*, pure white snow dots the homes and streets. Behind these façades lies the underbelly of America. As often happens in film noir, things eventually go bad for the femme fatale. Suzanne drives her blood-red car to the local television station to retrieve her teen documentary tapes, which contain evidence that she put the youngsters up to the murder, only to learn that the police have been there before her.

Russell, the third member of the teenage trio, is a homophobe. He is played by Casey Affleck (brother of Ben who also appears in *Ocean's Twelve* [2004], *The Assassination of Jesse James by the Coward Robert Ford* [2007], and *Gone Baby Gone* [2007], directed by his brother) and is a fully-realized character; a piece of him represents a segment of America that fosters a violent hatred for gays. Russell spews obscenities about AIDS and vile phrases like "Hershey Highway."

When Jimmy is arrested for Larry's murder, there is a poster of John Travolta as Tony Manero in *Saturday Night Fever* (1977) in his room. Although Jimmy is a heavy-metal kid sporting a mullet (until it is cut short for him when he is jailed), the macho disco king, with all his swagger and cool, would be an idol to pathetic Jimmy Emmett.

As mentioned, a gay reference occurs when, after the murder, Suzanne is angry with Lydia because she refuses to accept that their "friendship" is over. She tells the clueless girl she has lesbian tendencies. This is said to viciously attack the girl verbally. Lydia is underdeveloped emotionally, like the two boys, and has not developed her sexuality. She is a fringe person in the world of high school and wants to be accepted. Lydia sees Suzanne's earlier attention as a sign of friendship and perceives Suzanne as a role model.

What does a gay person look like? Van Sant has achieved a high level of realism in his portrayal of characters, both gay and straight. Here he's indicating that society jumps to stereotypical conclusions in terms of sexual orientation. His masterpiece in this realm is *Milk* (2008), which is peopled with a wide range of gay characters; the message is that people are people, some are outgoing and up-front about whom they are, and others are not. It is the emotional life of the character that interests Van Sant.

This is a script that Alfred Hitchcock could have directed, but, of course, with a completely different subtext. The master of suspense had an indelible impact on American and international filmmakers. It is possible Van Sant and Buck Henry had Hitchcock's sardonic approach and interest in the criminal persona in mind.

Suzanne is swamped by reporters and paparazzi (one reporter is played by Joyce Maynard) as she leaves the courtroom during her murder trial. This is another aspect of the fame she seeks. Suzanne talks to us in narration about how responsible she was in speaking to fellow journalists about the case, which gave her the opportunity to elaborate on her "story" to convince "her" public of her innocence.

At the end of *To Die For*, the screen is transformed into countless small boxes containing Suzanne's image. This audacious application of style had been achieved earlier by Norman Jewison (*In the Heat of the Night* [1967], *Jesus Christ Superstar* [1973], *Moonstruck* [1987]) and his editor, Hal Ashby, in *The Thomas Crown Affair* (1968). In *To Die For*, the multiple images are an homage to the Jewison film, experimental films, and the theme of becoming famous on TV. Suzanne's life has exploded; she is internationally famous, but not in the way she planned.

Although *To Die For* is set in Little Hope, New Hampshire, it was actually shot in Ontario, Canada, a popular industry practice to save money. In many films, this corporate decision fails miserably in terms of establishing a sense of place. Here, in *To Die For*, the viewer never suspects the switch.

GOOD WILL HUNTING (1997)

Good Will Hunting is the film that placed Gus Van Sant on the national and international cinema maps. Based on an original screenplay by Matt Damon (*Mystic Pizza* [1988], *All the Pretty Horses* [2000], *The Bourne Ultimatum* [2007]), and Ben Affleck (*Dazed and Confused* [1993], *Pearl Harbor* [2001], *Gone Baby Gone* [2007]), it is the story of a South Boston prole, a "Southie" who is a math genius with behavioral problems who conquers all to be with the woman he loves. Van Sant would revisit a revised version of this theme later in *Finding Forrester* (2000) (in which Matt Damon has a cameo).

The screenplay credit for Matt Damon and Ben Affleck lands on a shot where the two are walking. They are shown from the waist up, and the viewer can admire their handsome male beauty. This is not a gay film like *Mala Noche* (1985), *My Own Private Idaho* (1991), or *Milk* (2008), but it is a fine example of the homosexual gaze.

On the Angelfire Web site, Derek P. Rucasi dissects this phenomenon:

> Although a stylistic convention of the classic Hollywood film format, the male gaze is apparent in non-Hollywood films as well as in blockbusters. More analytically, the homosexualized male gaze follows conventions rooted within Hollywood origins. This brings into question the difference between the heterosexual male gaze upon a female and the homosexual gaze upon a male. It would only be reasonable to assume that homosexual filmmakers capture the mise-en-scene differently than heterosexual male filmmakers. And even within the classic Hollywood format of filmmaking conventions, a homoerotic gaze can be focused from male to male in a heterosexual context.

Until women were empowered to direct films, the world of cinema was to a large degree the domain of the heterosexual white male. There were exceptions, such as directors George Cukor (*Little Women* [1933], *Camille* [1936], *Travels with My Aunt* [1972]), Edmund Goulding (*Grand Hotel* [1932], *The Dawn Patrol* [1938], *Of Human Bondage* [1946], *Nightmare Alley* [1947]), Mitchell Leisen (*Death Takes a Holiday* [1934], *Hold Back the Dawn* [1941], *Bedeviled* [1955]), Irving Rapper (*Now, Voyager* [1942], *The Glass Menagerie* [1950], *The Miracle* [1959]), Arthur Lubin (*Buck Privates* [1941], *Phantom of the Opera* [1943], *Francis in the Navy* [1955]), and James Whale (*Frankenstein* [1931], *Bride of Frankenstein* [1935], *The Man in the Iron Mask* [1939]).

Although there is no gay content in *Good Will Hunting*, the male bonding between the young male characters can be viewed as a homosexual theme. There is the issue of the homosexual gaze and the film's openly gay director. Matt Damon, as the lead, is on-screen through much of the film. In several scenes, he has his shirt off. The principle of the homosexual gaze is at work. Van Sant is looking at two attractive men and his sole objective is to cinematically portray them as characters in a movie story. This principle of the homosexual gaze does not suggest that Van Sant is necessarily attracted to the young men on-screen or off. It is just the way a gay man would look at an attractive man, the same the way a heterosexual looks at an attractive woman. Watching *Good Will Hunting*, the viewer is following the intricate story and relationships, but there is a subtext hidden below the surface of this successful crowd-pleasing film. It is a fact that it was directed by a gay, not straight, man. Van Sant was perfect for this assignment because of his distinctive cinematic skills, his uncanny ability to direct actors, and his fascination with youth and youth culture. Gus Van Sant is also a man who remains forever young, sporting the same hairstyle for decades, loving contemporary music, and retaining a fascination with youth's society. All this combines to make a strong directorial package for Gus Van Sant's first box office success. *Good Will Hunting* was budgeted at around $10 million in 1997. It made $273,000 during its opening weekend in the United States and to date has grossed $226 million worldwide.

The film's look, provided by production designer Melissa Stewart (who worked in various art department jobs on Van Sant's *Drugstore Cowboy* [1989], *My Own Private Idaho* [1991], *Even Cowgirls Get the Blues* [1993], and *To Die For* [1995]) and cinematographer Jean-Yves Escoffier (*Gummo* [1997], *Rounders* [1998], *Cradle Will Rock* [1999]), is rich with saturated colors and an environmental design sense perfect for the story and characters. Like all great directors, Van Sant has a vast knowledge and command of the crafts and understands that a film is written not only by the screenwriter but by the cinematographer, the production designer, and the sound, music, and myriad other professionals who work on making any film. For Van Sant, who edited his early student work and his first feature, as well as the films in his experimental period, it is editing that is the final rewrite of a film. (No one knows who made this statement first, but the concept is most often contributed to Carol Littleton [*Body Heat* (1981), *The Big Chill* (1983), *Beloved* (1998)]). "The most important element to me is the script," Littleton told David Chell for his book *Moviemakers at Work*, "because editing is essentially rewriting. It's the final rewrite."

This multilayered film, with its many characters, themes, and subplots, is especially well edited. Curtiss Clayton, who had co-edited *Drugstore Cowboy* (1989) with Mary Bauer, edited *My Own Private Idaho* (1991), co-edited *Even Cowgirls Get the Blues* (1993) with Van Sant, and edited *To Die For* (1995), was not available to edit *Good Will Hunting*, so the director turned to master editor Pietro Scalia, who has worked with Oliver Stone, Bernardo Bertolucci, and Ridley Scott, among others. "I met Gus in Toronto about three weeks before they started shooting," Scalia explains. "I admired Gus and was looking forward to meeting him. He responded to the fact that I had worked with Bertolucci. He was a big admirer of Bernardo's work. He had watched *La Luna* (1979) and *The Conformist* (1970) over and over again. He asked me if I wanted to go see a movie with him, and Matt, and Ben. We went to see *Inventing the Abbotts* (1997). It was a great evening and I returned to L.A. and a day or so after I was hired."[37] Van Sant who had edited his own films and collaborated on one with Curtiss Clayton did not do any hands-on editing for *Good Will Hunting*.

"He just loves the process," Scalia continues. "He knows it's a form of either writing or painting for him. For me, it was one of the most pleasurable editing experiences I ever had."

The film was edited in Van Sant's home, as Scalia details:

The assistants were in the living room and my cutting room was in the library, in the study next to the kitchen. It was very relaxed. He would have coffee and sit with me. He would bring his guitar and play some music. Gus is very quiet. He would sit there but he knew exactly what I was doing so it was easy to get his reaction on something—he was always there. He's a very economical guy—he knows when he has his material. It wasn't excessive. Many set-ups but not many takes of the various set-ups—there was a lot of variation and he also let the actors do a lot of improvisations, changing things as they were happening. He has a very fluid style. There was a lot of spontaneity from the performer and from the camera. There was a real elegance in Jean Yves' camera movements and composition, and the colors. I loved the material I was getting.[38]

"Matt and Ben knew the characters so well," Scalia continues:

They would change a few things here and there, improvise—change the dialogue. There was a lot of color and variation in the takes. When I got the material from Robin Williams[39] [who plays a therapist engaged to "cure" Will so he can move on to live his life as a math genius] I noticed that he would do a lot of takes. Gus did 3, 4 takes of the same set-up but with Robin Williams he would do 5, 6, 7, even up to 9, 10 takes. He usually had a good performance in the very early takes. I called Gus and said, "Why are you doing so many takes?" He said, "It's because Robin asked me to do another one." "But," I said, "you usually have it in take two." He said, "Yes, I know." I said, "So I will concentrate on the early takes. I like them better—they're more raw, more real." He said, "Yes, you're right, I like those as well." As an actor, Robin, being a perfectionist, he was trying to improve and know the material better, but what was good about the early takes was an uncertainty—acting by the seat of your pants, improvisational material which is very real and that was the key to the performance. As the takes would progress it would become, not as natural, just as perfect, but it wouldn't have the same quality. When we screened the cut for Robin in San Francisco he commented, "You guys did a great job; I just remember there were some other takes. No, no, no, you guys did the right thing—you picked the right choices, it's great."[40]

The intercutting on *Good Will Hunting* is especially intricate. "Gus and I spent a lot of time specifically in the first act." Scalia explains:

> We knew we had to establish not only the story and the characters and get the ball rolling, but the key to how the events of the other scenes following that would be determined by the first act. In one of the versions of the script the Robin Williams character was introduced early on. We knew in our gut instincts in terms of storytelling that that was not right. He's a star but in terms of story he should come in when the story requires him to come in (around 35 minutes into the film). At one point we see him in his room drinking; it doesn't make sense to introduce a character if he can't relate to anything. We had to concentrate on Matt and Ben's friendship and the boys and how they move around. Another key element was Skylar's (Minnie Driver)[41] character [a woman whom Will falls in love with and with whom he wants to spend his life]. The way she was structured in the script she would disappear half-way through the middle act. We also had to space her out, to understand the importance of her character and the truth that she would tell him, and also the other side—the balance on Robin's character, the other truth that he would balance so it was about forming bonds, forming relationships and trust. I shifted also her storyline towards the end a little bit as you progress dramatically, so when he had to make a choice about seeing the girl or not it becomes really intense. Once you set the groundwork it's easy to jump back and forth to where you want to be and decide how long you want to play a scene. When Ben saw the film he was not happy about the structure simply because he saw that his scenes were cut shorter and somewhat restructured because the dramatic weight was slightly shifted toward both the girl and the professor. The intercutting in between scenes was to keep everyone in the air—keep them bubbling along. We do have an emotional progression with Matt.[42]

Van Sant made excellent use of reaction shots. Often, a shot of a character reacting can say more than a shot of the actor speaking. As Michael Kahn[43] explains in *Selected Takes: Film Editors on Editing,* "There are cause and effect relationships and one cut should be as a natural consequence of another that leads to another. They're invisible cuts. One cut calls for another. If reactions aren't true, it hurts the reality of the scene. An audience senses when something is not true."[44]

Two characters in particular were used to comment on the action and the other characters in a scene, as Scalia reveals:

> The professor's assistant Tom played by John Mighton, in his only fictional film screen performance to date; a real mathematician and founder of Junior Undiscovered Math Prodigies, he was also technical advisor on the film. Van

Sant dressed him in black and called him "the shadow"; he brings something even if it's a tiny piece of drama in terms of being jealous about being defensive. These are good human touches—it's good story telling. If you have a friend Billy McBride played by Cole Hauser sitting around the table—it's nice to cut into it in making him part of the scene. When Matt is introducing Skylar to his friends he takes them to the bar and he's telling the joke about a police officer and this cruiser and you have Casey always interrupting Ben. There's a lot of takes and a lot of improvisation, so I had to weave it together, shorten the joke a little bit which went on too long. Casey interrupts him. And Billy McBride, "Shut up let him speak"—he's reacting to Will, listening, Skylar listening. Then when the scene switches to Skylar telling her joke you see reactions on Will. "How are his friends going to react?" "Is she going to pull this joke off?" The camera is continuously moving around. I call it "cutting behind the scenes" it seems like it's natural but there's a lot of sound work, a lot of dialogue work done. It's cheated behind their back. The camera moves around it and I'm behind it literally. To keep the rhythm of the language of how people normally talk, how they overlap is to weave together the performances to make it sound natural but you don't see that, you just see a conversation. It's a lot of takes and a lot of intricate, detailed sound work. Sometimes even when they overlap you make very surgical cuts on the end of words or an answer. You add the ending of one sentence to the next so you can come around and have that actor finish on screen with that line even though half of that line was off-screen behind an actor's back over somebody else's reaction. So cutting behind in order to keep that feeling of participating can be part of it. Everybody is just as important.

The way Gus shoots there's a lot of thought behind the shooting. "We're going to do this, a master. . . ." There's a lot of design, camera movements—an overall design of how he pictured the scene.[45]

Good Will Hunting was released by Miramax. During that time, Harvey Weinstein, who owned the company with his brother, Bob, was notorious for taking a director's cut after the director left and radically recutting the picture. As Scalia recalls, "No he did not. When we first screened it in New York for Miramax Harvey Weinstein loved it. He said, 'We've got to preview this right away!' So we set up a preview screening in New Jersey and it got a huge response. Harvey said, 'These numbers are better than *Pulp Fiction* (1994), better than *The Crying Game* (1992)—this is great stuff!' He left us alone. He didn't recut it. Gus went back and did some more fine-tuning and trimming, but Harvey Weinstein did not get involved at all."

The lilting and magical score by Danny Elfman, who had written the music for *To Die For* (1995) and went on to work with Van Sant on his postmodern *Psycho* (1998) and *Milk* (2008), is another example of Van Sant's affinity for music. As Pietro Scalia observed:

Besides being a musician, Gus has a musical sense. You must see the musicality in the images and once you have that you create rhythm, music will make it so much sweeter and better. It's the cutting *to* a specific piece of music. It's cutting the film then looking for the right pieces of music. I had some of Danny Elfman's previous music in my library that I laid on the temp track but Gus also brought in Elliot Smith, the songwriter from Portland. Gus gave me a CD with his music. I loved his album and there were many songs that were also key to getting a feel to the soundtrack. We tried the Beach Boys, all kinds of music; Gus loves music and as we would edit he would play music for me. We would try it on but Elliot Smith's music was an integral part. Then he wrote original songs for us and that's why the soundtrack feels organic and part of the movie.[46]

The final running length of *Good Will Hunting* is 126 minutes. That's not excessively long, but many scenes were deleted during the editing process. "Sometimes a piece just doesn't fit in anymore," Scalia explains. All the scenes in the bars were quite long. At one point, a whole different sequence was shot for the opening that showed the Saint Patrick's Day Parade in Boston.

The "deleted scenes" feature on the DVD shows many scenes that were cut out or shortened. The Saint Patrick's Day original opening was done on the fly. The boys wore hats because the haircuts hadn't been decided yet; they'd just arrived on location. They weren't in their characters yet, as well.

"Bar Cat Joke" was to follow the parade opening and show the local color in a bar. It was the last scene removed from the film. The joke took too long to tell, and it did not advance the plot.

"Will Does Math" showed Will doing math, first on paper and then on the wall of his apartment. Damon had to learn and memorize complex math formulas by rote—he didn't understand them but could execute them.

"Sean on Roof at Night" was used to get the Williams character in the film early, as was previously stated. The decision to wait almost 35 minutes was gutsy and right for the complex story.

"Will and Lambeau Do Math" was Tom the assistant's big scene. He was given a line at the end. The scene was cut because Will and the professor had three scenes working together, which was redundant.

"Will Sees Hypnotist" details Will's faking going under hypnosis and posing like a statue.

"Lambeau with Recruits" shows how the professor, a former academic math star, is hot again because of his charge. One of the recruiters is played by one of the film's producers, Lawrence Bender (*Pulp Fiction* [1994], *From Dusk Till Dawn* [1996], *Kill Shot* [2008]). The scene was cut to keep the time clock down.

"Chuckie Meets Recruiters" is the same scene as the one in the film, which was recut from this long version. Van Sant had never made a film with so much conversation, and he found it a refreshing challenge. By keeping the dialogue scenes short and intercutting sequences, he succeeded, along with Scalia, in achieving a lively pace with good dialogue and intriguing relationships.

When director Elaine May[47] was in postproduction on the infamous *Ishtar* (1987) and needed to shorten the film, a scene would be removed, the film screened for the editing crew, and a vote taken. The process was repeated as necessary. Van Sant took a page from the Elaine May playbook on *Good Will Hunting*. "Skylar and Chuckie Talk" was the scene in question. In it, Skylar visits Chuckie to talk about her predicament with Will. He knows the boy better than anyone. The scene is funny but shows yet another relationship, and it doesn't further the story—the cinematic Golden Rule.

"Construction Site" had already been established in a scene with the guys at work, so that was the reason it could go.

"Pudge Fish Card" depicts Will and his doctor talking about baseball and his departed wife. It was intercut with Skylar leaving on a jet plane. Van Sant and Scalia tried to keep it in, but rearranging of other scenes made it impossible.

Will is interpreted as a math whiz Golden Boy in a scene where he is bathed in golden light, captured by Escoffier's camera. An image of Will writing on a mirror represents introspection for an emotionally bottled-up boy. A shot of his eyes reminds the viewer of the Leonardo da Vinci quote "Eyes are the window of the soul."

One of the major themes of this feel-good movie is that you can do anything. Will's breakthrough in his doctor's office sends him the message that he can do anything he wants to do. Will doesn't really want to work in astro-mathematics at this point in his life—he wants to live. He learns this lesson from the therapist. The film ends with Will driving to Skylar in the car his buddies constructed for him out of spare parts. It is love and life that he wants now. He has learned this from the therapist, and the doctor has learned from Will that he has to stop pining for his dead wife and maybe find love again. This is another of the film's themes about the teacher/student relationship. When it works well, both come away as better people.

At the outset of the film, the professor ends the term by announcing a contest about solving a complex theorem that is chalked on a large board outside his classroom at MIT. None of the students can solve it, but Will, a janitor swabbing the halls, easily comes up with the answer. When he gets into legal trouble, the professor comes to his rescue. To stay out of jail, he must see a therapist and work with Lambeau on his extraordinary math skills. Although Will is self-taught, he outshines even the man who becomes his mentor.

The nature of mentorship is three-fold in *Good Will Hunting*. The professor teaches him about math and opportunity; the therapist opens the door to living a life; and Skylar teaches him about love. The boy, an orphan, has been physically and mentally abused, which accounts for his out-of-control behavior and explains why he is tied up in knots emotionally.

Van Sant on occasion throughout his career and in this film utilizes the helicopter shot, a bird's-eye or God's-point-of-view shot that is very cinematic and imparts information that no other shot can do as well by invoking a physical reaction in the viewer's psyche.

A fight scene is shot in slow motion. Van Sant uses the technique to investigate the scene's action, much like an experimental filmmaker. We see pain, violence, and beauty here. We feel the weight of the punches and observe in micro-detail the ballet-like movement inherent in the thrashing bodies. A song on the soundtrack begins to blur aurally to get inside the head of the participants and to allow the viewer to experience the event.

In a Harvard bar, Will takes on a student who is also vying for Skylar. The young man, who thinks he is cool, projects a condescending attitude toward the working-class. Ultimately, Will wins Skylar's number (the holy grail of pick-ups) and lets the hot shot know he's won by slamming the paper with Skylar's telephone number onto the bar window and asking if he likes apples. When the reply is yes, Will retorts, "How do you like them apples?" Will appears cocky and confident, but all of this, we learn in the analyst's sessions, is a defense mechanism.

"*Good Will Hunting* was one of those experiences that just came together," Scalia concludes. "Gus had a sense of calmness in his work with the actors who trusted Jean-Yves, the production designers, the producers—everybody was on the same page. It was very relaxed—there was nothing, no turmoil and the great thing about it was that people responded to it and it did well for Miramax."

Good Will Hunting and *Finding Forrester* (2000) are about mentoring. Van Sant was mentored by William Burroughs and learned by screening the film work of Andy Warhol, Alfred Hitchcock, Stan Brakhage, and many, many others. In turn, Gus Van Sant has mentored countless filmmakers and audiences through the visual and honest storytelling brilliance of his films.

Good Will Hunting was a blockbuster for a director who rejects such visibility. It's the film for which he will likely be most remembered. The oeuvre of Gus Van Sant is wide and vast; he can do almost anything and does. Everyone needs a break, and, for Van Sant, *Good Will Hunting* was his. He took good advantage of this gift.

5

Going Hollywood (Sort Of)

PSYCHO (1998)

Gus Van Sant's copy of Alfred Hitchcock's *Psycho* is an experiment carried out before he became a truly experimental filmmaker with *Gerry* (2002), *Elephant* (2003), *Gus Van Sant's Last Days* (2005), and *Paranoid Park* (2007).

Hitchcock's *Psycho* (1960) is a verified American classic psychological thriller that opened a new dimension in horror. It is the forerunner of splatter and gore films, and—amazingly—it was shot in black-and-white with a small TV crew from *Alfred Hitchcock Presents* (1955–1962).

The psychological thriller is a film in which the characters not only are battling physical enemies but are guided by the sanity or insanity of their own states of mind. Alfred Hitchcock was a pioneer in this genre, having earlier directed *Rebecca* (1940), *Suspicion* (1941), and *Spellbound* (1945).

Splatter movies were literally invented by Herschell Gordon Lewis (*Two Thousand Maniacs* [1964], *Color Me Red* [1965], *Something Weird* [1967]) with his film *Blood Feast* (1963). The harebrained plot concerns an Egyptian caterer who slaughters women with a blade so that he can use the parts to resurrect an Egyptian goddess. It can be assumed that Lewis had viewed Hitchcock's enormously popular *Psycho*.

Gore films were also a Lewis invention, with such titles as *A Taste of Blood* (1967) and *The Gore Gore Girls* (1972). Gore flicks are similar to splatter movies in that they feature gore, gore, gore, and buckets of blood.

Psycho is based on the true story of Ed Gein, a dangerously deranged serial killer who murdered a slew of people in the 1940s and 1950s. Robert Bloch (*The Cabinet of Dr. Caligari* [1962], *Strait-Jacket* [1964], *The House That Dripped Blood* [1971], and literary work including *Skeleton in the Closet and*

Other Stories, This Crowded Earth, and *Spiderweb*) wrote a novel about the grisly goings-on of Ed Gein's pitiful life—aptly named *Psycho.*

In the 1960s, the baby boomers and Gus Van Sant witnessed the Vietnam War and the summer of peace and love and then watched the Age of Aquarius crumble into chaos after the bloody Rolling Stones concert at Altamont in 1969. Van Sant experienced the rise of social movements such as Gay Liberation and the woman's and the Black Panther movements.

Van Sant was highly influenced by the 1960s but would make *Mala Noche* (1985) in the 1980s, well after the America New Wave had come and its filmmakers had "blown it."[1] Van Sant would bravely lead international cinema in another kind of New Wave, nicknamed queer cinema, of which *Mala Noche* was a forerunner and *My Own Private Idaho* (1991) was considered the masterpiece.

Hitchcock's *Psycho* was a popular and controversial film in its time. It led into the explosive and mind-expanding 1960s and was a harbinger of the American New Wave. Hitchcock, along with other aging mavericks such as Robert Rossen (*Body and Soul* [1947], *All the King's Men* [1949], *The Hustler* [1961]), Billy Wilder (*Some Like It Hot* [1959], *The Apartment* [1960], *Kiss Me Stupid* [1964]), and John Huston, made intense, powerful, and, at times, challenging films. *Psycho* was the critics' darling and an international milestone.

The story of Hitchcock's *Psycho* initially focuses on Marion Crane (Janet Leigh), who works in a real estate office and steals a large sum of cash from a client to use to foster her relationship with her lover. She runs off with the money and is unexpectedly, brutally murdered by motel clerk Norman Bates (Anthony Perkins).[2]

Killing off a star early in a film was shocking and practically unheard of—it influenced a number of future films such as *Scream* (1996), directed by Wes Craven (*Last House on the Left* [1972], *The Hills Have Eyes* [1977], *A Nightmare on Elm Street* [1984]), which tried to top the master when Drew Barrymore,[3] a bona fide star at the time, was murdered in the opening moments of the film. Michelangelo Antonioni's landmark film *L'Avventura,* also released in 1960, may or may not kill off the female lead, who disappears while swimming in the ocean while her friends are on board a yacht, but, as in *Psycho,* after the audience becomes attached to her, she is gone, never to return.

The remainder of Hitchcock's *Psycho* revolves around Crane's boyfriend, Sam Loomis (John Gavin), and Marion's sister, played by Vera Miles (*The Searchers* [1956], *The Man Who Shot Liberty Valance* [1962], *Separate Lives* [1995]), who track down the killer and learn what has happened to their loved one at that seedy motel.

The success of *Good Will Hunting* (1997) placed Van Sant at the top of the directors' heap. He received a slew of offers, many rip-offs of *Good Will Hunting.*

Among the stacks of scripts delivered to his office were remakes of films whose titles were owned by the studio. Making French films into U.S. productions (e.g., *Three Men and a Baby* [1987]) was, at that time, the Hollywood fashion, but remakes of American titles were picking up steam. One of the projects offered to Van Sant was a remake of Hitchcock's *Psycho*. Surprisingly, a new generation had not seen the film. Even many members of Van Sant's cast and crew were not that familiar with the iconic thriller.

A book could be written alone on the reasons and motivations Van Sant has offered to interviewers and the press for his decision to remake *Psycho*. He was sticking his neck out, and the decision threatened to incur the wrath of film buffs everywhere with choices like shooting on color stock rather than the stark black-and-white of the original. The least believable and most outrageous of his long list of reasons was that he wanted to experience what Hitchcock saw when he looked through the viewfinder. Well, Hitchcock storyboarded every shot of his films and "made them" (in his mind) before shooting. Hitchcock disliked the production process and expected the design and camera teams to replicate the boards. So he probably rarely looked through a lens, maybe in his earliest days in a career that spanned six decades. Other reasons had to do with pacing of the film, making the relationships believable, and—the pièce-de-resistance—his wish to poke the *Psycho*philes in the eye by creating new shots that were intercut with the original images. Film buffs and critics continue to call Van Sant's *Psycho* "a shot-by-shot remake," never mentioning that, while that is largely true, there are added shots and changes. Van Sant shortened the psychiatrist's end-of-the film explanation about Norman Bates's psychosis, put in the Van Sant signature moving clouds, and even had Norman Bates masturbating while looking through a peephole at Marion undressing for her shower. This author's favorite is a shot of a seemingly naked woman with a black mask and g-string on, turning her head as if she could see private investigator Arbogast being maimed on the staircase. It was as if a Kubrick fan were trying to combine *The Shining* (1980) with *Eyes Wide Shut* (1999).

Van Sant made the critical decision to update his film to 1998. He worked with the original scenarist, Joseph Stefano (*The Naked Edge* [1961], *Futz* [1969], *Two Bits* [1995]), to cut lines, make relationships believable, and give the project a late 1990s patina. The master of macabre hadn't liked the long explanation of the psychiatrist, so Van Sant decided that cutting it was "justified." Also, Hitchcock had to face the studio and the censors, especially in the shower scene, and brilliantly managed to break new ground in explicit screen violence; that censorship issue was no longer relevant, giving Van Sant more leeway.

The famous title sequence with thick black lines crossing against white is replaced by green, interpreted by some as the color of sickness and death.

The story begins at 2:43 P.M., just as in the original. The opening shot is a panorama of the city; it then tracks into the room where the secretive lovers have just finished their afternoon delight. The shot is accomplished using modern cinema technology unavailable to Hitchcock. (Just imagine what Sir Alfred could have done with a Steadicam!)[4] Although Janet Leigh (*Little Women* [1949], *Houdini* [1943], *The Manchurian Candidate* [1962]) had short hair teased up, Anne Heche (*The Juror* [1996], *Donnie Brasco* [1997], *John Q* [2002]) has a short layered haircut that seems like an homage to Jean Seberg in *Breathless* (1959). Viggo Mortensen (*Carlito's Way* [1993], *A History of Violence* [2005], *The Road* [2009]) looks unkempt, like a 1960s hippie, while John Gavin (*Imitation of Life* [1959], *Spartacus* [1960], *Thoroughly Modern Millie* [1967]) is a preppie. The sound design includes the moans and groans of another couple copulating in an adjacent room.

The bra worn by Leigh turned heads because of the actress's ample bust size (depending on which Web site you consult, it's a 34 or 36C.) Heche, in her tangerine lingerie, appears to be less well endowed. In 1960, it was a scandal to see a major Hollywood star in a brassiere. By the late 1990s, this was a common sight, as was upper or full-figure nudity. The relationship between sex and violence has been part of movies since their inception, but Hitchcock expanded the connection between the two, and Van Sant worked within the standards his times allowed, while still being loyal to the original.

At one point, Anne Heche wears a pink dress, a color associated with homosexuality. Pink lipstick, which is very 1960s, is also worn. The actress had a very public relationship with comedienne Ellen DeGeneres (*Coneheads* [1993], *EDtv* [1999], *Finding Nemo* [2001], her own daytime television show [2003–], and *American Idol* judge [2010]). Heche was living a lesbian lifestyle, then later became heterosexual and married a man. Having a gay actress in his film (playing straight, as so many gay and lesbian actors did throughout film history) helped to connect this film to Van Sant's Gay movies *Mala Noche* (1985), *My Own Private Idaho* (1991), and *Milk* (2008) and to single scenes of homosexuality in *Elephant* (2003) and *Gus Van Sant's Last Days* (2005).

Van Sant found a very clever way to do his and Hitchcock's cameo. It is assumed that Van Sant often made cameo appearances in his films to pay homage to his cinematic master. In the Hitchcock film, Sir Alfred is outside the realty office where Marion works; he is wearing a big cowboy hat. In the Van Sant update, the director is talking to a man who looks like Hitchcock in the original movie.

Hitchcock's only child, daughter Patricia (*Stage Fright* [1950], *Strangers on a Train* [1951], *Skateboard: The Movie* [1978]), played the other woman in the office in the Hitchcock version. In Van Sant's film, Rita Wilson (*Sleepless in Seattle* [1993], *Runaway Bride* [1999], *Auto Focus* [2002], and married to Tom Hanks) plays the role.

During the scene in which Marion decides to pack up the money and leave, she is wearing a green bra; Leigh wore black to insinuate that she was a bad girl. There is the tangerine color in the room and a blue bed. There is a bird on the window, relating both to Norman's stuffed varieties and to another

Hitchcock classic, *The Birds* (1963), of which there is a remake in the works for 2011, directed by Martin Campbell (*GoldenEye* [1995], *The Legend of Zorro* [2005], *Casino Royale* [2006]), with Michael Bay (*Bad Boys* [1995], *Pearl Harbor* [2001], *Transformers* [2007]) as one of the producers.

The driving sequences are technologically better than the original. Hitchcock's use of rear-screen projection was always poor and especially unbelievable in *Psycho*. The audio montage of the voices Marion hears talking about her is repeated, but with more aural depth and a mix with just the right echo to sound as if they are playing inside Marion's head. James Remar (*48 Hrs.* [1982], *The Cotton Club* [1984], *2 Fast 2 Furious* [2003]), who was in *Drugstore Cowboy* (1989), does a fine job in the famous trooper scene.

James Legross (*The Rapture* [1991], *Mrs. Parker and the Vicious Circle* [1994], *Zodiac* [2007]), from *Drugstore Cowboy* (1989), plays the car salesman, and Marion is carrying a tangerine-colored parasol. This is a new touch. Leigh didn't need shielding from the sun, but Heche looks very stylish with the prop. Van Sant's objective here is to create the right color palette as he collaborates with the trinity of his director of photography (Christopher Doyle), his costume designer (Beatrix Aruna Pasztor), and his production designer (Tom Foden [*The Cell* (2000), *One Hour Photo* (2002), *Matchstick Men* (2003)]) to find the right look for the characters, the content, and his directorial point of view.

Driving at night in pouring rain created an effective scene in the Hitchcock version; here, with color, Van Sant is able to have the Bates Motel sign glow. The inside of Norman's office is orange, connecting it to the bathroom at the car dealership, which is also painted orange. There is also blue in Norman's office, another reference to *A Clockwork Orange* (1971), and there is pink, the color associated with the gay rights movement.

The famous Bates house has a different architecture and/or is photographed to highlight its structure and texture differently than in the original.

Marion signs the register as Marie Samuels (perhaps named after the New York socialite or perhaps a coincidence) and is shown to her room by the murderous Norman, who is especially nervous about the bathroom during his tour.

The bathroom as a room has appeared in countless films since the beginning of film. In comedies and dramas, this private room has been explored for its comedic and dramatic qualities. Film critic Roger Ebert wrongly stated that there was a bathroom scene in every Kubrick film. Shower scenes are not as prominent, but one in Val Lewton's (*Cat People* [1942], *The Curse of the Cat People* [1944], *Bedlam* [1946]) production of *The Seventh Victim* (1943) has a forerunner of the Hitchcock scene. This one is between two women (giving it lesbian overtones) and has a threatening quality. No murder takes place, but one would be hard pressed to argue that Hitchcock had not seen the scene. Actually, Val Lewton himself was a master of the thriller, the psychological thriller, and the horror film.

The bedspread in the bedroom is green like money. Marion puts the wad of bills into a newspaper and folds it up. She hears screams coming from the Bates house as clouds move quickly past it. Hitchcock or not, moving clouds in the sky are a Van Sant autograph.

The stuffed birds are in this version and as chilling as in the original. Norman is a troubled and deeply disturbed young man. Marion sees this but is too wrapped up in her own problems to react. As mentioned, the film ends with a psychiatrist analyzing Norman, who dresses up in woman's clothes to "be" his mother. The doctor doesn't agree with the suggestion that Bates is a transvestite, but a case can be made for it. Could this be another reason Van Sant was attracted to this project? This gay subtext is a key element in the story and makes this another gay project from Van Sant. Also of interest, Anthony Perkins, who forever shaped the character was bisexual. He was married to Berry Berenson, the sister of *Barry Lyndon* star Marisa Berenson, but by most accounts lived a predominately gay lifestyle.

The acting, as in virtually all Van Sant films, is fine and well watched over by the director. The acting in the Hitchcock original is good, although, unlike Van Sant, Hitchcock generally had a disdain for actors. Van Sant loves actors and understands the important contribution they bring to a film.

There are three books on the subject of the shower scene in Hitchcock's *Psycho*. They are *Alfred Hitchcock and the Making of Psycho* (1990) by Stephen Rebello, *Behind the Scenes of Psycho, the Classic Thriller* (1995) by Janet Leigh with Christopher Nickens, and *Psycho in the Shower: The History of Cinema's Most Famous Scene* (2009) by Phillip J. Skerry.

Here are some excerpts. First Rebello:

> Hitchcock also told several interviewers that he had his makeup and special effects men devise a blood-squirting rubber torso prop that went unused. It makes for a good anecdote, but—since Hitchcock preferred understatement and often boasted about never intending to show the blade of the knife puncturing flesh—only an anecdote. Certainly no surviving member of the crew recalled such a prop. "It wasn't his way of doing things," asserts Jack Barron. "He tended to show things after the fact, blood going down the drain and such. Not the precise spot where the blood spurted from the body." But when the film was released, sharp-eyed audience members swore that they saw the knife blade pierce a naked midsection just south of the navel. The frame-by-frame blowup book on *Psycho* by Richard Anobile published in 1974 validated their claim.[5]

Now Janet Leigh:

> On *Psycho*, Mr. Hitchcock hired a body double, a professional artist's model who was accustomed to being nude . . . she was paid $400 a week, one week guaranteed. He used [her] to see how much of the body outline the camera would pick up behind the shower curtain, to test the density of the water—what

level of water force would read well and yet not obscure Marion. But she was not on camera during the shower scene. At the end of the murder, Norman wrapped the corpse in the shower curtain and dragged it out to the car. That was the only shot I was not in. Hitch showed me that no one could see who it was, so there was no need for me to be bounced around. I totally agreed.[6]

Joseph Stefano:

He [Hitchcock] knew he would never get away with frontal nudity, but he thought he might squeak by with a high overhead shot of Marion lying over the tub. For this shot he used a model. But her buttocks were seen. The incredible thing was that's the scene right before this one was when he went to your [Janet's] eye and it was heartbreaking. There was no sex connected to it at all. There was this beautiful person whom I cared about all through the movie up to this point and she was lying there dead. But no deal. It was the only angle from the shower sequence that was cut.[7]

And now Skerry analyzing the shower sequence and talking with Van Sant's editor Amy Duddleston. Note that Skerry refers to Norman (Bates) as Norma when he is dressed in drag as his mother:

"We got all the shots as they are in the original. We cut it the exact way it was cut originally. But there was something not quite right with it." I [Skerry] claim that the shower scene is four minutes long and contains sixty shots. Van Sant's version is four minutes and seventeen seconds long and contains seventy-one shots. The additional shots are of two types. The first is material that Van Sant adds to give the scenes his own stamp (e.g., two shots of clouds and one shot of Marion's pupil dilating as she is dying). The second type is made up of shots that are additions to ones Hitchcock used in the original. Van Sant adds two shots of Marion's feet wading in the bloody water of the tub. These added shots are in keeping with the more explicit presentation of violence in the film. . . . Van Sant also lengthens the vertiginous camera move as the drain dissolves into Marion's eye. . . . Because of a synching problem, Herrmann's music comes in a beat or two late when Norma pulls open the shower curtain. In viewing the first dub, Van Sant and Duddleston realized the problem but liked the result. In our interview, Duddleston said to me, "That was a beautiful mistake. It was a happy mistake." Because most of the audience knows the scene, the tardy arrival of the music is oddly effective.[8]

The shower sequence in *Psycho* is arguably among the most brutal, violent, and bloodcurdling sequence ever put on the screen.

Following are some thoughts on the Gus Van Sant remake:

- Color was a bad idea—too gory—and the color of that vital body fluid was more orange than red.

- Heche was a good choice for a contemporary Marion. The Jean Seberg brush-cut was perfect for 1998. Heche isn't as well endowed as Leigh, who has said in print that it was God's blessing to her. The hype and rumors prior to the release of Van Sant's *Psycho* promised more nudity because that's what Hitchcock would have done if he hadn't had censors breathing down his neck, but that turned out not to be the case. The only exception is Heche recreating a shot that Leigh's body double, Marli Renfro, had executed (but that Hitchcock did not use) in which her naked derriere is exposed.
- The music, based on the original Bernard Herrmann score, was spot on.
- The casting was on point in some places and off in others. The worst selection was Viggo Mortensen—not because he doesn't resemble John Gavin but because his characterization does not create sympathy or empathy in the viewer.
- There was only one Anthony Perkins.
- Gus Van Sant and Julianne Moore both made the mistake of making it seem that Lila Crane, Marion's sister, was a lesbian. It was good for press but detracted from the story after Marion's murder.

Van Sant's *Psycho* is copied with diligence, but that seems to be the argument against it. Paintings are copied by amateurs learning to draw and paint, but this director (also a painter) was a seasoned pro by this point in his career. Should films be copied in the same manner as paintings are in the art world? Painters can say they are reliving the original artist's brushstrokes and technique. The filmmaker can say the same, but what purpose does it serve other than bringing the old to the new? Van Sant seemed to be untouched and unrattled by the criticism spewed at him, but was it worth it? The film made a slight profit. The worldwide gross to date is $32 million; the original budget was estimated at $20 million.

The debate as to which *Psycho* is better, Hitchcock's black-and-white original or Van Sant's color and narratively altered color copy, will persist. The original is remembered as a classic American film, and the shot-by-shot copy (with a few changes) was accepted by a new audience upon its release in 1998. The debate as to which is "better" will continue, but both films will be there for audiences to compare. And respect for two great filmmakers who took a chance and put their reputations on the line will last. In the final analysis, it is impossible to say which film is better—this depends on one's taste and age—but it will be a bad sign of the times and a forecast of a gloomy cinematic future if this trend keeps up What are new filmmakers going to remake next, *Citizen Kane* (1941)?

FINDING FORRESTER (2000)

To the comparatively few who have viewed *Finding Forrester,* it is a neglected cinematic gem. The process started when superstar Sean Connery and the well-established director Gus Van Sant began talking about a new project.

Van Sant was asked to direct *Finding Forrester*, featuring Connery (*Dr. No* [1962], *The Hill* [1965], *The League of Extraordinary Gentlemen* [2003]), a star considered by women young and old to be "the sexiest man on earth" (winner in 1989 of the *People* magazine competition, coming in, at age 59, as the oldest person to win the title).

This was Van Sant's second "prodigy" film. *Good Will Hunting* (1997) raked in a lot of cash for the studio and producers, so *Finding Forrester*'s Connery, Jonathan King (*54* [1998], *Bruno* [2000], *Dreamgirls* [2006]), Laurence Mark (*Black Widow* [1987], *Jerry Maguire* [1996], *I Robot* [2004]), Rhonda Tollefson (*Just Cause* [1995], *Entrapment* [1999]), Dany Wolf (*Psycho* [1998], *Elephant* [2003], *Gus Van Sant's Last Days* [2005]), and Columbia Pictures were expecting a big payday. The budget of *Finding Forrester* was estimated at $43 million, a hefty price tag at the time for a non-blockbuster movie. The U.S. opening weekend take was a paltry $743,056. By 2001, the film had grossed $51.7 million, not enough to bring any kind of real wealth to the participants. More people have seen the film on video and DVD than saw it during its initial release.

This was Gus Van Sant's first opportunity to direct a megastar and to make a film about black youth culture. There was also the theme of education and going to high school, this time an upper-class private school.

Both protagonist Will Hunting, in *Good Will Hunting* (1997), and Jamal Wallace, in *Finding Forrester*, read voraciously. Will reads about philosophy, math, history, and the sciences; Jamal reads novels and short stories. Will is a math genius, and Jamal is a student of English studies and a writer with uncanny gifts.

Finding Forrester concerns a reclusive writer, William Forrester (Sean Connery), who is based on two real-life recluses. One is J. D. Salinger, who like Van Sant, was drawn to young people and youth culture (Salinger wrote *The Catcher in the Rye, Nine Stories, Franny and Zooey*, and *Raise High the Roof Beam Carpenters: An Introduction*); the other is Thomas Pynchon, the author of *V, The Crying of Lot 49, Gravity's Rainbow, Vineland, Mason and Dixon, Against the Day*, and *Inherent Vice*.

Like Salinger, Forrester is a reclusive writer who identifies with adolescents. Also, he continues to write, sells some books, and archives some work, without appearing anywhere in the general public eye. Like Salinger, the Forrester character sues to block a biography or book written about him. Pynchon is principally the model for the character's writing style.

Forrester's big book is named *Avalon Landing*, a doorstop World War II novel about a man changed forever by his harrowing experiences, for which Forrester wins a Pulitzer Prize. *Gravity's Rainbow* is 784 pages and won the National Book Award; it is a metafictional romp through World War II. (Pynchon sent harebrained comedian Professor Irwin Cory [1914–] to accept the award. He left the attendees in stitches, as this line testifies: "But we have no paranoia, and Mr. Pynchon has attained and has created for

himself serenity, and it is only the insanity that has kept him alive in his paranoia.") Other writers can be considered models for William Forrester. In Ray
Bradbury's *Dandelion Wine,* a character who has written only one book is
named William Forrester. Like Ralph Ellison, Forrester likes to watch boys
play basketball; in Van Sant's film, Forrester does so, peering out his window
through a pair of high-power binoculars.

Regarding Jamal Wallace, one can't rule out that his surname is a reference
to David Foster Wallace, whose big book *Infinite Jest,* first published in hard-
cover in 1996 by Little Brown, put him on the metafictional-postmodern
literary stage. Wallace, who committed suicide in 2008, was one of Van Sant's
favorite authors, and the director once was interested in turning the 1,079
page novel (including voluminous footnotes) into a motion picture.

Finding Forrester is a commercial film, but Van Sant begins it with a self-
referential moment. A young man holds high a camera slate with the inscrip-
tion "B1 Take G1 Roll 309 Ext. Day A Cam." Van Sant is letting us know
that we are watching a movie. This is a dangerous notion with a film that
must engage the audience through story and characters. *Finding Forrester* is
a feel-good film, a drama with irony and comedy—a dramedy.

As the credits roll, a montage of a black neighborhood and its denizens
unfolds. At this point, the film appears to be about a black neighborhood,
but the audience needs to wait until after the credits to learn that the film is
also about Forrester, high in his apartment building, looking down through
his window at the young men who play basketball on the ground below.

Ghetto culture is represented in many ways, including through music. The
young man holding the clapboard becomes a rapper, and Jamal's brother
Terrell is played by hip-hop legend Busta Rhymes (Trevor Taheim Smith Jr.),
who, in addition to his musical talents, has acted in *Who's the Man* (1993)
and *Shaft* (2000) and has contributed to the soundtracks of many films.

Van Sant explores new cinematic territory here—the Bronx in New York
City. In this Van Sant film directed outside Portland, the director captures
the sights, sounds, and feel of the city like a native. Van Sant had spent time
in New York as a young man and other times, exploring painting and the
bohemian, hippie, and punk cultures. Van Sant has a natural sensibility that
encompasses all the environments portrayed in his movies.

Van Sant's visual obsession with hallways continues here with the vestibule
of Forrester's apartment and the school halls that fascinated him in *Good
Will Hunting* (1997) and *Elephant* (2003). This may go back to his days as
a student, or it may symbolize a seemingly endless journey. Perhaps it is an
homage to experimental filmmakers Ernie Gehr (*Still* [1969], *Hotel* [1979],
Cotton Candy [2002]) and Michael Snow (*Wavelength* [1967], *Back and
Forth* [1969], *Puccini Conservato* [2008]). These filmmakers explore interior
space by utilizing various cinematic tools, most famously Snow's application
of the zoom lens during the production of *Wavelength,* which features Van
Sant supporter Amy Taubin.

As always, Van Sant is concerned with breaking down stereotypes. Jamal is a well-spoken, literate writer and avid reader of works by dead white men. His character challenges the old stereotypes of black adolescents as drug addicts and criminals so often present in mainstream movies.

The screenwriter, Mike Rich (*The Rookie* [2002], *Radio* [2003], *The Nativity Story* [2006]), is a graduate of Oregon State and worked for a Portland radio station KINK, where he was a news reporter. Rich named the character after his high school English teacher Mrs. Forrester. In 1991, his first screenplay, *Finding Forrester,* was awarded the Nicholl Fellowship in Screenwriting by the Academy of Motion Picture Arts and Sciences.

Forrester is a basketball and baseball fan. At one point in the story, Jamal uses his brother's contacts at Yankee Stadium to bring the reclusive Forrester to stand on the famed field. As in *Good Will Hunting* (1997), the therapist/teacher teaches the student, and the student reciprocates by teaching the teacher. Both boys help a troubled adult come out of his shell and his limited world into the larger social universe.

Another theme in both films is that knowledge is power. Both Will and Jamal use their gifts to seek their dreams and to escape the ghetto.

The jazz soundtrack by guitarist Bill Frisell (*La Scuola* [1995], *American Hollow* [1999], *The Mesmerist* [2003]) features a trumpet that is reminiscent of Miles Davis,[9] another prodigy. The music gives the film another dimension not directly connected with academia; jazz supports Forrester's old-school work, and rap represents the new school, represented by Jamal and his friends.

Jamal gets the opportunity to enter a prestigious prep school, where he is one of the few minority students, and is hounded by Professor Robert Crawford, played by F. Murray Abraham (*Amadeus* [1984], *Mighty Aphrodite* [1995], *Perestroika* [2009]), who is jealous of the boy's talents and ultimately accuses him of plagiarism, forcing Forrester to come out of his reclusive state and stand up for Jamal.

The script has just the right psychological underpinnings to explain why Forrester has stayed in his apartment for almost 50 years since his whirlwind of a novel arrived on the literary scene. This is best demonstrated in a sequence in which Jamal takes Forrester to Madison Square Garden, a sports and music arena. They accidentally separate, and Forrester panics, hiding in a cubby space as the crowd swirls by him. This fear of crowds and the outside world is a form of agoraphobia. The confident and, at times, self-assured arrogance displayed by Forrester inside the womb-like comfort of his apartment breaks down as the man experiences a florid panic attack once out of his milieu.

Michael Pitt (*Hedwig and the Angry Inch* [2001], *The Village* [2004], *Silk* [2007]), who would later portray Blake, based on Kurt Cobain, in *Gus Van Sant's Last Days* (2005), plays John Coleridge. He is a friend of Jamal's and Jamal's paramour Claire Spence, played by Anna Paquin (*The Piano* [1993],

X-Men [2000], *Blue State* [2007]). Coleridge is also mentally tortured by the mean-spirited Professor Crawford, who tries to stump the befuddled boy with a question concerning Samuel Taylor Coleridge, who wrote "The Rime of the Ancient Mariner" and "Kubla Khan." He is saved by Jamal, who tells him just to say his name! Crawford is an angry hack who failed as a writer and wields his power to demotivate the students—a sort of literary villain played by Abraham with great charm, complexity, and ill temper. In reality, there is a Robert Crawford, who has been a literary professor and poet in Scotland, Connery's birthplace.

Before Jamal becomes part of his life, Forrester has his world in order. A young man from his publisher comes regularly with groceries and sundries so that the cloistered writer can shut out the world around him.

After a cat-and-mouse struggle, Jamal gets Forrester to mentor him. The old man still writes on a typewriter, and one exercise designed to help Jamal write involves back-to-back machines, with Forrester pounding away to teach the boy to just start writing. Jamal gets it, and they duel away. Throughout, the typewriter brings its own nostalgia and rhythmic "music" to the film.

To show that he understands youth culture, Forrester delivers the memorable line "You're the man now, dog" to suggest, in his charge's dialect, that Jamal has learned to write in his own voice.

Claire is the daughter of the wealthy Dr. Spence, played by Michael Nouri (*Flashdance* [1983], *American Yakuza* [1993], *The Proposal* [2009]), who is on the school's board. At first, he makes it very clear that he does not want Jamal with his daughter. It's possible that veiled racism is behind this decision but more likely it is an issue of class structure, another theme from *Good Will Hunting* (1997). Van Sant judges his characters by their inner being and their artistic and personal achievements, not by class. More often than not, Van Sant films explore lower- or middle-class society, rather than the world of the rich and well connected.

Another window on the world for Forrester is his three TVs, which he often watches simultaneously. He employs another teaching device by watching *Jeopardy!*[10] with Jamal as they both compete for the "questions" along with the contestants. Like Thomas Pynchon, Forrester is intrigued by information on myriad subjects.

Plagiarism is considered by society as a particularly shameful exercise because ideas and intellectual property are valued as accomplishments that define the creator.

As part of his "education," Jamal is given a short story from Forrester's file and told to copy it word for word. Forrester has kept and catalogued everything he has ever written—a treasure trove of literary manna to anyone who can get his hands on it. The old master explains that by copying a work (a painting or a movie, like Van Sant's *Psycho*), one helps the personal creative juices come out, leading to original writing. Jamal's two mentor/teachers, contemporaries Forrester and Professor Crawford, clash in philosophy and methods of tutoring the boy in their separate venues. Jamal is asked by Forrester to copy letter by letter one of the old man's stories; through the boy's own invention, he finds a way to imprint his literary signature on the work. Unfortunately, Crawford has a photographic memory and recognizes Forrester's use of language and application of literary style and accuses Jamal of plagiarism.

The school has enrolled Jamal not only because of his intellectual skills but because it needs a good basketball player and Jamal fits the bill. To further bolster the class distinction, Jamal gets into a heated rivalry with another black player who comes from a well-heeled family.

The concept of a duel is a thematic thread in the film. Jamal duels mentally with Forrester and Crawford and physically with the black basketball player. *Finding Forrester* and *Good Will Hunting* (1997) share the idea of young men struggling to find their identities. In both instances, they achieve their goals through epiphanies. They must be their own people, not a collage of those who have influenced them.

Bill Frisell's rendition of "Somewhere over the Rainbow" brings hope to Jamal that the struggle within him and his struggle with society will one day be over. Van Sant understands how to layer the narrative and thematic communication of his films by utilizing the soundtrack music and effects to the fullest. In *Finding Forrester*, as in Van Sant's *Psycho* (1998), there are the sounds of a couple making loud love. In *Psycho*, they come from an adjoining room in the hotel during the opening scene; in *Finding Forrester*, they come from Jamal's room as he tries to write. The heavenly voices of a choir are another Van Sant aural signature that is used in *Finding Forrester*. There is also the slow-motion sound of a heartbeat during a basketball game at the prep school, which may have been inspired by Sam Peckinpah's *The Wild Bunch* (1969), in which a recording of normal speed heartbeat is heard during the opening shootout as tension builds to the first gunshot. The cover of Forrester's legendary book *Avalon Landing* sports an airplane. At one point in the film, the sound of an airplane plays over the image, taking us inside Forrester's past.

Like most Van Sant films, this one takes advantage of the dramatic monologue when Forrester opens up and tells his backstory. It involves World War II, his dead brother, who is buried in the Bronx, a nurse, and how everything changed. Sean Connery, in a career of wonderful performances (and don't forget he's the best, and for most the only, James Bond), gives one of his best as Forrester—cranky, vulnerable, wise, and righteous. His work was nominated for a Satellite award, given by the International Press Academy.

Forrester sits at his window and peers at birds through his binoculars, just as he watched the boys play basketball This could be a reference to Hitchcock's *The Birds* (1963), which has been remade by director Martin Campbell with Naomi Watts and George Clooney and is to be released in 2011, or to *Psycho* (1960), remade by Van Sant in 1998.

The production design by Jane Musky (*Blood Simple* [1984], *Glengarry Glen Ross* [1992], *Notorious* [2009]) captures the Collyer Brothers-like hoarding of the hermit Forrester.[11] The apartment is cramped, filled with books on shelves and stacked up everywhere. The film is set in the modern day but looks like a period film when the scene is in the Forrester apartment. The furniture, appliances, everything looks like it has been frozen in time.

The cinematography by Harris Savides (*Birth* [2004], *American Gangster* [2007], *Whatever Works* [2009]), who has become Van Sant's long-time collaborator, is dark but never noirish. The lighting and compositional style in the apartment and the school emphasize the venerable quality of the environments. Savides, a native New Yorker who attended college at the School of Visual Arts, in downtown New York, doesn't go for the cliché or copy other New York cinematographers such as Gordon Willis (*Klute* [1971], *Annie Hall* [1977], *The Godfather* trilogy [1972, 1974, 1990]), who shot in the city for a decade with Woody Allen; Tom DiCillo (*Underground U.S.A.* [1980], *Stranger Than Paradise* [1984], *Living in Oblivion* [1995]), or Andzej Bartkowiak (*Prince of the City* [1981], *Family Business* [1989], *A Stranger among Us* [1992]). Savides doesn't go the documentary-style route as Boris Kaufman (*12 Angry Men* [1957], *Splendor in the Grass* [1961], *The Pawnbroker* [1964]) did in *On the Waterfront* (1954) or the stylized look of countless Hollywood cameramen who shot in New York during the Hollywood studio era. Savides uses a dark palette, natural light, and a camera style that doesn't call attention to itself except during a slow-mo basketball sequence, slow-motion photography being a Van Sant trademark. There is also a wide use of the color green, here alluding not to death or the landscape but to the claustrophobia of Forrester's apartment and the crowded city streets. The city doesn't look familiar in this film; it is shot so that the viewer can discover this unique town as Forrester rediscovers it. Earlier in film history, this was accomplished by cinematographer Adam Holender, who at the time of photographing *Midnight Cowboy* (1968), a homosexual story by the gay filmmaker John Schlesinger, had only recently arrived from his native Poland. As an outsider, Holender was able to "discover America" with the fresh eyes of an immigrant. Savides also applies orange light to impart wisdom, intelligence, and art to *Finding Forrester*.

Coverage in *Finding Forrester* is plentiful, unlike in some Van Sant films, mainly the experimental ones, which utilize a minimum of shots and camera positions.

Early in the film, Forrester finds a series of chap books filled with writings in Jamal's backpack, which was left behind when the boy was dared to enter the apartment by his friends. Jamal later discovers the Forrester has gone through each one and in bold handwriting has written notes and corrections.

Substance abuse is a theme in *Finding Forrester* as it was in *Mala Noche* (1985), *Drugstore Cowboy* (1989), and *Good Will Hunting* (1997). Jamal's father, who left the family, was a drug addict (he does not appear in the film). Drinking and pot-smoking are part of the lifestyle in *Mala Noche* and *Drugstore Cowboy* is *about* drug abuse. In *Good Will Hunting* it is suggested that the therapist may drink too much. Forrester always has a drink at hand.

The photograph of a young William Forrester is hung on the back wall of Professor Crawford's classroom. In fact, the picture is of a young Sean Connery striking a pose similar to that of J. D. Salinger in a popular picture taken around the time *Catcher in the Rye* was published in 1951. The photograph is one on a wall of pictures of literary greats throughout time, reminiscent of the wall of Italian American heroes in Sal's Pizzeria displayed in Spike Lee's incendiary *Do the Right Thing* (1989), whose production was designed by Wynn Thomas. Crawford's wall is part of his reluctance to accept the present (like Forrester); although he goes outside, he is also a literary recluse, but, instead of seeking refuge in an apartment, he chooses a classroom. The two men have a real history. Back in the day, Crawford tried to publish a book on Forrester (he admires and is jealous of *Avalon Landing*), but the author put a stop to it. Both men have tempers and pride themselves on not losing control (although Crawford loses it with Jamal when he throws him out of his classroom for being insubordinate), but, in the tradition of don't-get-mad-get-even, Crawford uses words as swords and actions as gunfire. He does not like to have his authority challenged by *anyone.*

Catcher in the Rye, with its story of adolescence and longing, would make a perfect film project for Van Sant, but the rights were unattainable while Salinger was alive (and may still be now that he has died, depending on his will). Salinger originally wanted films made of his work, but Hollywood badly botched an adaptation of his short story "Uncle Wiggly in Connecticut," renamed *My Foolish Heart* (1949), for which the famed Epstein brothers[12] wrote the script and Mark Robson[13] served as director. Although it received an Academy Award nomination, it was brutally panned by the critics. Over the decades, many have tried to get the rights or to make a film out of this classic coming-of-age novel, including Samuel Goldwyn, Marlon Brando, Jack Nicholson, Tobey McGuire, Leonardo DiCaprio, Billy Wilder, Harvey Weinstein (he could give it to Van Sant!), Steven Spielberg, Terrence Malick, and Robert Downey Sr.

Holden Caulfield, the central character of *Catcher in the Rye,* has been thrown out of prep school (Jamal attends a prep school, and Will Hunting never did too well with conventional school). Holden goes to a psychiatrist after having a nervous breakdown; Will sees a therapist.

Finding Forrester is set in the Bronx, and Van Sant went to the New York City borough where Stanley Kubrick grew up to shoot his film *Killer's Kiss* (1955). Kubrick, like Forrester and Jamal, went to Yankee Stadium. Kubrick was there in the daytime to see a game and sat in the seats, rather than standing on the field. On cue, Jamal's brother throws a switch that pours the lights onto the legendary field. When the brother thinks it's time to leave, the night returns to darkness, symbolizing the fragility of a fantasy realized.

Even though Forrester has struggled against severe panic attack because he is outside for the first time in decades, the experience, he tells Jamal, has been one of the best evenings of his life.

In *Good Will Hunting* (1997), Will has two mentors. The professor is laid back and mentors Will by giving him math problems. The therapist mentors Will by challenging him, defying the boy, going head-to-head with him, and searching for the truth. Forrester mentors Jamal by badgering and support-ing the boy at the same time. He gets Jamal to see that writing isn't purely an intellectual exercise. He stresses that writing must come from the heart, then go to the head. The writer should not think but just write—"just do it."[14] The most important lesson Jamal learns from Forrester is to write for himself, to write the book he wants to read, as Van Sant makes the films he wants to see. In a rooftop basketball sequence, the sky is saturated blue, and clouds are dotting the landscape. Here the shot is conventional but framed for the sky. Not every director would compose this way—it is another ex-ample of Van Sant putting his imprint on every film he directs. Thunder and rain are also elements in the sound design; they are prevalent in many of the Van Sant films.

A fault of the film is its lack of definition of the time frame. Is this the 1970s? Some hairstyles seem to point to that decade, but the African American boys are not sporting Afros. Michael Pitt's Coleridge has long hair, but so do young men in the 21st century. This doesn't hurt or harm the film, but it does leave the audience wondering. If the viewer is trying to figure out when a story is taking place, he is distracted and not totally entering the world of the film he is watching.

A party at Claire's apartment contrasts wealth with the near-poverty of Jamal's family and the decaying environment in which Forrester hides from the world. Jamal gives Claire a present, a signed copy of *Avalon Landing* that Forrester had given him.

A student of film and an admirer of Stanley Kubrick, Van Sant presents one Kubrick shot in his film that includes is a center figure or object counter-balance on either side. This compositional concept has been borrowed and imitated by a generation (or two) of young American filmmakers as an ele-ment of motion picture grammar and homage.

Photos of Forrester's family present his backstory, which he also tells to Jamal. Bill Frisell plays "Somewhere over the Rainbow" on his guitar. The song, written by Harold Arlen and E. Y. Harburg for *The Wizard of Oz* (1939), is a classic, and the rainbow is a gay reference (*The Wizard of Oz* is full of gay inferences and a favorite of the community). It is a poignant mo-ment in *Finding Forrester* without being overly sentimental. Van Sant has a warm heart but knows that going over the top emotionally destroys the fabric of a screen character and cinema story.

Forrester, inspired by Jamal, decides to see the world. While traveling, he dies of cancer. He has kept his disease a secret from the boy to keep the mentorship unencumbered. Jamal learns about it from Forrester's lawyer, played in a surprise cameo by Matt Damon, further linking *Finding Forrester* with *Good Will Hunting*.

Finding Forrester was edited by Valdís Óskardóttir (*The Celebration* [1988], *Eternal Sunshine of the Spotless Mind* [2004], *Mr. Lonely* [2007]). She talks about how she first met Gus Van Sant. "I was working with Harmony Korine on *Julien Donkey-Boy* (1999) in New York and one day he came in with Gus because he wanted Gus to see a couple of scenes from the film."[15]

Óskardóttir explains how she got the assignment to edit *Finding Forrester*.

Harmony had an idea of a film he wanted to do. It was three short films written by him but should be directed by three different directors, shot by the same DP and edited by the same editor. Gus was going to direct one of the films and he decided to go ahead and do his film. So I went to Oregon for a month and edited the short film and during that period he was talking to Sean Connery and Columbia Pictures about *Finding Forrester*. I thought of asking Gus if he needed an editor for that film but decided not to ask. I told myself that if he wanted me as an editor on *Finding Forrester* he would contact me and he did or Dany Wolf his producer did and I read the script. I liked it a lot and that was that.

During the shooting of *Finding Forrester* in Toronto, I asked Gus on the early stage of the editing how he wanted me to cut a scene I was wondering how to cut and he said, "You're the editor, you'll figure it out." After the shooting the editor's cut was finished; he was in the editing room during the days I was editing. He sat on the sofa and played his guitar or read books or worked on his computer. He never interfered while I was working, meaning that he didn't talk to me or tell me what to do and how to do it while I was working on something, but waited patiently until I was finished and then we talked and we talked a lot. He didn't do any physical editing but he was there with his sharp, clever mind whenever I—or the film needed him. I was told some years later that he had said to a director that asked him how it was working with me: "She likes to be the skipper in the editing room." I guess that's true. I like having things my way while I'm working and Gus had the mentality and generosity to give me the space I needed. But that doesn't mean that he didn't have opinions or knew what he wanted.

As one of the producers, Sean Connery was involved so he came into the editing and watched sequences while we were shooting and after that he came to the screenings and followed the editing process. So he was involved.

When asked about the shooting ratio, Óskardóttir responded, "I would say it was about 50 hours of material. At least we had everything we needed for making the film and not at any point did I think we needed something that wasn't in the footage. We had it all."

It was Rob Brown's first time acting in a film, but to Óskardóttir working on his scenes was no different from cutting an experienced actor. "There is no difference in cutting a first time actor; you do the same as you do with other actors and that is to look for the best performance."

When asked how Van Sant compared to other directors, this was the reply: "I don't want to embarrass the other directors I have worked with by telling you how Gus is compared to them or they to Gus. The only thing I can tell you is that they could learn a lot from him."

The film was cut on AVID.[16] "*Finding Forrester*" was cut in Portland, Oregon and Gus was sweet and concerned inside and outside the editing room."

Two editors, Valdis Óskardóttir and Pietro Scalia, talk about Van Sant in the same manner. There are few if any negative reports from the many crew members who have worked with Van Sant. The image of him playing guitar for his editors while they work is calming and very American. The troubadour runs deep in our history, as does the painter, writer, and filmmaker, making Gus Van Sant an important 20th- and 21st-century figure.

Antonioni Meets P. Adams Sitney vs. Kurt Cobain in Disguise While Paranoia Strikes Deep

GERRY (2002)

When Stanley Kubrick's *2001: A Space Odyssey* was released in 1968, it was called the most expensive experimental film ever made by a major Hollywood studio. Kubrick was not as much an admirer of the avant-garde film as is Van Sant; Kubrick knew his film history and had seen many experimental films. Van Sant's passion for the cinematic road less traveled led him to a $3.5 million movie about walking, loneliness, male bonding, and murder out of love in which both characters are named Gerry and the title, *Gerry,* is used as an adjective.

The ostensible subject of *Gerry* is driving and walking. The method to portray the "action" is the long take. In the Internet article "Notable Use of the Long Take in Motion Picture Films," Jeffrey Sward defines the technique this way:

A long take is a continuous shot in a motion picture with no cuts, photographed from a single camera. Generally long shots run several minutes. In order to ac-commodate changing scenery or moving actors, the camera is often on a dolly or studio crane. The Steadicam is often used in long takes after its invention in the 1970s. Long takes are rare because of their relatively high expense and complexity. Long takes require extensive technical coordination among the camera operators, lighting technicians and actors. Long takes are also unforgiv-ing of mistakes, requiring a retake from the beginning. The time involved in ex-tensive planning, coordination and retakes is costly in labor dollars. Culturally the population has become accustomed to cuts in motion pictures, so there are no continuity reasons for long takes. However, when done well, the long take is often an object of beauty as well as cinematic craftsmanship. The long take is the director's and cinematographer's *éclat, raison d'être, tour de force, sine qua non,* and *ipso facto.* The term "long shot" is often used to mean "long take." More often "long shot" refers to a scene where the camera is positioned to take in a large area such as the actors included with their surroundings. The term "long cut" is often used to mean "long take." More often "long cut" refers to the longest version of a motion picture containing the fewest cuts.[1]

Movies cited by Mr. Sward include, *The Best Years of Our Lives* (1946), directed by William Wyler; *Breathless* (1960), by Jean Luc-Godard; *The Gang's All Here* (1943), by Busby Berkeley; *Royal Wedding* (1951), by Stanley Donen; *GoodFellas* (1990), by Martin Scorsese; *Gun Crazy* (1949), by Joseph Lewis; *Lady Be Good* (1941), by Norman McLeod; *Broadway Melody of 1940* (1940), by Norman Taurog; *The Player,* (1992), by Robert Altman; *Rope* (1948), by Alfred Hitchcock; *Touch of Evil* (1958), by Orson Welles; and *Will Success Spoil Rock Hunter* (1957), by Frank Tashlin.

Although these filmmakers have ventured into the use of the long take, none are associated with the technique as much as these master filmmakers: Michelangelo Antonioni, Béla Tarr, Miklós Jansció, Theo Angelopoulos and Abbas Kiraostami, Aleksandr Sokurov, and Andrei Tarkovsky.[2]

Gerry concerns two men named Gerry who drive to a wilderness trail, get out of their car without any real hiking gear, and begin to walk. When they see a group of hikers pass them by on the trail, they make the fatal decision to go off-road. *Gerry* is loosely based on a true story of two men who got lost in a vast landscape in which one kills the other to end his friend's suffering. The improvisations and narrative development evolved through inventions by Casey Affleck (Gerry), Matt Damon (Gerry), and Gus Van Sant.

Gerry follows the real-life story with some additions, such as a scene where Casey Affleck's Gerry finds himself on a monolith-like rock but doesn't know how he got up there or how to get down. Van Sant talked to Rob Blackwelder of the SPLICEDwire Web site about this scene.

> From the very beginning Casey was going to be the one that gets on the rock, so he somehow became the authority on what the rock was supposed to look like. . . . He wanted a rock in the middle of an open field. Just a round rock, so it would be like, how did he get on top? . . . This one . . . was discovered by a PA. . . . I loved it. I thought it was incredible, and it was so incredible that Casey felt like he couldn't say no because we'd looked at like 15 other places.[3]

During the feature-length experimental film, Van Sant pays tribute not only to long-take avant-garde masters like Michael Snow but to Kubrick's *2001: A Space Odyssey* and the seminal trip film *Easy Rider* (1969). The Kubrick nod is the rock scene; the Fonda/Hopper film is referenced by several camp-fire scenes in which Damon takes the role of Wyatt/Captain America and Affleck assumes the part of Hopper's Billy/Billy the Kid. The low-budget *Easy Rider: The Ride Back,* directed by Dustin Rikert, shot by Brian Lataille, edited by Michael J. Duthie and Andrew Robertson, and starring the relatively unknown Chris Engen as Virgil Williams, Sheree J. Wilson as Shane Williams, and Jeff Fahey as Wes Coast, along with a cast of more than 50, traces Wyatt's family from the 1940s to the present was released in 2009 in the United States in a limited run.

Whereas films like *The Wild Bunch* (1969) and *Natural Born Killers* (1994) hold records for the most cuts in their time, films like *Gerry*, with long takes, have the fewest cuts. The record goes to *Russian Ark* (2002) for one shot with a running time of 99 minutes and to *Rope* (1948), which is made up of 10-minute takes and is 80 minutes long.

Gerry was shot in Argentina and Salt Lake City, Utah. The locations were chosen for their varied topography and texture. The foliage and landscape in Argentina are linked to one of Van Sant's most employed colors, green, and the Salt Lake City ground is stone white. When the two locations are intercut, they become one vast environment. Green again represents death. It is the endless terrain that leads to Casey Affleck's Gerry's death, when the young man, tired and dehydrated, can't go on any longer. White is purity and endless bliss, but here it is too much for the Gerrys.

Does *Gerry* have a homosexual context? There are only two men in the film (not counting the passersby on the trail or the man and his son at the conclusion). Both boys, Matt and Casey, are pretty. The audience spends much, if not all their time, gazing at the Gerrys. There are close shots that allow the audience to gaze fixedly at their handsome and delicate faces. Even though these moments are rare and few and far between, overpowered by the large number of long and extreme long shots, the viewer becomes infatuated with their youthful beauty, as has the director who cast them. They stay close for warmth and to console each other. The strangling scene oddly looks like sex. Damon forces himself on top of Affleck's body and appears to be engaging in intercourse when he is really putting his friend out of his misery.

Gerry presents the most awe-inspiring and physically gorgeous application of Van Sant's signature images of large open skies with moving clouds, sometimes in slow motion, other times at high speed. Here, the sky represents beauty and danger, with heat and cold controlling the two doomed walkers. Often Van Sant calls in another director of photography to do this "second unit" work. This Hollywood term is an insult to Van Sant's results, which look to the experimentalists for inspiration. In *Gerry,* the photography is accomplished by master cinematographer Harris Savides, who may have shot his greatest footage ever on *Gerry* in terms of the epic scope in which he captured the environment and the relationship between space and the main characters—man's relationship to his universe. No Oscar was given to Savides, but he was nominated for a 2003 Independent Spirit Award for his photography on *Gerry*. A documentary included on the DVD release shows Savides at work. He is a large man, who is mainly seen sitting behind his camera connected to a huge boom with everything rolling on tracks laid on the unforgiving salt. Savides is heard asking for another take of a shot because he knows he can do better. He may be one of the only men who could shoot a remake of David Lean's *Lawrence of Arabia* (1962), another iconic film referenced throughout *Gerry*.

It is the photography of *Gerry* that provides a large share of its greatness. The use of light, movement, and composition are near perfection. There are many locked-off shots in *Gerry*, as well as tracking, dolly, handheld camera and Steadicam work. *Artform* magazine called the film "One of the Year's 10 Best Films!" while the more conventional *People* magazine proclaimed it "visually spectacular."

Returning to the question of what *Gerry* is *about*, viewers must experience and analyze specific scenes and shots to answer this question for themselves; different people may reach different conclusions. The most amazing set piece is a very long take in tight close-up of the two Gerrys walking side by side, Savides' camera photographing them in profile. The viewer becomes transfixed by their movement and whether one is ahead or behind the other. This shot is the litmus test of whether a particular viewer is ready for this uncompromising film. Some would find it a good time to walk out, whereas others are hypnotized by the cinematic notion of movement within a frame. Movement within the frame becomes part of the content and one of the thematic treads of *Gerry*. This shot is the seminal image of *Gerry*. It is visceral, startling, audacious, punishing, and without regret.

The Weinstein brothers[4] as film moguls have put their unconditional support behind Van Sant on many projects. Although Harvey Weinstein has a reputation for taking movies away from directors and recutting them, he apparently has great trust and faith in Gus Van Sant. Although they were the distributors and not the original financiers (who must have lost their shirts, as Van Sant Senior did on *Alice in Hollywood* [1979]), the Weinsteins are to be commended.

Roads have been featured in many Van Sant films, most notably *My Own Private Idaho* (1991). In *Gerry*, the opening and closing shots and some flashbacks within the structure present driving scenes on a two-lane road. The road movie theory has been previously discussed and applies well to *Gerry*. Here, in *Gerry*, the road takes on an existentialist modality. It's like the automobile version of Samuel Beckett's *Waiting for Godot* (1953); in fact, the entire film could stand as a cinematic variation of this literary giant's theatrical masterwork. Both works deal with desolation, longing, and spirituality and have two featured male characters.

This road is relentless and never-ending. It is first viewed from behind, photographed apparently from a following camera car. The camera gets close, then pulls back, gets close, then falls back, as we become fascinated with the image and wonder what this film will be about. Who is in the car, and why is it taking so long to meet the main characters? Because *Gerry* is an experimental film reminiscent of Marguerite Duras's[5] 1977 film *The Truck*, we will have to wait and put our hearts and minds in the hands of the director.

When *Gerry* was in release, audiences began walking out after a period of time and even this early in the film. Van Sant cuts to the interior of the car. Matt Damon's Gerry is in the passenger seat and Casey Affleck's Gerry is driving. They do not speak for a long time. They seem somber and on a mission. The windshield is dirty and smeared from the movement of the windshield wipers before the film started. The reverse angle is held for a long time. If the viewer didn't know initially that this was an unusual and challenging film, he would know it by now. *Gerry* is also about time and space, like a Kubrick film, so the flashbacks are of little help in determining how long the Gerrys have been out there. In what year does this take place? There is little to go on; the language, hairstyles, and clothing can fit into many time frames.

What happens after the film ends? As we watch Damon's Gerry, he seems to be shell-shocked, maybe thinking about how he's going to tell Affleck's Gerry's family what happened. What will he do with his life, and how has this experience affected his future? In *New Cinematographers*, by Alexander Ballinger, Savides comments on this dramatic and haunting sequence.

> That was one of the most technically demanding scenes in a movie of this size. We had to get a very small remote head called a Sparrow Head that we put in the passenger seat of the car. We intended to start the scene looking out the window and then panned all the way over to the driver. Then we panned back, but we couldn't use it because you need to cut from the driver looking at Matt in rear view mirror to Matt and it didn't work when you panned back to the kid and back, but it was a beautiful shot. Gus operated. . . . I wanted Gus to be there and watching it.[6]

Elements, the glass components cemented to each other that contribute to the magnifying and refracting of a lens, are visual design components in *Gerry*. Pink is one of the colors used, a reference perhaps to Van Sant's novel or the color of gay liberation. Originally considered a mistake by Hollywood moguls, revealing the lens elements during a shot was turned into artistic expression by Conrad Hall (*The Professionals* [1966], *Hell in the Pacific* [1968], *American Beauty* [1999]) in *Butch Cassidy and the Sundance Kid* (1969) and by László Kovács (*Psych-Out* [1968], *Five Easy Pieces* [1970], and *New York, New York* [1977]) in *Easy Rider* (1969). Savides has learned the beauty of this effect involving lens technology from these past masters; Savides controls it like a surgeon, placing the lightly colored circles exactly where they can be a part of the artful compositions.

Pietro Scalia, editor of *Good Will Hunting* (1997), is an admirer of Van Sant's experimental films. "I love *Gerry*. There's beauty and simplicity. It's poetry and as a filmmaker it's a luxury to do those kind of films and that Gus was able to get financing and collaboration from Matt and other actors to do those series of films. They are very personal and both very intimate and poetic and I love poetic cinema."

ELEPHANT (2003)

After *Gerry*, Van Sant continued his experimental film period with *Elephant*, which is loosely based on the Columbine massacre. On April 20, 1999, two students, Eric Harris and Dylan Klebold, entered their school, Columbine High, in Jefferson County, Colorado, armed to the teeth with weapons and ammunition. They shot and killed 12 students and a teacher. Twenty-three others were wounded. When they were finished with the slaughter, Harris and Klebold committed suicide.

The violence at Columbine is directly related to a new culture of American violence and death, which includes such tragic events as the assassination of President John F. Kennedy on November 22, 1963; the massacre in 1966 of 14 people and the wounding of 32 others by Charles Whitman, shooting from the tower of the University of Texas at Austin; the assassination of Martin Luther King Jr. on April 4, 1968; and the assassination of Robert Kennedy on June 6, 1968,[7] as well as the Vietnam War and the random violence across neighborhoods in the United States that transformed a population that, up until the late 1950s, rarely locked the doors of their homes to installing as many locks as they could afford.

Van Sant wrote the original screenplay inspired by Harris and Klebold's horror show and the youth culture of the times. *Elephant* features a young cast and, to a great extent, male beauty in the innocent and the guilty.

Fine Line Features and HBO films teamed up to present *Elephant*, which is a Meno Films and Blue Relief production. Meno Films was connected to Home Box Office, and Blue Relief Productions was owned by actress Diane Keaton, who is one of *Elephant*'s producers.

The first shot of the film can be interpreted as a short experimental film in itself. A fade-up reveals an aquamarine-colored sky with two telephone poles—one in the foreground, the second in the lower left of the frame. A streetlight is connected to a large central pole. The image reminds the viewer of a backwards flag, a possible political comment on the subject matter about to be revealed—the American education system in crisis. Throughout the credits, the image darkens until it is blue/black, and the streetlight comes on with its eerie green light. Here, green again signifies death.

The cast of young actors includes Alex Frost (*The Lost* [2005], *The Standard* [2006], *The Vicious Kind* [2009]), Eric Deulen (his only film to date), and John Robertson (*The Heart Is Deceitful above All Things* [2004], *Transformers* [2007], and *Wendy and Lucy* [2008]). Many of the other young actors have appeared only in *Elephant*, and many in the cast use their real first names for their characters.

Harris Savides is the director of photography for this, his third Van Sant film. Art director Benjamin Hayden had been in the art department for three Van Sant films (*Drugstore Cowboy* [1989], *My Own Private Idaho* [1991], *Even Cowgirls Get the Blues* [1993]) before becoming the art director of *Elephant*. Van Sant was the editor of his film. He has worked with several editorial collaborators, including Pietro Scalia and Elliot Graham, but like fellow independent filmmaker John Sayles (*Return of the Secaucus Seven* [1980], the gay-themed *Liana* [1983], and *Lone Star* [1996]), Van Sant likes to be in control of editorial matters. Producer Dany Wolf has worked with Van Sant on five films: *Psycho* (1998), *Finding Forrester* (2000), *Gerry*, *Elephant*, and *Gus Van Sant's Last Days* (2005).

The first section of the film is titled "John." A black card with white letters imparts the information. John is John McFarland (John Robertson). His father is played by Timothy Bottoms (*The Last Picture Show* [1971], *The Paper Chase* [1973], *The Man in the Iron Mask* [1998]). Bottoms is one of four brothers who became film actors. His presence here as John's drunk father is testament to the 11 films he made during the second golden age of American movies in the 1970s.

The first shot of the movie proper is an upward-moving shot of fall-colored leaves on a series of trees. The colors are bright and reflect the range of the season, also signaling that it is the beginning of the school year. The sky is a deeply saturated blue. The colors vibrate. The image looks like it could be from a David Lynch film, most notably *Blue Velvet* (1986).

Next is a full shot of a car being driven erratically (by Mr. McFarland) in a suburban neighborhood; he hits a car, almost runs into a bicyclist, gets too close to the curb, and then nearly hits a pole.

John has long, dyed-yellow blond hair that shoots out in sharp pointed shards and captivating green eyes. He is very pretty, innocent looking, and angelic. John has the kind of looks that many older gay men are attracted to. John is a student with a troubled father. He is wearing a bright yellow shirt with a black silhouetted bull in the center. According to the House of Names Web site, a bull on a coat of arms (and one can make an argument for the tee shirt being the modern equivalent) symbolizes "valor and magnanimity, bravery and generosity. The horns represent strength."

The sky does not match the opening distinctive shot. We already know we are watching not a conventional movie but a Gus Van Sant experimental feature film. John takes the keys and drives for his father. The camera favors Mr. McFarland as the light plays over his face and body.

The next section is "Elias" (Elias McConnell). In a long take, Elias approaches a field of leaves and trees carrying a still camera. He stops a teenage couple and asks to take their picture. The boy appears to be stoned and asks if Elias would like to get naked with them and take pictures. The girl seems to be the logical member of the couple and they walk a bit while Elias snaps a way. Elias asks the couple to kiss, and they oblige. When finished, the polite boy tells them he has to get to school and will make a print of the pictures for them. They walk off left, and Elias goes right. He walks away for a long time as we watch him move in the distance in a full and colorful shot.

John drives to school, and calls for help—someone to drive the drunken Mr. McFarland home. He is caught by the principal and ordered into the office, where they have a brief staring-down match. The doors of the high school are red—signifying the quintessential little red schoolhouse iconography that registers with millions of Americans and foreshadowing the blood that will flow later in the film.

Boys play football on a green field. Beethoven's "Moonlight Sonata" begins to play. Piano Sonata No. 14 in C-sharp minor was completed in 1801 and is believed to have been written for a 17-year-old countess student with whom the master was in love. It has been used in many films, including *Titanic* (1997) and *Moonlight Sonata* (2008). Vanilla Fudge keyboardist Mark Stein plays a dramatic rendition on the concept album *The Beat Goes On* (1968). "Moonlight Sonata," one of the most recognizable pieces of music in the world, has a calming but dramatic effect and a quiet sadness as it builds in power. Here Van Sant is setting the scene for the tragedy that will unfold over the 81-minute running time of *Elephant.*

Next section is "Nathan and Carrie" (Nathan Tyson and Carrie Finklea). The game continues. Michelle (Kristen Hicks), a rather homely young woman, enters the frame wearing sweats; her hair is long and very curly. There is a slow-motion moment as she looks up to the sky. She leaves. Nathan walks up to the camera and grabs his red lifeguard sweatshirt jacket, which was out of the frame. He puts it on and starts a long walk as the camera follows him in and out of the school. We see a hallway, stairs, and burnt-out windows as the Beethoven continues. The image is mesmerizing. The Steadicam follows him and eventually lands on three attractive teenage girls who stare at Nathan as he passes. They seem to like what they see. He turns in slow motion, then at sound speed, as he continues to walk down the hall until he meets his girl-friend, Carrie. They talk about class as the camera continues to follow from behind. They go into an office.

Back to the principal and John as if they have been sitting and staring for the whole time we've been away from them. John is told to get to class. It becomes crystal that *Elephant* is about many things—youth culture (Nathan passes by break dancers), the monotony of school, walking, camera movement, and, above all, time and space. All films utilize the passing of time. Some films take place in short periods of time, others longer, but it is the manipulation of time that is the director's control point for story, content, and visualization. Van Sant is fascinated, as was Kubrick in *The Killing* (1956), by multiple viewpoints and how things happen at the same time from different people's perspectives.

Many have observed that Kubrick was a director of time and space. Van Sant explores the space of the school rooms and the halls, making this exploration a significant element of *Elephant*'s content. Van Sant talked to Steve Head of the IGN Web site about Stanley Kubrick's influence in his own work.

> Kubrick's a big influence. In something like *A Clockwork Orange* (1971) he is trying to use the practical light. . . . In *Elephant* we basically used no lights; we never really adjusted. If we shot you, you would be lit by this window and we wouldn't put anything on them [pointing to the lights above and behind]. We would use these lights too; we would maybe leave them on or off but we didn't try and push the lights.

So *Elephant* is not a conventional film based on the Columbine massacre but a film about time and space—the trademark of the cinema. Of all the arts, cinema is best suited for this phenomenon. The frame, camera movement, design, spatial relationships, and the nature of how time unfolds are in the essence of the motion picture medium.

John walks down the hall and stops in a large room, where he begins to cry. The boy is full of tension because of his father and his getting into trouble with the principal because of him. A girl walks up to John and consoles him. She gives him a kiss on the cheek and leaves.

"Acadia," the third segment, deals with the notion of how you know whether someone is gay. For the aesthetic treatment of the scene, Van Sant uses the 360-degree pan. Acadia (Alicia Miles) walks into a classroom where a student/teacher discussion is under way. The students appear to be sitting in a circle. There is no master shot. The camera moves from person to person in 360 degrees, making it impossible to know whether the configuration of the blocking is rounding, oval, or otherwise. The students basically agree that it is impossible to tell whether someone is gay by looking at the person. When someone seems to have a direct answer in the affirmative, that person is cut off by the majority. The story of a farmer who couldn't tell if the rams he had were gay is brought up as an argument to prove that there are no real parameters to determine whether one is gay or straight. The viewer is challenged by the circumstance and the context to determine if any of these students are gay. Van Sant understands the nature of human curiosity. One boy has on two earrings—a youth culture phenomena, not a clue to sexual preference. In earlier times, an earring could be a signal to others that one was gay. During the 1970s, a colored handkerchief worn hanging out of a jeans pocket could signal that someone was gay and whether he was interested in picking someone up.

The 360-degree pan is a highly cinematic device. The staging is crucial to its success. The camera is moving steadily (it can rest on a person or object for a time) around the filming area, completing a circle that ties together everything shown. Circles are a way of symbolizing life (remember the song "Circle of Life" in *The Lion King* [1994], written by Tim Rice and Elton

John) and creating visual harmony. Here the discussion is unified by the camera circling.

During the 1960s and 1970s, the 360-degree pan was a challenge to maverick filmmakers. Hollywood studio films did not embrace this element of camera grammar as much as European and American New Wave filmmakers did. The technical challenge is where to put the lights or reflecting boards. Also, the 360-degree pan makes itself obvious, unlike intercutting, dissolves, fades, match cuts, and other so-called invisible devices created to allow the viewer to enter the cinematic story and not be distracted by the filmmaker's vision. That all changed with the French New Wave and other European movements that celebrated the cinematic language in which the use of camera became a part of the story. Getting into and out of a 360-degree pan takes careful directorial planning.

Jerry Lewis (*The Bellboy* [1960], *The Nutty Professor* [1963], *Hardly Working* [1980]) takes pride in telling a story of a 360-degree pan he made as a director of *One More Time* (1970), the sequel to *Salt and Pepper* (1968), which was directed by Richard Donner (*Superman* [1978], *Lethal Weapon* [1987], *Assassins* [1995]). After carefully hiding the lights for the interior shot, working out the elaborate staging, shooting, and editing the shot into the film, Lewis concluded that the 360 just didn't work—it distracted from the whole. Although an inventive filmmaker in his own right, Jerry Lewis was a product of the Hollywood studio system. The shot was removed, put in a can, and labeled "Jerry's ego." Van Sant's application of the 360-degree shot here and in other sections of *Elephant* is not executed out of ego but is used to make an artistic statement. Van Sant is an American maverick of the third generation, following the elders, who include Orson Welles, Sam Fuller, and Robert Aldrich, and the second generation, John Cassavetes, Stanley Kubrick, and Francis Ford Coppola.

The "gay" 360-degree shot in *Elephant* appears to be homage to the "praying for the food we eat" sequence in *Easy Rider* (1969) and the use of this camera grammar in the films of Jean-Luc Godard and Werner Rainer Fassbinder. Michael Ballhaus, who was the director of photography on many of Fassbinder's early films, states that he and the late director decided to put at least one 360 in every film, as a challenge and an artistic statement.

Jean-Luc Godard, probably the greatest advocate of this technique, employed the 360 in many films, most notably *Weekend* (1967), in which he, as the maverick's maverick, does multiple turns of the circle.

In the fourth segment, "Eric and Alex," the killers are first shown before the title card, which is the strategy throughout *Elephant*—the characters are introduced, then identified by a card. Eric (Eric Deulen) and Alex (Alex Frost) are seen approaching the school ready to start the massacre with gear and weapons in tow. They pass John and warn him to "get the fuck out of here and don't come back."

Earlier, the central action of *Elephant* takes place. Elias and John meet in the school hallway. They chat, and then Elias asks John if he can take his picture. He does. During this, Michelle runs behinds Elias on her way to the library for her work session.

Michelle wears sweats because she refuses to reveal any part of her body. Her gym teacher tells her this must stop and that Michelle needs to be in shorts the next day, but for Michelle, her gym teacher, and many other teachers and students, this is the last day of their lives.

Nathan and Carrie get permission to leave the school premises for a period of time. They walk down the hall, revealed as dark figures lit by pools of light that favor Carrie.

In science class, Alex is pelted with spitballs. This kind of humiliation dumped on him by the jocks in the class is part of his motivation for the plan to harm and kill students and burn down the school.

Alex goes into the school bathroom to clean up. The room is bathed in the green light of death.

Now in the cafeteria, Alex looks around as a boy deliberately sly-raps him with his shoulder. Alex writes notes for the massacre plan. When asked what he's doing, he replies, "You'll see." At one point, Alex is standing and holds his head. He is overwhelmed by the hatred he feels.

Elias is liked by almost everyone in the school. He goes into the photo lab. At one point in the film, he is warned to watch out for a particular male who is known for "goosing" students, or touching their private parts. Many have reported similar occurrences during their high school darkroom experiences.

There is an intriguing close-up on Elias's hand as he turns the silver canister containing his negative and developing chemical. He turns the can back and forth repeatedly, to coat the entire negative, in a steady, constant movement, then takes off the cap and spills out the chemical. Throughout *Elephant*, Van Sant shows the process details of taking a still photograph and developing and printing the picture. So another thematic strand of the film is the nature of photography itself. The still photography represents the motion picture photography employed in the creation of *Elephant*. Process itself is a theme—the process of planning and carrying out the massacre, dealing with parents and school officials, education, youth culture, and male/female, female/female and male/male relationships.

Freeform jazz is played in this sequence when Elias walks down the hall. On cue, the music is dialed down and the dialogue track brought up when he says hello to someone, then the music goes back up to the feature the jazz. This sort of freeform jazz, made famous by John Coltrane and others, is a nod to the 1960s and early 1970s. It is unlikely that these students listened to that genre of music, but it is Van Sant's manner of continually linking the time period of *Elephant* to the 1960s and 1970s. Also, this form of jazz creates a dramatic tension when married to the image. The seemingly arbitrariness of the music is a strategy to convey the random nature of the senseless acts that will occur. Although the two killers have a plan, once the attack is under way, their toxic anger motivates their every move and deed.

There is a brief moment in this sequence that is reminiscent of *Gerry*. As Elias walks down the hall and a female student walks behind him, the viewer become transfixed about who is ahead and who is behind, just as the infamous shot in *Gerry* where Damon's and Affleck's heads are seen in close-up, moving back and forth as they walk in a long and relentless take.

After Elias hangs up his negative to dry, Michelle is in the girl's locker room. She puts her top on and does not take a shower, while the other girls talk about her. Michelle is self-conscious about her body and does not want anyone to see her naked. Michelle is reminiscent of a character from a Harmony Korine movie (*Gummo* [1997], *Julien Donkey-Boy* [1999], *Mr. Lonely* [2007]), the kid next door from an alien, alternate universe. Korine is friends with Van Sant, and they have appeared in each other's movies. Van Sant also was a producer on *Kids* (1995), written by Korine and directed by Larry Clark. Harmony Korine has dealt with gay themes, and, although he has had girlfriends, there have been rumors he is either gay or bisexual. Korine has also been linked with the Dogme 95 movement.[8] Van Sant has not made a Dogma 95 film, but he has long been fascinated by the rigorous cinematic manifesto school of filmmaking.

We enter Alex's home. It is brightly light, a nice house; we assume he comes from a good family. A wide-angle lens is used to increase the size of the room and to direct the viewer to the relationship between the subject and his environment.

In the darkroom, a yellow light fills the space; it is warm and comforting. A female student with a red sweater moves in next to Elias. This is ironic because, once the massacre starts, clothing will be soaked with blood.

There is a blue cast in the main room where photographs hang on the walls. It gives the shot a cool, night-like feeling. It is not night but day; by night many will be dead. Elias walks down the hall as the light goes from dark to bright and a flute plays—is there hope the worst won't happen? The second running of the shot of John taking a picture of Michelle jogging by occurs from another angle. When does this happen in the continuity of the story? Why is this moment so critical? At first we think Michelle is running from the killers, but, no, she is going to her school library job. The two boys, John and Elias, are good kids, friends who are gentle souls. Is shooting the still picture a metaphor? Is the camera analogous to a gun?

Throughout *Elephant*, the footsteps do not make much noise. In reality, they should be a little louder and heavier, but that would take away from the imagery and the floating feeling the viewer experiences, as well as a voyeuristic quality—that we are part of this story, walking through the school and feeling the danger that lurks behind each step, each corner, each doorway. Was there Foley work done on the film, the art of creating footsteps by walkers performing live in time with picture? Control is the power of the film director, the ability to control what we see and hear and when and how we see and hear it.

Green hall. Again, the halls in this film remind us of two structural film-makers, Michael Snow and Ernie Gehr, with whom Van Sant is familiar and whose cinematic experimentations he admires. Structural filmmaking, which was named by P. Adams Sitney,[9] is a form of experimental filmmaking in which the shape of a film is predetermined, often by utilizing a particular camera grammar such as a pan or zoom. The cinematic structure is the content and point of the work. Structural filmmaking came of age in the mid-1960s and finds its prehistory in Andy Warhol's *Sleep* (1963), *Empire* (1964), and other early films made at his Factory. *Wavelength* (1967), a film with what appears to be a continuous 45-minute zoom shot, is a celebrated example of struc-tural filmmaking, as is much of Michael Snow's work from the mid-1960s and 1970s. Other structural filmmakers include George Landow, Ernie Gehr, Joyce Weiland, Paul Shartis, and Tony Conrad. Structural filmmaking has its admirers in the critical, viewer, and filmmaking communities. It also alienates many who find the films strident and cinematically limited. Theorist P. Adams Sitney, who called the movement one of the most significant in the develop-ment of the avant-garde film, championed structural filmmaking.

Sitney observed that there was a group of experimental moviemakers who in the early 1970s were moving away from the work of Stan Brakhage, Sidney Peterson (*The Potted Palm* [1948], *Mr. Frenhofer and the Minotaur* [1949], and *Lead Shoes* [1949]), and others who worked in their style.

Is *Elephant* a structural film? It fits the definition. The aesthetics of the film are rigorous and boldly on view. The content is not necessarily "peripheral," which makes Gus Van Sant's experimental period so potent. He has taken content and themes that are part of his worldview and applied camera, sound, and editing strategies from the structuralists.

By accomplishing this, Van Sant has won more converts to the experi-mental film genre. He may have lost some fans who admired his more con-ventionally narrative films, such as *Good Will Hunting* (1997) and *To Die For* (1995), but Van Sant attracted a new generation looking for films that are daring and that reinvent the cinematic language. More film students and film buffs are exploring the work of experimental filmmakers. It works like the book blurb. If a reader likes a book that has been blurbed by authors the reader hasn't heard of, the reader is inspired to hunt down these scribes because they have been "endorsed."

To shoot in the halls, which are the signature images of *Elephant,* the Steadicam was used extensively, reports Savides.

> About two thirds of the film was shot on Steadicam. . . . I did some simple operating when we were not on it. We had a wheeled device made that would carry the Steadicam operator similar to the dolly used on *Gerry,* so he could

turn gracefully. The other was this weird rig that's used once when Alex is walking through the school. It's the last scene before he walks into the cafeteria.
It was like a long legged spider with a camera mounted in front of him and as
he's running down the hall it allowed us to do a 180 degree turn as the camera
spins around.[10]

Michelle is given the job of reshelving books in the library by a supportive
and kind teacher who tells her he's there for the young woman if she needs to
talk. The library is the place that later (can we say "later" with this flashback
flash-forward[11] structure?) she will die, and the books will be splattered with
her blood. The blood on the books is a metaphor for Alex and Eric's distaste
for education and for those smarter than they are.

   "Brittany, Jordan and Nicole" is the next segment of the film. The voices
of the three teen girls start over the reshelving shot. The shot that follows
Michelle is the second time we see Nathan enter and the girls admiring his
male beauty. The angle favors the door and contains a rainbow flare, a symbol of the gay liberation movement and the Rainbow Coalition supporting
peoples of all colors. This time, the conversation continues from the point of
the first showing. One of the girls tells her friends that Nathan's girlfriend,
Carrie, recently punched a girl for looking at her man.

   The eventual slaughter is bloody, violent, and a powerful reimagining of
the Columbine shootings. *Elephant* is the most popular and widely viewed
film of Gus Van Sant's experimental period. It mesmerizes and challenges the
viewer. In our time of cookie-cutter plots and character in most American
modern cinema, *Elephant* is a new model for what movies and cinematic
storytelling can aspire to.

GUS VAN SANT'S LAST DAYS (2005)

   With his third experimental film, part of what critics have labeled "the
Death Trilogy" (although the fourth avant-garde-inspired film, *Paranoid
Park* [2007], also deals with death, as does *Milk* [2008], which ends in the
assassination of Harvey Milk and George Moscone), Van Sant was beginning
to use the muscle and power he had accumulated over the years by having
the audacity to put his name in the title. Several directors had done this in the
past; the champion is Federico Fellini, who directed *Fellini's Satyricon* (1969),
Fellini's Roma (1972), and *Fellini's Intervista* (1987). Stanley Kubrick directed *Stanley Kubrick's A Clockwork Orange* (1971), maybe to send a message that he didn't quite film Anthony Burgess's novel but instead filmed
his own directorial take on it. This name-over-the-title concept was born
out of the mind and ego of Frank Capra on *Mr. Deeds Goes to Town* (1936),
Mr. Smith Goes to Washington (1939), and his masterpiece, *It's a Wonderful
Life* (1946). In his 1971 autobiography *The Name above the Title*, the feisty
but depressive Italian American director explained that, to him, it is one man,

one movie. He believed in collaboration but was convinced that it was the director who made the movie, thus embracing the auteur theory conceptualized by the French New Wave critics and by Andrew Sarris in America. Capra didn't put his name officially into the title, but he made it clear that, in print, on the marquee, and on the film, his name came before anything else.

Van Sant was asked by Sean Axmaker of the GreenCine Web site why he made the film.

> Being from Portland, we sort of lived in the shadow of that music. . . . But I think that moment [Kurt Cobain's death] is where all of it just stopped abruptly. There was this big thing that came out of the sky and stopped alternative music. . . . It was so abrupt. . . . It was probably the impetus; the notoriety of this character and what it meant. That was probably one thing, having been part of something similar myself in Portland, having gotten something going and having stayed in Portland and having had an awkward relationship to my own city where I came from and having bought a house that cost a lot of money, which he had done. He had done these things that were similar. Living in L.A. some of the time, going back and forth, all that stuff. I guess I just drew parallels.[12]

Although the viewer is informed in a disclaimer that *Gus Van Sant's Last Days* was inspired by the life and final times of Kurt Cobain, it is a work of fiction in story and characters. Only devotees of the deceased musician would know how close to the truth the details are, but critics and audiences must have been surprised at Van Sant's audacity, after decades of quiet ownership of his work through skillful applications of form and content. The title curiously reads as if the film were about the last days of the director in terms of life and work. Van Sant's double meaning ties him to Cobain and, in middle age, an awareness of his own mortality.

The film is dedicated to Kurt Cobain (1967–1994), the leader of the legendary grunge band Nirvana, who committed suicide by shotgun on April 8, 1994, at his home in Seattle, Washington. He left his wife, Courtney Love,[13] and his almost-two-year-old daughter, Francis Bean Cobain.

The grunge music and lifestyle movement developed in Seattle, Washington, during the mid-1990s, inspired by the release of albums by Nirvana and Pearl Jam. Grunge music and the grunge lifestyle won favor with a group of post-punk bands in Seattle during the late 1980s. The most noted bands to develop grunge music include Nirvana, Pearl Jam, and Alice in Chains. A descendant of rock 'n' roll, grunge combines the extreme volume and distortion of heavy metal music with the aural power of classic rock groups such as Blue Cheer, Deep Purple, and Ted Nugent and the Amboy Dukes. It stresses power chords over a melodic approach to the guitar, the bass guitar, the drums, and the vocals. The lifestyle grew out of the underground reaction to baby boomers who had grown up to become yuppies. The look of grunge combines the tee-shirt-and-jeans look of the 1960s hippies with the unkempt sartorial style of punk, with its ripped and dirty clothing and appetite for hard drugs.

The movie stars Michael Pitt as Blake, the Cobainesque character. The name Blake is a curious choice. It can be seen as a reference to the English poet, painter, and printmaker William Blake (1757–1827), who was considered a madman in his time, who is now seen as a literary and artistic genius, and who has been an influence on artists in every medium; or to the ragtime piano player Hubie Blake (1887–1983), who made his impression on society through his music and his longevity. Another possible reference is film director Blake Edwards (*Breakfast at Tiffany's* [1961], *The Great Race* [1965], *That's Life* [1986]), who is married to actress/singer Julie Andrews but has long been considered by media insiders to be either gay or bisexual.

The principal actors, with one exception—Ryan Orion, who played Donovan—used their real first names. Asia Argento (*Demons 2* [1986], *Queen Margot* [1994], *Love Bites* [2001]) is the daughter of Italian horror master Dario Argento and a cinema director in her own right (*L'Assenaio* [2001], *The Heart Is Deceitful above All Things* [2004]). Lucas Haas (*Witness* [1985], *Music Box* [1989], *Alpha Dog* [2006]) and Scott Patrick Green (*Washington Man and Myth* [1999], *Cthulhu* [2007], and *Feast of Love* [2007]) also appear in the film. Green also has a long association with Van Sant, having worked on seven of the director's films in various capacities, from assistant to still photographer to actor. Van Sant even went so far as to name a character for the actor whose full name is Ricky Jay, and who appeared in many David Mamet–directed films including, *House of Games* (1987), *Homicide* (1991), and *The Spanish Prisoner* (1997), and who plays a private investigator in *Gus Van Sant's Last Days*.

Once again, HBO put its resources behind a Van Sant film, but this time Diane Keaton did not produce. *Gus Van Sant's Last Days* is a production of the Meno Film Company, which handled *Elephant* (2003) and *Paranoid Park* (2007). Run out of Portland, Oregon, the company's name has a gay subtext, as in "Men, oh!"

Gus Van Sant's Last Days has a simple plot and fewer cinematic bravura flourishes than Van Sant's other experimental films, but it is the most difficult one to enter and to follow as a viewer.

Blake wanders around the vast property around his castle. He mutters to himself, skinny-dips, and plays music in his studio. Two couples are living in the mansion, later including a friend who is searching for Blake to save his life. Blake's wife shows up to get him to safety, a Yellow Book salesman sells him an ad, and twins try to entice Blake and later Donovan to join their religion. Diving deeper into despair, Blake writes out an elaborate suicide note, shoots himself in the head, and is found by a gardener. The film ends with law enforcement and medical personnel dealing with the deadly scene.

For a director who eschews computer graphics interface (CGI) and flashy visual effects except when they are necessary to the story (as for the layers of hats in *Drugstore Cowboy* [1989]), Van Sant came up with a brilliant and beautiful image for Blake's death. We are told, depending on one's religion, that upon death, our soul leaves the body and goes up to heaven or down to hell. The Catholic Church and other religions consider suicide a sin. It is also a crime.

The shot is the clothed dead body of Blake lying on the floor of the music studio. A ghostly image appears. Blake, stark naked, steps out of his body and climbs up a wall—out of frame. The image was created by Illusion Arts, founded in 1985 by Syd Dutton (*Glory* [1989], *The Age of Innocence* [1993], *The Fast and the Furious* [2001]) and Bill Taylor (*The Thing* [1982], *The Addams Family* [1991], *The Shadow* [1994]). Over the years they have produced images for many Van Sant films including *Finding Forrester* (2000) and *Milk* (2008).

Van Sant looks to cinema magicians when he needs a shot that cannot be executed by the production crew. Van Sant does not make action movies or "special effects" flicks but knows what imagery can best tell a story at a given point.

Blake's escape out of his rock 'n' roll nightmare is presented from his perspective. The nakedness is his return to purity—almost an Adam before he eats the apple. Blake surely has sinned enough to desire redemption. The moment is transcendent in the way Paul Schrader wrote about the transcendental films of Robert Bresson, Carl Th. Dreyer, and Yasujiro Ozu,[14] but here Van Sant transcends the reality of what came before. Like Jean-Luc Godard, Van Sant is a cineaste who picks and chooses his influences for any given moment in a film and ensconces them in his directorial vision.

The moment is also a relief for the viewer after psychologically and physically enduring the tedium and pain of Blake's tortured life. If a motion picture is made up of moments, then this one may surpass all the others in the Van Sant oeuvre.

Van Sant makes yet another allusion to *Easy Rider* (1969) when the wandering Blake goes from day to night and in the evening builds a campfire. There is not a Captain America or Billy to talk to—only himself. Blake's inner monologues, along with his muttering, singing and talking to himself, demonstrate what the drugs and the rock 'n' roll lifestyle have done to destroy this young man. Kurt Cobain was a growing young man with promise and artistic ambition. If *Gus Van Sant's Last Days* were a conventional biopic, the rise and fall would be clearly part of the storyline. This film, like Kubrick's *2001: A Space Odyssey* and Robert Bresson's *Pickpocket* (1959), is an experiential event. Van Sant is interested not in show-and-tell but in having the viewer experience the event before him.

A biopic is a film that dramatizes the life of a real person. This genre is notorious for adding characters and compressing characters for dramatic reasons. Recent biopics include *Before Night Falls* (2000), *Joe Gould's Secret* (2000), *Pollack* (2000), and *A Beautiful Mind* (2001).

Michael Pitt inhabits Blake/Cobain, as Ben Kingsley[15] did with Gandhi, De Niro with Jake La Motta, and Sean Penn with Harvey Milk in Van Sant's *Milk* (2008). The performance represents a deep understanding of the character and the dark side of the rock 'n' roll hero. He is an antihero who does not play to the screen or to the audience but lives the actions of a searching, desperate man who has lost his way physically and spiritually. With his long, stringy blond hair, scruffy beard, and trashy clothing, Michael Pitt merges the interior with the exterior—the sign of a trained actor who puts together all the pieces of a character to shape a performance.

Two set pieces are featured in the film. Both represent life as it is, as opposed to the strange and nihilistic happenings in and around Blake's castle. The first is the appearance of Thadeus, a Yellow Pages salesman played by nonactor Thadeus A. Thomas. The large African American man has surprising presence and acumen. Thadeus at first appears to be all business, a trained professional who goes through his routine regardless of the circumstances. He treats the ruined surroundings and their devastated and stoned-out resident as if everything were normal. The beauty of Thomas's performance is that he is able to play the text of scene while at the same time projecting that he recognizes all is not well. His patter allows him to ignore Blake's bizarre behavior and reactions. He presses on, but the viewer can clearly see that Thadeus understands that he has an odd one as his current customer.

The humanity of Thadeus comes through when he asks the practically collapsed-in-his-chair Blake if he is all right. The defining moment comes when Thadeus leaves and forgets his Yellow Pages book samples, demonstrating a concern for the troubled young man. Even in his shattered state, Blake manages to sign up for another run of his ads for a company that sells auto parts. This is never explained in the film and adds to the complexity of Blake's eccentricity.

Like John Cassavetes in fictional features or the Maysles brothers in documentaries, Van Sant gets remarkably lifelike and compelling performances out of nonactors. By using the right person with the right personality and presence, a director can inject reality into a scene or a film by having the nonactor playact and be himself at the same time

The other event is the arrival of twin evangelical men, Elder Friberg #1 and Elder Friberg #2, played by identical twins Adam and Andy Friberg, also nonactors. The short-sleeved, clean-cut young men arrive at the castle and are greeted and let in by the character Donovan. The choice to use a fictional name rather than the actor's real name, Ryan Orion, seems to be a nod to the singer/hippie/conjurer Donovan Leitch. An iconic 1960s figure, Donovan is said to have made rain disappear during an outdoor concert. His music, which embraces youth culture and drug use (the psychedelic kind), serves as a historic landmark in the movement from rock 'n' roll to the alternative, punk, and grunge musical movements. So the name Donovan gives *Gus Van Sant's Last Days* another subtle level of reference and meaning.

The young men talk about their spiritual leader as Donovan chides them about Jesus and wine and they talk about keeping their bodies healthy. The brothers play their scene straight ahead, showing no reaction to the sinful environment they have entered. The scene is about spirituality, an important human need that Blake has abandoned; he is nowhere to be found.

Although the story is principally about Blake's deterioration and loneliness, the intrusion of the private investigator has the ironic ability to turn the narrative, as it is, into a jokey crime drama. As he is driven around to the castle and other locations on the hunt for Blake, Ricky Jay, as the P.I., tells outlandish stories and shares his philosophy about his job. Here the film resembles the work of Zen cinema master Jim Jarmusch (*Stranger Than Paradise* [1994], *Night on Earth* [1991], *Broken Flowers* [2005]). The goofy characters who take themselves so very seriously and the unreality of reality make life in *Gus Van Sant's Last Days* seem off-balance and yet centered in its own universe.

The complex sound design complements and augments the plight of the main character. Again a train engine is heard in the exterior scenes. Also heard are birds and the vocal performances by Michael Pitt. Church bells and a clock bell are incorporated aurally, as well as voices. Leslie Shatz (*Bram Stoker's Dracula* [1992], *Masked and Anonymous* [2003], *I'm Not There* [2007]), a frequent collaborator of Van Sant's, created the soundscapes. Shatz worked on *Even Cowgirls Get the Blues* (1993), *Good Will Hunting* (1997), *Psycho* (1998), *Finding Forrester* (2000), *Gerry* (2002), *Elephant* (2003), *Paranoid Park* (2007), and *Milk* (2008). At the 2005 Cannes Film Festival, Shatz won the grand prize for his sound work on *Gus Van Sant's Last Days*.

For the second time in his career, Van Sant's cameo in this film is aural; he is one of several phone voices who try to talk sense into the obstinate Blake.

There is a self-referential moment when the P.I. finds a substance in the house and says, "Look how it's starting to crystallize, cellulose nitrate, same stuff as film stock. This is eventually going to implode, crystallize and implode." The reference is to nitrate stock, which was used during the silent era and up to the point that safety film was created, in 1948. The constant danger that nitrate film might explode was a fear that back-in-the-day filmmakers and projectionists had to face. This line also can be interpreted as a metaphor delineating the mental state of Blake, who is gradually coming apart mentally.

Harris Savides again was the cinematographer, and his photography is yet another aspect of content in the film. There are many features to his results here: flawless compositions, bold yet delicate camera movement, and the magic of cinema light, showing a lot or just enough or plunging the viewer into darkness. The cinematographic set piece in *Gus Van Sant's Last Days* is a long slow backtracking shot[16] during which Blake plays slow music. It took many takes and intricate work by the camera crew to pull this off, as demonstrated by a DVD special devoted to this achievement, as well as a top shot taken but not used in the editing room.

There is even an homage to Van Sant's artistic hero, Andy Warhol. On more than one occasion, Donovan puts on a vinyl record and plays The Velvet Underground's "Venus in Furs," sung by Lou Reed. The droning quality of the production relates to the song Blake is creating throughout the film. The band, which was decades ahead of its time, was taken under Warhol's wing, and he featured them in his multimedia performance art show "Exploding Plastic Inevitable."

Van Sant shot his Kurt Cobain movie in Garrison, New York, at the Castlerock estate. The location is isolated and weathered by time. If the art department had found a suitable area in Portland, Oregon, it would have been convenient but not as visually perfect and disturbing. The estate does not look like the actual Cobain home but reflects rather Van Sant's image of a rock 'n' roll crib.

The clothes, by Amy Roth (her mother, Ann, is a renowned costume designer who worked with the director on *Finding Forrester* [2000]), are lived-in and accurate reflections of 1970s rock chic.

Gus Van Sant's Last Days is a musical biopic in the experimental genre that contains a gay scene between two of the musicians. Like Oliver Stone, for whom Van Sant almost worked on the former's unmade project on Harvey Milk, Van Sant is obsessed with history, but not in a political sense. The films of Gus Van Sant track cultural history—where we've been and why. Viewed together, they form a body of work that evolves in style and storytelling and in its view of our youth and adult culture.

PARANOID PARK (2007)

Van Sant's fourth film during his experimental period, *Paranoid Park* is an existential[17] mystery about the murder of a railroad security man. "Paranoia strikes deep—into your heart it will creep," sung by Stephen Stills of Buffalo Springfield in "For What It's Worth," is not heard in the film, but it surely captures the spirit of *Paranoid Park*.

Rap music, graffiti, break dancing, and skateboarding are part of American and worldwide youth culture. Throughout his life and career, Van Sant has had his finger on the pulse of cultural movements. From his days as a student and throughout his career, he has stayed forever young. Is it the Peter Pan syndrome, embodied by Steven Spielberg and the late Michael Jackson? Gay culture, like most of society, is dominated by youth. In the final analysis, Gus Van Sant keeps the adolescent in him alive because he has the mind of a complex and diverse artist.

Paranoid Park deals with extreme skateboarding, an underground sport in the suburban, rural, and ghetto areas of America that has its roots in the surfing communities of the 1950s, which looked for alternative ways to "surf" when the waves in the ocean weren't cooperating. In the 1960s, hippies and others made their own skateboards, using a board and wheels from roller skates. It was a cool way to get around. The tricks and moves fully developed in later decades were in their infancy back in the 1960s. The first manufactured boards were created and sold in California. By the 1970s, skateboards went high-tech, improving maneuverability which led to the movements and tricks of today. The skater could now perform turns and lifts. There was an organized sport with competitions that began in the mid-1960s, but carrying and riding your skateboard became part of American youth culture. As the newer boards allowed flips and airs, the parks where many kids skated faced liability claims because of the injuries incurred by thrill-seeking boarders. By the 1980s, skating on ramps became possible and trendy, making skateboarding in public parks and streets more dangerous. In New York's Central Park, members of the public were happily entertained by watching the superstars of the street sport maneuver in and out of a long series of pylon cones. By the 1990s, however, law enforcement and governmental agencies went to war with the outlaw boarders, issuing fines and summonses. Eventually, groups formed and built their own illegal skateboard parks, and boarding became part of the hip-hop culture. Skaters began taking over street rails, ramps, and anything they could ride the board on while performing daring feats of ground surfing. The outlaw parks were hounded by the authorities, and the underground skaters searched for hidden areas to build a skate park. The movement became part of the punk aesthetic and lifestyle.

Prior to *Paranoid Park,* several movies featured skateboarding, including the 1965 short film *Skaterdater, Grind* (2003), *Lords of Dogtown* (2005), *Gleaming the Cube* (1989), *Trashin'* (1986), and *Dogtown and Z Boys* (2001).

In 2007, *Paranoid Park* was awarded the 60th Anniversary prize at the Cannes Film Festival.

Paranoid Park has grossed to date only $486,201, but it has a fierce cult following and is considered by many critics and others to be Van Sant's best film. In it, the director takes his experimental style, nurtured in *Gerry* (2002), *Elephant* (2003), and *Gus Van Sant's Last Days* (2005), and gives the film a dark, elusive, mysterious, and haunting narrative structure.

Paranoid Park is an IFC (the Independent Film Channel and Center) production in connection with MK2 Productions, a French and American film company; the French wing handles production, while the American part is in charge of distribution. Other productions by MK2 include *Chocolat* (1998), *Taxi Blues* (1990), *Three Colors: Red* (1994), *Gabbeh* (1996), *The Piano Player* (2001), and *10 on 10* (2004). Films distributed include *Chaos* (1984), *Betty* (1992), and *The Oak* (1992).

The opening of the film contains a sky shot and shows cars rapidly moving over a green bridge. This sky is ominous and sets the mood for the murder mystery aspect of *Paranoid Park.* The green signals death.

The music is a compilation of the work of various artists, including Nino Rota[18] and Elliot Smith (an indie singer songwriter from Portland, Oregon, known for his folk, rock, and punk music and for bringing the local music community together before his suicide, in 2003, at age 34).

There is dramatic/mysterious music that again speaks to the murder and then, in avant-garde tradition, a nonsegue shift to music from a Fellini film. Some of Nino Rota's musical cues originally written for films directed by Federico Fellini were placed by Van Sant in unexpected moments in *Paranoid Park*. A circus theme is prominent. The Fellini film scores drawn from include those for *Amacord* (1973) and *Juliet of the Spirits* (1965). The connection between Van Sant and Fellini, Fellini and *Paranoid Park*, and the Italian circus music is not readily comprehensible to the viewer. Van Sant's strategy seems to be instinctual rather than intellectual, because the various combinations of music throughout the film work on a visceral level.

Some observations and guesses:

- Van Sant is an admirer of Fellini and Rota and two of the films referenced.
- *Juliet of the Spirits* is one of the great experiments in film color and dream narrative. It has a psychedelic quality to it.
- The life of the main character Alex (Gabe Nevins) is a "circus"; he is caught in a whirlwind of intrigue, angst, and accidental crime.
- The clash between the music and the story create a frisson, which represents Alex's confusion.
- The music represents conflict—should Alex confess to the murder of a railroad security man?

Van Sant, along with a handful of filmmakers, is skilled in forging music and images.

Paranoid Park has a very complex narrative structure. The film takes place in a time continuum. Alex is writing a journal of what happened in Paranoid Park, a skateboarding facility where the members of the cultural underground go to skate and to hang out with like spirits.

Van Sant, who adapted the novel of the same name by Blake Nelson, of Portland, Oregon, a writer of adult, young adult, and children's literature whose books include *Girl* (1994), *Gender Blender* (2006), and *Destroy All Cars* (2009), is interested here in nonlinear narratives. The film incorporates the cult of skateboarding as a way to enter the alternate youth lifestyle while exploring experimental narrative forms and thematic invention. Through the script and in the production and editing processes, Van Sant has shaped this haunting meditation, another contribution to the so-called Death Trilogy.

Cinematographer Christopher Doyle, who photographed Van Sant's shot-by-shot re-creation of *Psycho* (1998), has also been associated with Wong Kar Wai. His credits include *Chungking Express* (1994), *Made* (2001), and *Lady in the Water* (2006). His cameo as Alex's uncle is a tribute to this fine cinematographer. Although the role is small, Doyle looks the part and, although a nonactor, is believable in it.

Alex sports a long and fringy Beatle haircut. He does not have the traditional Van Sant long side part. This fits the boy's face and allows the director to cinematically meditate on the boy's features and expressions.

The casting and performance of Gabe Nevins (another Portland, Oregon, resident) bring a Bressonian quality to *Paranoid Park*. Robert Bresson (1901–1999) was a transcendental filmmaker who used nonactors, whom he called models. He did not require dramatically emotive responses but photographed the face to explore the inner being. Van Sant takes that lesson here, with haunting results. We see Alex's torment and peer into his soul. *Paranoid Park* is a spiritual film in that it investigates the conscience and moral fiber of its main character.

Is *Paranoid Park* a transcendental film? This concept was developed by filmmaker Paul Schrader (*Blue Collar* [1978], *Mishima: A Life in Four Chapters* [1985], *Auto Focus* [2002]). In his book *Transcendental Style in Film,* in which he studies Ozu, Bresson, and Dreyer, Schrader defines that cinematic phenomenon as a spiritual state with austere production values, performances that transcend the self, and seamless editing. Schrader's *American Gigolo* (1980) comes very close to embodying his intriguing and controversial thesis and features an ending that is a tribute to Bresson's *Pickpocket* (1959).

Here is an excerpt from Schrader's introduction:

> In motion pictures these constructs [of Transcendentalism] take the form of what Robert Bresson has called "Screens," clues or study guides which help the viewer "understand" the event: plot acting, characterization, camerawork, music, dialogue, editing. In the films of transcendental style these elements are, in popular terms, "nonexpressive" (that is they are not expressive of culture or personality); they are reduced to stasis. Transcendental style *stylizes* reality by eliminating (or nearly eliminating), those elements which are primarily expressive of human experience, thereby robbing the conventional interpretations of reality of their relevance and power. Transcendental style, like the mass, transforms experience into a repeatable ritual which can be repeatedly transcended.[19]

Paranoid Park meets all the requirements for a transcendental film. The highly literate Van Sant must be familiar with Schrader's theories and Bresson's films. As is his trademark, Van Sant makes the strategy his own by placing the film in the world of underground youth culture—employing many nonactors and a filmic style that places the viewer in a spiritual cinematic environment. The exception is the complex time structure, which pops back and forth. In this way, *Paranoid Park* seems to have taken a page from the Errol Morris playbook used for the experimental documentary *The Thin Blue Line* (1988), in which a murder case is presented in a flashback/flash-forward structure.

Paranoid Park does not apply the homosexual gaze as thoroughly and consistently as do *Good Will Hunting* (1997), *Elephant* (2003), and other

Van Sant films. Nevins is pretty and young and has the innocence of youth. It is the latter that Van Sant explores—the innocence of youth and the complications that threaten this young man because of his life circumstances. Gus Van Sant is young at heart, but not in the way that Steven Spielberg and George Lucas are—they remain adolescents at heart. Gus Van Sant is less interested in the Peter Pan syndrome and more concerned with making the point that it is youth that is the future—their culture becomes our culture.

Using sound design as a tool for getting into Alex's head, as Frank Warner did in *Raging Bull* (1980), Van Sant and his longtime sound designer Leslie Shatz blend music that was rerecorded to play backwards, some of it with a dreamy character that may speak to the back-and-forth narrative, an at-first unintelligible voice, and a person speaking French. These experiments are in the tradition of *musique concrète*. *Musique concrète*, French for "concrete music," refers to an experimental form of musical composition that utilizes recorded sounds as raw material. Developed about 1948 by Pierre Schaeffer and others on his staff at a French radio station, *musique concrète* assembles various natural sounds recorded on tape or disks, producing a montage of sound. The sounds may be modified by being played backwards, compressed, or extended in length, by the addition of echo effects, or by alternations in pitch and vibrancy. The completed composition is the result of the gathered and structured sounds into an artistic work.

This music works on the viewer subliminally and connects with the image, drawing the audience into the picture. Sound designer Walter Murch (*The Godfather* [1972], *The Conversation* [1974], *Apocalypse Now* [1979]) was the first to use the term "sound montage" for his early credits; he did so because he was working nonunion and couldn't use the more formal title "supervising sound editor," which was popular at the time, although it was later changed to "sound designer." In *Sound-on-Film: Interviews with Creators of Film Sound,* he adds depth to the art Van Sant and Shatz were exploring in *Paranoid Park.*

> One of the main influences on me was the desire to somehow bring film and Music Concrète—the fun of assembling all these real sounds in an unusual context and yet having a visual reason for doing so. . . . Pierre Henry and Pierre Schaeffer [were influences] . . . [as a teenager] I had a tape recorder attached to my radio. I came home one night, turned on WBAI, and I couldn't believe what was coming out of the radio. It wasn't electronic music like Ussachevsky of the Columbia-Princeton Music Center or the Theremin introduction on the Long John Nebel radio show . . . the sounds were all real sounds . . . it was an album put together out of various compositions . . . they spliced sounds together, turned them upside own and backwards, and speeded them up.[20]

Home movies are once again used in a Van Sant film. There are images of the skateboarders flying through the air and the park; these evoke memo-

ries of Alex and the viewer and also present the beauty of the sport. Van
Sant, who has created many short films, treats the "flyers" segment as a self-
contained short film on skateboarding.

There are many beautiful images in *Paranoid Park*. A boy runs in a field
with a dog, Alex walks through the grass, and a shot of a boy in a large field
is framed as if it were in a Western movie.

Van Sant repeatedly returns to Alex sitting on a bench and writing the
story of *Paranoid Park*, a journal suggested to him to help him get the whole
ugly incident out of his mind.

Voice-over is introduced when a friend tells Alex to go to Paranoid Park.

Slow motion is applied to some of the shots of the boarders boarding
and to the home movies. Van Sant takes an overused technique (especially
on television) and utilizes the correct grammar just as a writer uses the right
adjective or verb to tell a story.

It would be simplistic to say that the story of *Paranoid Park* is told in back
story, although on the surface it appears that way, but this is a film the interested viewer should see multiple times so that the mysteries of the shifting
time frame become evident.

As in *Good Will Hunting* (1997), *Finding Forester* (2000), *To Die For*
(1995), and *Elephant* (2003), Van Sant probes the world of school life and
hallways. Where does Van Sant's obsession with school environments come
from? They are an integral part of youth culture. They are universal (except
for those who are home-schooled); everyone has good and bad memories of
the years spent getting an education. Halls have particular resonance. Many
former students have painful memories of walking through an endless system
of connecting halls, going from class to class, getting lost because of the
sameness, forgetting what class and room are next. This is a seminal element
of development; although the time we spend in high school is important for
our lives and careers, the experience leaves scars.

Alex is in class when he is called to the principal's office. The camera
follows him through the hall in both front and back view. "I Can Help" is
on the soundtrack. The song was written by Billy Swan; in it, a man tells a
woman he will be there for her. Alex is going to be asked if he can "help"
with a police investigation. He can't "help" because to do so would implicate
him in the accidental murder of a train yard security guard. The police can't
"help" because they just want to solve the crime and arrest the perpetrators.
A detective tells Alex and later other skateboarders during a visit to the high
school that he can "help" solve the crime if they will "help" him. Van Sant
plays the song for its rhythmic and storytelling qualities, which bring texture
to the sound and images.

The detective is Asian, which plays into the stereotype of the inscruta-
ble Chinese detective made famous by Charlie Chan[21] (who was played by
Caucasian actors). Here Detective Richard Lu is acted by Asian actor Dan
Liu in his first screen role. Once again, Van Sant is playing with stereotypes.

This is what the audience wants to see, but the character is far more complex than Charlie Chan or Mr. Moto.[22]

Paranoid Park now shifts into the crime genre. Liu is formal at first, calling the park the Eastside Skate Park and not using the street name, Paranoid Park. He is playing good cop with Alex, trying to get on the boy's good side. Alex appears to be in a fog because his mind is trying to process his situation. He answers the detective's questions and lies when necessary. When caught in an illogical statement, Alex backtracks and comes up with another story. The detective, not to tip his hand, is waiting for his moment and doesn't demonstrate any real emotion.

The scene is not a typical integration sequence. It's more like real life—boring and pedantic, a long search for the truth without a "Perry Mason moment."[23] Emotionalism is the road for most crime films and especially for television shows like *The Shield* (2002–2008), in which the subject breaks down in an outburst of emotion. *Paranoid Park* has Zen quietness and is focused not on action but on the inner workings of the mind and soul.

Another home movie montage, this one of the skateboarders performing tricks. Van Sant concentrates on the love of the action. There is a language and a grammar to the skateboarding names for the stunts and tricks. Just as Van Sant knows the language and elements of cinema, these skateboarders know the elements of their cultural practice. It is more than a hobby. They are kinetically aware of what can be done with a modern skateboard.

The youths deal with the outlaw aspect of skateboarding. A shot of a policeman writing up a skateboarder for illegal application on city property demonstrates this. Paranoid Park is an avenue for getting past all of the legal restrictions on the rights of skateboarders. The policeman's face is blacked out, a tabloid image. This may be a documentary shot and the filmmakers didn't have permission to show his face, or perhaps the shot was staged and presented as a graphic image of reality. *Milk* (2008) treats the documentary footage of gay men being rousted in a bar in a similar fashion. The "censored" image in both films is startling and effective. As an avant-gardist, Van Sant knows he can use found footage, mistakes, anything to make an artistic statement or manipulate the image in any way to make a point.

Why is the park nicknamed Paranoid Park by its denizens? Paranoia is an unfounded or exaggerated distrust of others and can sometimes reach delusional proportions. The paranoia of the skateboarders manifests itself in constant suspicions, rather than in full-blown delusions.

Are the skateboarders paranoid because they fear they are being persecuted by law enforcement and a largely hostile public? There is drug use in this culture, and substances like marijuana can leave the taker paranoid. Finally, Alex is inwardly paranoid because he is being watched by the police who think he is connected to a murder. He is also experiencing fear because of his feelings about whether he was responsible, in a moral sense, for the security man's murder. Guilt and fear don't clearly register on Alex's face; they come from inside in the Bressonian tradition. The park is the real Paranoid Park in Portland, Oregon, where the film was shot.

Now Alex is in his room writing on the journal. The impression is that this is a life project he must continue. This can be seen as a reference to Robert Bresson's *Diary of a Country Priest* (1951), a film about acceptance in which a young priest is not accepted by his parish and records his feelings in a journal. The subtext of *Paranoid Park* is partially about nonacceptance and rejection. Youth culture throughout the ages has rarely been accepted by the powers that be. (To a certain extent, the 1960s were an exception, with some over-30s wanting to join in on the celebration of youth and freedom offered by that magical decade.)

Alex's father is played by Jay "Smay" Williamson, a professional skate-boarder in his only known film performance to date. He questions Alex about the journal, and the boy blows him off. Alex is on a mission to rid himself of his secret guilt. Alex's dad and his uncle are played by two professionals in cameo roles, recalling Van Sant's use of nonactors (as did Robert Bresson and John Cassavetes) and his respect for "the real thing" in his movies.

Paranoid Park also concerns a secret. Alex is troubled by this. He lies to protect the outlaw arena but also searches for redemption and relief from his guilt, which he achieves through his journal.

Alex goes to Paranoid Park with his friend Jared (Jake Miller, in his only known film performance). It is their first time. Jared finds the courage and skates, but Alex feels he's not a good enough skater and watches the proceedings.

The park is illegally built and is the home for the fringes of society—train-hoppers, guitar punks, skate-drunks, and throwaway kids. Van Sant has long been interested in the rejects of society, those living outside the law.

A row of skateboard jumpers shot in slow motion is lyrical and poetic and speaks to what Alex in subtext wants to be—an artist. It also reflects Van Sant's point of view as someone who is captivated by the beauty of youth. This view is the opposite of society's—Van Sant is nonjudgmental toward youth society.

Paranoid Park is a film of repeat shots or actions or what seem to be repeats of shots or actions. Jared repeats a line about coming to the park another day. Shots of Alex seem to repeat, but as the viewer gets deeper into the spiritual aura of the film, he is unsure whether he has seen the shot before or just one like it. Alex is trapped within a time continuum. Moments of his life circle around him and are expressed through the film's nonlinear storytelling style, in the script, and in the final rewrite during the editing process.

Alex has a hottie girlfriend, Jennifer, played by Taylor Momsen, who had been in as many as six movies before working with Van Sant, including *How the Grinch Stole Christmas* (2000), *Spy Kids 2: Island of Lost Dreams* (2002), and *Hansel and Gretel* (2002). Jennifer is pretty, a well groomed and put-together teenager. She is a virgin and a bit of a Valley Girl. Because of his predicament, Alex cannot live up to her demand for his total attention. She also seems too sexual and too popular for him. What is she attracted to? The answer never comes. Van Sant understands the teenage girl's psyche. She finds him cute. He often says the wrong thing to her because he is more inside his own head than in reality. When confronted, he lies, and she believes him.

Back to the scene at the bench; Alex continues to write in his journal. This seems to be the only time he is totally alive. He is on a spiritual mission.

Alex skates over a long bridge to get to Paranoid Park. It is a "bridge" between society and the underground. He goes to the park by himself. There is a large crowd watching the skateboarders. They are all attracted by the spectacle of the hard-core freaks expressing themselves.

Van Sant complicates and layers the structure of the film by bringing two different time frames together with a sound overlap. Alex is sitting on the bench and in a voice-over a voice from a Paranoid Park scene is heard. Is Alex writing about this moment now? Is he so all-consumed by working through his emotions about the accidental murder that time has converged on him and the viewer?

At the park, a man who will remind the viewer of a cross between Henry Rollins[24] and Gus Van Sant asks Alex if he can skate with his board because the boy is just sitting there. The man and his friends live at the park.

Alex is at home changing his clothes after the murder. He is wearing only his boxer shorts. He takes a cleansing shower shot in slow motion to emphasize the spiritual nature of this action. In *Psycho* (1960, 1998) the shower is a place of danger and murder. In *Paranoid Park*, the shower is a refuge from the cruelty of the outside world and a temporary moment of peace and absolution from sin.

Van Sant contrasts the two halves of society by using two locations. The park is the netherworld, suburbia the straight world.

Alex goes to a coffee shop with a girl who is his friend. She would like to be romantically involved with him but accepts her situation and is a caring friend who happens to be a girl. She knows something is wrong with Alex but is not yet able to find out what it is. She looks like an average young teenage girl; she is not particularly seductive but is cute, with a warm face and disposition. She does not have a perfect body like Jennifer, who only wants Alex to eradicate her virgin state. She finally, through honest, probing questions, gets Alex to admit something has happened.

Alex tells the girl that he has broken up with Jennifer. His reasons are dictated by his spiritual crisis.

Van Sant explores the problems facing suburban teens, including divorce.

The school hallway, shot in slow motion, shows students trapped in the morass of angst and boredom of school. Alex runs into Jennifer. The Fellini music is playing. Jennifer is angry that Alex spends so much time with Jared. They don't appear to be broken up, as previously established.

Alex shops for a suit. The scene is photographed with a handheld camera in cinéma vérité style.[25] Jennifer tries on dresses. They appear to be shopping for a prom. This scene causes déjà vu in the mind of the faithful Van Sant viewer, because it is reminiscent of the scene in *To Die For* (1995) in which Suzanne Stone Maretto tries on bras and panties in front of Lydia Mertz, a teenage girl Suzanne later accuses of having lesbian tendencies.

Alex buys a new skateboard because he has thrown the other into the water after the accidental murder.

Alex and Jared are in a car; the camera captures the scene in slow motion. As Jared scrutinizes Alex, speed metal music plays.

Alex is sitting on the bench and writes "Paranoid Park" in his notebook again.

Alex walks through a field; the moving grass can remind the viewer of the shots in Terrence Malick's *Thin Red Line* (1998) of soldiers slowly moving through high grass to get to the enemy machine gun nest.

Alex again enters his room; he is writing and speaking to the viewer via voice-over.

A conversation repeats.

A news report is heard.

The murder mystery deepens and widens in scope.

Alex is in a library checking a newspaper to see if there is a mention of the murder. There is a photograph of the victim.

Back at school, a student is arrested, for smoking pot or for something else. A corn dog is eaten in the cafeteria as an announcement comes over the loudspeaker asking particular students to come to the office. They are all skateboarders.

School hall. The skateboarders walk in a line to the office. They look like the men at the end of Peckinpah's *The Wild Bunch* (1969) as they walk to what will be their death. One of the boys skates to his destination. A skateboard is an extension of a rider's body. Skateboarders take the boards everywhere they go—they are both transportation and personal expression.

Detective Lu comes to a classroom to address the boys. He tells them the police want the skateboarding community to help solve a murder. He calls the park the Eastside Skateboarding Park; they call it Paranoid Park. They are on opposite sides of society.

He questions the boys, including Alex.

He shows them a photograph of a decapitated man for its shock value.

Lu and Alex engage in eye-lock. This is a battle of wits.

Alex writes on the bench as dreamy music plays. The writing process propels him into a different mindscape.

Alex pukes in the school bathroom. In *Elephant* (2003), there is a scene in which several teen age girls go into bathroom stalls to throw up as a way of purging themselves after eating as a way to maintain their anorexic quest for thinness. Alex purges himself to try to get the murder out of his mind.

At this point, *Paranoid Park* switches to the Errol Morris strategy. We now are shown what happened that night in the train yards. Alex and the man from the skate park are in the train yard to ride the rails. This is a connection to Van Sant's first feature-length film, *Mala Noche* (1985), in which the Mexican men sneak onto a freight train to get from one place to another. This is part of an American tradition that goes back to the Great Depression of the 1930s, when men rode the rails in search of food, money, and jobs. There is also a long hobo tradition in America, homeless men and women who go from city to city, state to state, via the trains.

Alex wanted to partake of this outlaw experience and is taught by his new mentor, who has lived off the land in a 21st-century style and reached back to an earlier time in the country's history whose ways he has now incorporated into his lifestyle.

As they climb up to the moving train's open car, a security guard spots them and takes off on foot after them, wielding a large handled flashlight. When he catches up to them, he pounds Alex with the flashlight handle. A train is coming on another track next to the guard. Alex gets the flashlight away from the doomed man and smashes him, propelling the guard backward. The train runs over him, severing his body.

The viewer now knows that this was not premeditated murder but a form of self-defense, even though Alex was breaking the law. It comes approximately 45 minutes into the film. Those who have been following the complex narrative closely now know what they have been watching for roughly the first half of *Paranoid Park*.

This seminal event in Alex's young life is shocking and emotionally overwhelming. It sheds light on his unfolding behavior.

In a startling nightmare image more fitting for a gruesome horror film, the security guard is shown crawling with no legs. It is bloody and graphic and is like no single shot in any other Van Sant movie.

Back to the stare-down between Detective Lu and Alex in the classroom. Was this event what on Alex's mind as the detective talked to the class? Did the stare-down trigger this memory in Alex? Is this a flashback? Van Sant has created one of the oddest crime films in movie history.

Murder and guilt bring Dostoyevsky to mind, especially his masterwork, *Crime and Punishment,* written in 1866. The book was adapted for the large and small screens many times between 1935 and 2002. Robert Bresson's first color film, *Une Femme Douce* (1969), is based on Dostoyevsky's short story "A Gentle Creature," written in 1876.

Alex is running in the rain.

In high-speed cinematography, a thunderstorm is shown over the bridge.

In voice-over, Alex talks to himself.

Alex has blood on his jacket, which relates to the earlier scene in which he takes off his clothes.

Alex throws his old skateboard into the river.

Marching or circus music is heard, as is the voice of an announcer of some sort.

The structure of *Paranoid Park* can be compared to the art movement of Cubism, in which objects are broken into parts and then reassembled in an abstract form. Another art form that may have influenced Van Sant is deconstruction, the practice of breaking down a literary text into its smallest parts in order to understand its complexity, working method, and multiple meanings.

Moments of the film, such as the horror shot of the dismembered man crawling, connect to surrealism, a movement based on artistic presentation of dreams and other flights of fantasy.

The shower scene is repeated. Now the viewer understands the true meaning of Alex's need to cleanse himself. The scene is longer and is photographed in slow motion.

This is not a spontaneous performance. Van Sant has worked very hard with Nevins to get him to display the right expressions and meanings. A little is a lot in this style, which is why, although Bresson's films are very austere, they are deeply emotional for those who "read" them in the spirit in which they were made.

When Alex has his shirt off, there is no feeling of a homosexual gaze coming from Van Sant. Alex is young and in trouble, and such a point of view would be inappropriate and contrary to the spirit of the film.

Skateboarders run themselves and their boards up and down the walls of a tunnel. The scene is spiritual, as in Bresson's *Pickpocket* (1959), which observes without judgment the art and craft of picking someone's pocket. Here it's the art and craft of skateboarding as witnessed by an innocent eye that is simply watching the skateboarders do what they do. Some boarders angry, others joyful as they bring their personal ethical system to the act. Here the viewer is put in a position to see through different eyes.

Alex's voice-over sounds like the voice of a real teen, not an actor. He speaks with no dramatic inflection.

Alex repeatedly tries to reach his dad by phone. A recorded voice tells him to have a happy citizenship day (a holiday created by Congress in 2004). There is irony in the state of citizenship in Alex's confused psyche.

Alex stares and thinks. Thinking is a very hard state of mind to act and photograph. Here it takes a nonactor to make it believable to the viewer.

It is raining. Alex awakes and comes back home, telling his off-screen mother that he was at an "Expo . . ." He lies to her. When she is shown, it is from a distance and in a back view.

Alex is at a restaurant. His friend who happens to be a girl is with a friend of hers who also seems to find the vacant Alex attractive. This girl has doe-eyed makeup and is pretty but empty.

Alex walks around a mall as the Fellini music plays. The camera focus shifts.

Alex goes into Rebel Skates and buys the new board seen earlier.

The structure and point of view of the film all reflect Alex's viewpoint: how he sees the world now that he has been involved in a murder, accidental or not.

Alex is like many teenagers—a good boy who is attracted to the dark side.

Alex, Jennifer, and others ice-skate at a rink.

Alex and Jennifer move through the garage of a house to the pool area and then to a bedroom, where she is sexually aggressive with him. Alex is passive. They have intercourse, and Jennifer is elated she is no longer a virgin; she phones a friend to announce the event.

A group of boarders sits in a hot tub circle discussing the police.

The locker area in the school is a place Jennifer and Alex usually run into each other. This time she asks him if he got the condoms so that they can have more sex. He lies to placate her.

Alex is with his dad, who tells his son he's not coming back home—his marriage to Alex's mother is over. The scene is shot with selective focus, signifying that the boy is inside his own head, which visualizes Alex's lack of mental focus. The focus in on the dad as he apologizes.

Jennifer is dressed as a cheerleader. Fellini music. Jennifer and Alex begin to argue, and there is no sound at all. The camera is on Jennifer's face, as it was on the childlike, clownlike face of Fellini's wife, Giulietta Masina, in *Juliet of the Spirits* (1965). Taylor Momsen, who plays Jennifer, has the face of a young waif.

Alex has broken up with Jennifer. Is it because of the sex? There are no real answers here. His male friends think Alex has made a bad decision because Jennifer is so sexually alluring.

Coffee shop. Alex tells his friend who is a girl that he can't relate to anyone. She likes Alex. She tells him she's against the war. What war? We are not given that information but assume it is a war that was in progress during the year of *Paranoid Park*'s release.

Alex is lying down on his driveway. The girl rides up to him on her bike. She gives him a ride. He is on his skateboard and holds onto the back of the bike. There are three circles caused by the elements of the lens—another reference to *Easy Rider* (1969), photographed by László Kovács.

The girl tells Alex to write a letter about what's bothering him. That's the person to whom Alex has been writing to all through the running time of *Paranoid Park*. She tells him just to get out what is bothering him out of his system. He doesn't have to send the letter. Or he can send it to a friend—like her.

Alex is home. It's revealed that he has written it to her. He stops, does a little guitar playing.

Alex burns the letter. It brings to mind the burning of the sled at the conclusion of Orson Welles' masterwork, *Citizen Kane*, in 1941. The fire in *Paranoid Park* is held for a long time.

School. The class shown in the beginning of the film returns. Alex is tuned out.

Slow-motion montage of skateboarders. The beauty of the action. A skate-boarder makes a jump.

Cut to black.

Paranoid Park has concluded.

The credits tell us that the film was shot on location in Portland, Oregon.

End of Gus Van Sant's experimental film period.

7

The Mayor of Castro Street

MILK (2008)

Harvey Milk (1930–1978) was the first openly gay man elected to a political office. He and San Francisco Mayor George Moscone (1929–1978) were shot in cold blood by disturbed San Francisco board supervisor Dan White (1946–1985). A biography and documentary covered the tragic story. Director Oliver Stone wrote a script, "The Mayor of Castro Street," which he was to produce but not direct. His film *JFK* (1991) had infuriated the gay community by portraying a crazed group of homosexuals as involved in the assassination of President John F. Kennedy. When word spread that Stone was involved in a film about Harvey Milk, there was once again outrage from within the gay community.

In July 1992, Warner Brothers hired Gus Van Sant to direct the biopic, with Robin Williams in the title role, but Van Sant and the studio parted company in 1993 due to creative differences. Other directors were attached to the project over the years, including Bryan Singer;[1] actors who were considered for the lead included Richard Gere (who played a gay man during the Holocaust in Martin Sherman's 1979 play *Bent*), Daniel-Day Lewis (who played a gay man in *My Beautiful Laundrette,* released in 1985) and James Woods.[2]

Eventually, Van Sant came back to the project with Sean Penn as Harvey Milk and a tremendous supporting cast that included James Franco (*Spider-Man* [2002], *City by the Sea* [2002], *Pineapple Express* [2008]), Emile Hirsch (*Alpha Dog* [2006], *Speed Racer* [2008], *Taking Woodstock* [2009]), Josh Brolin (*Grindhouse* [2007], *American Gangster* [2007], *W.* [2008]) as Dan White, and Victor Garber (*Light Sleeper* [1992], *The First Wives Club* [1996],

Legally Blonde [2001]) as George Moscone. Many would agree that it made sense to have an openly gay director at the helm of *Milk*, but Van Sant's accomplishments, overwhelming credentials, and masterful moviemaking are what qualified him for the project.

Stylistically, Van Sant has never made a film quite like *Milk*. During his career, Van Sant has worked through many artistic periods and in many visual and cinematic storytelling styles. *Milk* followed his four experimental films, *Gerry* (2002), *Elephant* (2003), *Gus Van Sant's Last Days* (2005), and *Paranoid Park* (2007). *Milk* is an epic examination of Harvey Milk and the times in which he lived. Van Sant drew on all his filmmaking abilities and philosophies to make the film—including his experimental period.

It is the scope and texture of *Milk* that gives the movie size and weight. Historically, the film was researched to the nth degree and received assistance from living witnesses of the true story. The actors inhabit their roles—the proof is in their performances and in the pictures of the actual people they play that are shown during the movie's closing credits. The environments are meticulously rendered. Van Sant and his design team captured the zeitgeist of the time and left a history lesson for the ages. There is some artistic license afoot in *Milk*, as filmmakers feel they must tinker with the story or characters, but Van Sant is more than respectful in preserving history and the times that are depicted.

The title sequence is a mini-documentary on how gay men were treated back in the day. Black-and-white archival footage depicts police raiding gay bars and arresting homosexual men. The victims are humiliated by being handcuffed and rousted into police vans. The footage is grainy and raw. One man seated at a bar gets tired and angry at being photographed and hurls his drink at the camera. The men are a cross-section of America. Some "look" gay to the public, while others appear to be average Joes. This entrance into the secret world of the back-in-the-day gay community is shocking because of the candor of the footage, showing men who are not allowed to be themselves under arrest for being who they are. This history lesson sets up the film's major themes, especially the lack of equality for homosexuals. Change has to come, and the film will be about the man who singlehandedly incited such change and gave his life in the process.

In the introductory footage, black censorship bars, as seen in old tabloid papers, are added to block the faces of the damned—a powerful and postmodern way of displaying America's shame in criminalizing a large portion of its population. This segment is a prelude to the film proper, signifying that we are about to see a motion picture of epic importance.

In 1978, the year of his assassination, Harvey Milk sat down in his kitchen and tape-recorded his story. This narration is recalled throughout the 128-minute running time of the film and is highly effective in personalizing Milk's feelings and emotional makeup as he works his way up the political ladder and plunges into the heart of the political beast, inspiring and motivating his gay "brothers and sisters." This narrative thread always reappears at the right time in the story, keeping the viewer aware that it represents Harvey Milk's last will and testament.

The kitchen table shot has a stillness about it, a single, medium composition of a private matter that the viewer is allowed to observe. Harvey Milk recounts his life in a kitchen captured in saturated color. His tapes are numbered as he reads from a yellow legal pad. Sean Penn's performance is remarkable throughout the film, but in these moments he underplays the character, speaking in a quiet but steady tone. He is a gay man, a politician, a historian, and the voice of America's conscience. This is certainly a shopworn cinematic narrative device, but it is so effective in this instance that it transcends gimmickry and allows the viewer to witness the last hours of a man who changed social and political history. The silence in the room, along with the weighty presence of Harvey Milk, channeled through Sean Penn's inhabitation of the character, recalls Samuel Beckett's *Krapp's Last Tape*, in which a man looks back on his life and records his reactions to his past. The walls of Milk's kitchen are green, again symbolizing death—a life cut short.

Van Sant returns to this shot at key moments and at points where Milk's private presence at this time in his life is warranted. The voice-over is played over color documentary footage, as well as docudrama[3] and re-creation executed by the production team.

In the film, Penn sports a prosthetic nose. His hair is cut perfectly for all the time periods in the film. He received much praise for this performance, including the best-actor award from the Screen Actor's Guild and the Academy Award for best performance by an actor.

Like all great directors, Van Sant utilizes the crafts brilliantly.

- *Screenwriting:* This is a true story, and the screenplay with few exceptions is loyal to the actual people on whom the film is based as well as to the times they lived in and the locations in which they lived.
- *Directing:* The film is masterfully directed. It's an epic motion picture but with few shots, not a dense montage. It attains a perfect relationship between form and content.
- *Cinematography:* The lighting captures the times, and the compositions convey the grandeur and spectacle of the moment. The color is saturated, but skin tones are naturalistic. There is little camera movement and many full shots.
- *Production design:* Castro Street comes to life—details within details, perfect extras, protest signs, storefronts, political landmarks, and buildings.
- *Editing:* The film has just the right pacing; shots hold long but are the perfect length for the scene and the moment. While most filmmakers edit films as if the shots were aimed and fired at the audience with a machine gun, Van Sant times his choices with grace and passion.
- *Hair and make-up:* Thanks to great research and execution, everyone looks like they were in the 1970s; mullets, shags, and close-cropped looks all

reflect the style of the gay community during the artistically relevant but so-cially and politically nightmare-engulfed 1970s. While many directors at the time and since have put the wrong haircuts on their 1970s characters, Van Sant has a photographic memory for the way he and his friends wore their hair and what their faces looked like. He has done his research.

- *Costumes:* It's been said many times that the 1970s were a fashionista's nightmare. In *Milk* the clothes are rendered in color and cut to a T. Every-one looks real, not over-the-top, as on *That 70's Show* (1998–2006) and in countless bad movies that aim tore-create the 1970s.
- *Music:* The range of tunes and melodies from period records played to establish and complement the time of the film are touching and nostalgic but flawed by too much old-school Hollywood scoring provided by long-time Van Sant collaborator Danny Elfman. There are too many themes. The music plays when the actors are talking and are carrying the emotional load. Music should heighten emotions, not stifle or overplay them in these moments.
- *Archival research:* The footage, stills, and newspaper clippings are all perfect. They were found and created by the art department under the watchful eye of Van Sant and his team. Scratches have been digitally added to make the footage look aged.

When Milk kisses Scott (James Franco), he does not make cinema history. The first major male-to-male kiss was between Murray Head (*The Family Way* [1966], *White Mischief* [1988], *Lovers of the Nile* [2002]) and Peter Finch (*The Nun's Story* [1959], *Far from the Madding Crowd* [1967], *Network* [1976]) in *Sunday Bloody Sunday* (1971), directed by John Schlesinger, a gay director. Audiences found it shocking at the time, which was during the early days of the gay liberation movement. Did Harvey Milk see this film? Did Van Sant see this film? It doesn't matter because the impact of this lip-lock between the younger man and the older one was tremendous and bled lots of talk and ink. The audience and society in general were ready for it, even if they didn't think so. Of course, the Anita Bryants of the world (a story well documented in *Milk*) screamed and shouted, demanding *Sunday Bloody Sunday* be taken off screens and banned forever, but the cinema didn't budge in its conviction.[4]

Back to one of the few flaws in the film—Van Sant and Danny Elfman's decision to use the wall-to-wall scoring approach of past Hollywood mas-ters such as Franz Waxman, Erich Wolfgang Korngold, Max Steiner, Dimitri Tiomkin, and Miklós Rózsa.[5] Here it gets in the way of the deep emotion communicated by the actors. Instead of allowing the inherent drama to un-fold organically, the music (albeit in a sophisticated manner) is most often what the industry calls Mickey Mousing—a term for times when the music mimics the screen action and the same feelings or emotions aurally.

Sean Penn goes beyond the Hollywood stereotype of a gay man. His arms are loose and flowing at times, and his vocal inflections are just the slightest bit lispy, but the result is an actor physically and psychologically capturing the openly gay political activist who was Harvey Milk.

The ensemble cast, another nod to old Hollywood, is filled with great character performances: Emile Hirsch as Cleve Jones, Diego Luna (*Before Night Falls* [2000], *Y Tu Mamá También* [2001], *Open Range* [2003]) as Jack Lira, Lucas Gabeel (*College Road Trip* [2008], *High School Musical 3: Senior Year* [2008], *Rock and Roll Forever* [2009]) as Danny Nicoletta, and James Franco in an amazing performance as Milk's lover, Scott Smith. Each plays his character and expresses his homosexuality with an emphasis on character development and story.

If *Milk* doesn't have a single signifying image, there are many shots of Penn as he talks passionately to his political and activist team or to crowds that have gathered on the street to hear him speak and lead them. There is certainly a signature line. "My name is Harvey Milk and I want to recruit you!," a line actually spoken by Harvey Milk in life, suggests a military metaphor in the war against homophobia.

The tapes being recorded are, we're told, to be played only in the case of Milk's assassination. Like Dr. Martin Luther King, Harvey Milk knew he wouldn't live out a normal life. It was his final dedication to the movement. If the disgruntled and mentally disturbed government official Dan White hadn't assassinated Harvey Milk, someone else would have.

The actual news clip of the historic press statement by Dianne Feinstein, president of the San Francisco Board of Supervisors (and now a U.S. senator), that Harvey Milk and Mayor George Moscone had been shot dead is shown in the film. In this manner, the film may still have some DNA from Oliver Stone's original involvement; the clip gives gravitas to this critical moment.

Castro Street in San Francisco, which was re-created in its 1960s and 1970s glory by the art department, was where many of the events in Harvey Milk's life occurred. It is like Christopher Street in New York, a block, a "zone" where gays can congregate and be themselves, but at the time gays were "imprisoned" by this neighborhood and the city's limits in space and tolerance for those who danced to the beat of a different drummer.

Experimental filmmaker Bruce Baillie created *Castro Street* (1966), a short film that portrayed the mood and ambiance of this down-market but highly significant area. The Castro movie theater, still in existence, was, in the 1970s, a vital film repertory house that showed Hollywood classics. The audience, filled with an abundance of gay people, cheered and booed their reactions during the screenings—it was a lively counterculture institution. When *Milk* was premiered at the Castro, the audience, many old-timers who had known Harvey Milk and many of the participants wept openly at the powerful re-creation of the history of their lives.

Van Sant continued to make the right aesthetic choices on a scene-by-scene, shot-by-shot basis. An important meeting between Harvey and his team is photographed in a single long take to tie everyone together and to emphasize the principle that they are one. This technique had been applied by Dennis Hopper and director of photography László Kovács (*Five Easy Pieces* [1970], *Shampoo* [1976], *Ghostbusters* [1984]) during a key scene in a Van Sant favorite, *Easy Rider* (1969), in which the members of the hippie commune form a circle and give a blessing for their food. Here, in *Milk*, the camera moves in 360 degrees. Van Sant commands his camera, manned by longtime collaborator Harris Savides, to move through the scene, revealing everyone in the room listening and reacting to Harvey Milk's strategy ideas.

Like the gay character Andrew Beckett in another brilliant performance about a homosexual, played by Tom Hanks in *Philadelphia* (1993), Harvey Milk loved classical opera. This may be another gay stereotype, but it is a part of the culture. (A contemporary opera, *Harvey Milk* [1995], was composed by Steward Wallace to honor the slain leader.) The opera *Tosca* (1900), composed by Giacomo Puccini, is dramatically utilized in *Milk*. The story of *Tosca* follows an escaped political prisoner and a woman who aides him; both are brutally murdered. The death scene is used to score Harvey Milk's last moments.

Earlier, as Milk listens to opera at home and at the opera house, he, like Andrew Beckett, expresses his passion by conducting in the air with dramatic and graceful movements of his arm, an image that stays with the viewer long after the movie has concluded.

To capture the scope of the times, Van Sant, as did Oliver Stone in *JFK* (1991), brilliantly incorporates stock footage. Stone integrated it with the created footage shot in many different camera formats and altered the famous Zapruder film[6] to make a political point and to create an aesthetic of pointillism (by optically zooming in and increasing the grain), which transforms the hard-core realism into Shock Art.

Van Sant utilizes stock footage to provide historical and political background that would have been less effective if re-created in live action. Van Sant, relying on his own sense of aesthetic application, utilizes the technique of stop-motion photography,[7] which communicates the feeling that the viewer is watching a moment in time. As always, there is a postmodern and experimental film aesthetic to these aspects of the film.

Milk is a culmination of a career of filmmaking that has embraced the personal, the commercial, the experimental, and influences from art history from the 1960s and 1970s to create a biopic, a popular Hollywood genre. Then and now, it merges form and content to capture the life of an important historical and political human rights figure and the times in which he lived. Taking a nod from the Oscar-winning documentary *The Times of Harvey Milk* (1984), directed by Rob Epstein (*Word Is Out* [1977], *The Celluloid Closet* [1995], *Paragraph 175* [2000]), Van Sant spends much of his artistic time on *Milk* getting the cultural and environmental atmosphere right as if a cinematic time machine had taken the film back to the 1960s and 1970s, then filtered what it "saw" through a fervent creative temperament that is Gus Van Sant.

Again, Van Sant adds a self-referential aspect to a film. Harvey Milk ran a functioning photography store that became his political headquarters. The store sold Kodak film, which is prominently displayed throughout the film. Several characters, including Milk, take photos of reportage and capture the street happenings of the Castro. The result is a photographic record of gay life and the birth of gay liberation in San Francisco, portrayed on film in and for the movie. Kodak is synonymous with motion pictures. Although there have been other film stocks used in America and abroad, it is Kodak that is principally associated with motion-picture-making in the United States.

There is also a theme of transformation. Milk realizes that he has not done anything with his life and in middle age becomes an activist. He goes from being conservative in his haircut and his fashion sense to being a long-haired, jeans-wearing hippie and then moves on to being clean-shaven and wearing a suit after losing his bid for public office.

Another brilliant aspect of Sean Penn's remarkable performance is that he captures the changes in Harvey Milk from the emotional and intellectual depths of the character. Van Sant has always been a director who, like William Wyler, Ingmar Bergman, Elia Kazan, and Martin Scorsese, elicits great performances from his cast. *Milk* represents the height of his powers; every role is played with great depth and range of character and is loyal to the person portrayed and the life and times in which the story takes place.

The shooting style of Van Sant and director of photography Harris Savides varies. It depicts epic scenes in one shot, limiting the coverage so that the camera eye can easily be an observer to history; it also employs a personal and experimental as well as a documentary style that supplements the real documentary stock footage used in the film. *Milk* is a hybrid of Van Sant's techniques throughout his career, which was the logical and the correct vision to apply to this subject—a man who represents change.

Milk is also an overtly personal film. As a gay man, Van Sant gets deeply involved in the story, which is a part of his life. Every minority relates to the struggles that broke the barriers of an America that was not yet ready for true equality. So *Milk* is about social and political change as well as a portrayal of a group (like the civil rights movement, and the women's movement) that makes the journey from being in the closet to being out and from being passive to fighting for equality in mainstream society.

Milk is also about the radicalization of an individual. Harvey Milk tells his team and anyone who will listen that it is time to seize the moment. Inspired to action by the Stonewall Riot of 1969 and the savagery and humiliation heaped upon gays by the police, Harvey Milk decides that change comes from within. He preaches that gays should come "out of the closet," be honest and proud of their sexual preference, and stop going to the bath houses and other underground activities. He also addresses the hippie lifestyle many gays adopted in the 1960s and urges them to stop smoking pot. His philosophy was "Anything for the movement."

The lighting becomes more modeled in the kitchen diary/tape/narration sequences as the film progresses and Harvey Milk's life becomes more complicated. When he finally is elected to office, the weight of responsibility is expressed in a more textured shooting approach. The style reflects the content.

As the film indicates, there was much opposition to Harvey Milk and his movement; two opponents stand out dramatically and a third is represented in stock footage. State Senator John Briggs, played with fervent intensity by Denis O'Hare (*21 Grams* [2003], *Michael Clayton* [2007], *Charlie Wilson's War* [2007]) is a fierce opponent of any sort of gay rights bill. Milk and Briggs debate, scheme, fight, and represent the two forces pulling at the country's value system. The stock material of Anita Bryant presents her as a force of nature. She is a singer and orange-juice pitchwoman who during the 1970s was a conservative whirlwind, leading her own movement and preaching that homosexuality was a sin and unnatural. Van Sant made the right decision not to go the docudrama route here and have an actress portray Bryant; the reality of the clips brings verisimilitude to the film. It educates the young, who may not know who she is, and packs a visceral and emotional punch for those who lived through that time; at the height of her fame (or infamy), Bryant a figure one either revered or hated.

The third major adversary is Dan White, the failed politician who assassinated Harvey Milk and Mayor George Moscone. Josh Brolin also inhabits his real-life character and plays him from the inside and out. Physically he looks very much like Dan White, and he successfully builds White's overwhelming negative emotions to a frightening conclusion. Dan White was a loser who couldn't stand failure. He was not able to negotiate like the silver-tongued Harvey Milk. Milk took defeat in stride and tried harder the next time; Dan White turned to violence.

The death of Harvey Milk does not come as a surprise for many viewers. The true story is widely known and is foreshadowed in the film. What Van Sant and scenarist Dustin Lance Black (*The Journey of Jared Price* [2000], *Something Close to Heaven* [2000, short film], *Pedro* [2008]) accomplish in *Milk* is a Greek or Shakespearean tragedy of grand proportions. Harvey Milk is a doomed figure like Martin Luther King Jr. Like King, Milk fueled a worldwide movement for change that continued to grow after his shortened life.

Few Hollywood films have portrayed the intimate lives of gay characters as well as *Milk*. Along with presenting a portrait of the public man, *Milk* investigates Harvey Milk's love life in a manner that takes the position that, in the main, gay relationships are very little different from heterosexual ones. Harvey Milk is shown in two major life partnerships. The first is with a younger man, Scott Smith (James Franco), who is with Harvey at the beginning, when he is yearning to do something meaningful with his life. The relationship eventually breaks up because of Harvey's obsession with his cause. Milk's relentless commitment to politics and his activism ultimately burn out the sweet and compassionate Scott. He leaves still loving Harvey but unwilling to be in a relationship where there is no give and take. James Franco gives a remarkable, multidimensional performance, for which he was nominated for an Independent Spirit Award for Best Supporting Male.

The second major relationship is with the high-maintenance Jack Lira, played to the hilt by Diego Luna. Jack is one of the walking wounded and is very dependent. Unlike Scott, Jack demands an undue amount of emotional attention and plays the role of a needy spouse, throwing tantrums over petty issues. The relationship ends tragically, with Jack committing suicide because Harvey has come late for dinner one too many times.

Milk was highly recognized by the Hollywood community. Released in the year of *Slumdog Millionaire* and *The Wrestler*, *Milk* was a competitive force and garnered many Academy Award nominations and awards. The best original screenplay Oscar went to Dustin Lance Black, and a statue was handed to Sean Penn over Mickey Rourke in *The Wrestler* (Rourke beat Penn at the Golden Globes). Oscar nominations also went to Van Sant for best director, Danny Elfman for best music, Josh Brolin for best supporting actor, Danny Glicker for best costume design, and Elliot Graham for best film editing—and the film also got the big one, a nomination for best picture of the year. Penn went on to win the Austin Film Critics Association award, tied with Rourke for the Boston Society of Film Critics award, and won the best actor award from the Broadcast Film Critics, the Dallas-Fort Worth Critics Association, the Los Angeles Film Critics Association, the National Society of Film Critics, the New York Film Critics Circle, the Palm Springs International Film Festival, the San Francisco Film Critics Circle, the Screen Actors Guild, the Southeastern Film Critic Association, and the Vancouver Film Critics Circle.

Throughout *Milk*, Van Sant relies on stock footage of actual television reports by NBC's Tom Brokaw and by the CBS legend the late Walter Cronkite as they reported on the vote on gay rights legislation in San Francisco. The film, because of the detailed and beautiful researched script by Dustin Lance Black and Van Sant's direction, follows not only the complications of the American political system but the human impact of the drive for equal rights for gays and the fervor on both sides of the issue.

In the film, Sean Penn delivers a monologue—an important feature of a Van Sant film. This one is a speech that Milk gave after failing to win passage of the Briggs initiative.[8] He tells the assembled crowd that he is angry, and he acknowledges that the crowd is angry. Milk was a stirring speaker like Malcolm X,[9] who could rally large groups to action. This is just one of the nuances of Penn's performance that emphasizes the complexity of Harvey Milk.

Nothing Van Sant had directed previously prepared him for the scope of *Milk*. There are many impressive scenes involving large crowds and a large ensemble cast to manage. Van Sant supplies a limited number of shots for many of the group scenes, a classical approach more European in genesis than American. Savides' immaculate sense of composition brings a David Lean sense of the saga to a modestly budgeted film (approximately $15 million) for a period film with meticulous and extensive re-creation.

The structure of *Milk* plays longer than its 128-minute running time. So many facets are covered that a lesser filmmaker would have taken 2½ to 3 hours. In a daring narrative element, Dustin Lance Black and Van Sant hold off the appearance of the Dan White character for almost 45 minutes into the storyline. Black and Van Sant take their time and probe details, setting up Milk's background, his rise to power, and the growth of the gay liberation movement. Dramatically, they create narrative tension, regardless of whether the viewer knows the outcome.

Much of *Milk* is photographed with a static or locked-off camera. When necessary, Van Sant and Savides employ a handheld documentary-style camera; they do this in the "I'm angry!" speech, which produces a visceral effect.

The bilevel storytelling—Milk talking into his meticulously catalogued tapes, to be played posthumously, and the narrative proper—keeps the film alive, both in real time and in flashback. Factually, the story is told in back-story, but Van Sant's adroit handling of time and space make the viewer forget he is watching a rigorous structure. It is broken down by a steady flow that maintains both narrative strains, releasing viewers from structural rigidity and putting them into a time-space continuum—a cinematographic time-machine tripping back and forth into time—that is rarely achieved by filmmakers.

Even Cowgirls Get the Blues (1993) had a lesbian theme and many lesbian characters; that film was a black comedy, and, in it, Van Sant painted story and characters with a broad cinematic stroke. *Milk* has one major lesbian character, Anne Kronenberg. The part is played by Alison Pill (*Pieces of April* [2003], *Dear Wendy* [2007], *One Way to Valhalla* [2009]), who began appearing in movies in her pre-teens. Here she plays the real-life young lesbian woman who "infiltrated" the gay boys club of Harvey Milk's coterie. Kronenberg, who is portrayed as possessing an indefatigable intelligence and confidence, strides into the photo store and tells Harvey Milk that if she were his campaign manager, he would win his upcoming race for a position on the San Francisco Board of Supervisors. He brings her into the "family" because she promises to get him in the papers. She succeeds in gaining newspaper endorsements, and any trepidation of having a "girl" around is dissipated.

In a commercial sense—and this film was intended for a wide audience, unlike Van Sant's four experimental films—having a female character is good for the demographics of a major release.

Once again, Van Sant pulls the slow-motion camera out of his tool box. An example is a scene where a young boy takes a long walk towards Milk. The slow-motion application to this shot builds organic tension. What is this boy's mission? When he encounters Harvey Milk, who is on the street campaigning, he hands the activist a flyer for his opponent, Dan White. This is one of several foreshadowing moments in the film. The other takes place on a night when Milk turns paranoid because of death threats he has received. He hears footsteps and sees a strange man following him. Thinking the worst, he becomes anxious, suspicious, and frightened until he reaches the photo store, where Cleve Jones, memorably portrayed by Emile Hirsch, is waiting for him. Ironically, Hirsch received lavish critical acclaim for his role in the Sean Penn–directed *Into the Wild* (2007).

Van Sant is narratively astute at creating dramatic tension in a film where the main character's demise is revealed at the outset, as in Brian De Palma's *Carlito's Way* (1993) and *The General* (1998), directed by John Boorman. His ability to forge the aesthetic with content makes this daring trope successful. In lesser hands, the audience would be thrown out of the film and left wondering why the image has slowed down, rather than understanding (as they do in an Alfred Hitchcock film) that the boy in the first example may be connected to the handwritten murder threats. Finding the right slow-motion frame rate for the moment is the cinematic key to success here.

Sex scenes in *Milk* between Harvey and Scott and later between Harvey and Jack Lira are shot directly and communicate that sex is sex and plumbing is plumbing. A gay kiss is shown not for shock value but as human expression.

Throughout the film, Van Sant presents cards that contain information about time, place, and events, such as "District Elections, November 7th, 1977." In the art of the biopic and docudrama, facts and reality are crucial. Equally crucial is the balance between facts and dramatic license. By and large, Van Sant succeeds in adhering fairly to the facts while presenting a personal dramatic valentine to Harvey Milk and the history he shares with the gay rights movement. *Milk* harnesses the power to convert those who have been unexposed to gay men or who are misinformed about how gays live. The fight for equality is part of the human struggle—one in which humanity takes two steps forward and one step back, making slow progress.

The director boldly applies an experimental and or surreal moment, like the hats falling in *Drugstore Cowboy* (1989). In *Milk,* there is a magical realism[10] moment when the card punch holes from the voting process are shown floating through the camera frame.

Local news coverage of the election is also utilized to supply verisimilitude and to emphasize the immediacy of the media—another Van Sant theme, most visible in *To Die For* (1995). When a national news story breaks, it is the local station or affiliate that is on the scene first, often with a reporter with deep background who has been following the story all along. There also is a passion in this reporting that does not get passed down to the national news, which has traditionally reported the events that affect the nation either in an objective style and as humanely as possible or with a slant known to the loyal viewers. By covering the gamut from local to national news, Van Sant and his scenarist communicate the scope of the story. Van Sant is always interested in multiple views of the same story or action, as was Kubrick in *The Killing* (1956), Tarantino in *Pulp Fiction* (1994), Todd Haynes in *Velvet Goldmine* (1998), Orson Welles in his masterpiece, *Citizen Kane* (1941), Oliver Stone in *Nixon* (1995), and, in the granddaddy of all American film, D. W. Griffith in his apologist classic, *Intolerance* (1916).

Harvey Milk is shown through a prism of many views and perspectives. There is the strait-laced, button-down Harvey, the hippie, the suited politician, and the naked lover. He is presented as a man in a relationship, a leader, a motivator for his massive cause, and a one-on-one recruiter who beseeches people to join the movement one person at a time. Harvey Milk is presented in debates, formal and informal, on television, and in on-the-spot interviews as events occur and explode. He was a man of the moment and a person of humor and culture.

Sex and power are connected. When Harvey Milk wins his seat, Cleve Jones and another man aggressively engage in oral sex, much as a heterosexual duo might feel strong sexual impulses during times of celebration and elation. The moment is raw but discreet—this is not *Mala Noche* (1985) or *My Own Private Idaho* (1991). When Cleve "goes down," that action is enough to get the point and emotion across. Again, this is not the cliché of the homosexual as promiscuous and indiscreet but the essence of the power/sex quotient.

The relationship between Dan White and Harvey Milk was fraught with repressed anger on White's part and the need to be the negotiator and big-tent figure on Milk's. They viewed each other as adversaries until they both won seats on the county board of supervisors. Then they began to jockey for position and power. Harvey Milk was thick-skinned about fighting for issues; he didn't take political confrontations personally. White did. He was overly sensitive and took everything to heart. One could even say he suffered from paranoia, which ultimately led him to murder Milk and Moscone. This also is the stuff of classical drama. Both men are doomed because they are in each other's path, like Macduff in Shakespeare's *Macbeth* or the characters in Sophocles' *Oedipus the King*.

Dan White desperately tries to fit in, inviting all the supervisors to his son's baptism. The only person to show up is Harvey Milk, out of consideration and for political reasons; Milk understands that, in politics, alliances that include people from all sides of the spectrum are important. Negotiations between Milk and White to support each other's pet projects and bills break down because Dan White won't budge and Harvey Milk has strong principles. The narrative structure widens the gap and brings the two men closer to tragedy and personal disaster.

Harvey Milk is also in conflict within his own political machine. When working on defeating Brigg's Proposition Six, which was designed to bar gays and lesbians from teaching in the California public school system, Milk is angry at the print campaign, which does not contain the word "gay." His anger is symbolized by his throwing the flyer into a fire, an image that recalls the conclusion of *Citizen Kane* (1941) and Van Sant's own *Paranoid Park* (2007). Milk's anger is righteous, while White's leads to physical violence. Dan White is a ticking time bomb just waiting to explode because of his feelings of lack of self-worth. At White's trial, his lawyers used the "Twinkie defense" to support a theory that nutritional deficiencies caused by his diet, which was heavy on junk food, caused him to lose his sanity.

Humor is a necessary component in a drama or biopic. The tragedy of Harvey Milk and the steps he took to rise, only to fall and rise again, triumph because Milk and his tribe play hard and work harder. There is a running gag about pushing a birthday cake in Harvey's face, which goes back to silent comedy and always gets a laugh. Scott is the first to do this, and others make it a tradition. When coupled with Penn's infectious smile and quiet, strong voice, it builds a three-dimensional portrait of the real man.

Another foreshadowing of Harvey Milk's eventual tragic end is that four of his personal love relationships end in suicide. He finds partial redemption when he talks a young gay out of killing himself and tells him to leave his oppressive home, in which his parents are going to have him medically and psychologically "corrected." Gays and lesbians are born, not made.

Stock footage of Governor Jerry Brown of California and President Ronald Reagan present views of the Prop 6 controversy in docudrama style and add to the film's credibility. Montages based on the theories and work of Russian film director and theorist Lev Kuleshov (*The Project of Engineer Prite* [1918], *The Death Ray* [1925], *The Great Consoler* [1933]) convince viewers that what they are seeing on screen is "real"; they see the stock footage and the docudrama re-creations not as two different elements but as part of one fluid cinematic story.

Harvey Milk often said he would never make it to 50; he was shot by Dan White at age 48. A series of events leads to the assassination. Dan White quits his position on the Board of Supervisor because he has made no lasting political capital. He is rejected by Mayor Moscone when he asks to be reinstated. This loosens White's grip on reality and causes him to shoot the mayor dead. He then blames Milk because of his deep-rooted fears, prejudices, and delusions about American morality. Dan White thrusts himself into Harvey Milk's office, where he asks to speak to Milk in private. Milk excuses himself from his appointment and goes into another office, where he quickly realizes it is all over for him. The impact of Milk's death on the Castro district is rendered by a moving candlelight vigil. Tosca is replayed as part of a last vision. Milk's deep love for opera, which gave him peace in life, now marks his death.

Milk, like *Good Will Hunting* (1997), catapulted Gus Van Sant into the international spotlight. His story continues.

8

Short Films, Work as a Producer, Music Videos, Feature Film Segments, and Future Projects

SHORT FILMS (NOT DISCUSSED IN TEXT)

1967: *Fun with a Blood Root* is a 40-second animated film in which a man who is actually a flower bites another flower.

1971: *The Happy Organ* is a 20-minute film about a young brother and sister who leave the city for a weekend at the beach. Frank Zappa music is on the soundtrack. The title comes from a song by Dave "Baby" Cortez that is never heard during the film. There is time-lapse photography in this short with clouds, which became a trademark in Van Sant's feature films.

1972: *Little Johnny* is another 40-second film. This one is not animated and is shot in 16mm black-and-white.

1973: *1/2 of a Telephone Conversation* is a two-minute, 16mm black-and-white film.

1975: *Late Morning Start* is an attempt at nonlinear storytelling that Van Sant considers a good-looking film that is a failure.

1986: *Five Ways to Kill Yourself* is a three-minute black-and-white film that won the Teddy Award in the Best Short Film Category at the Berlin International Film Festival in 1987.

1987: *Ken Death Gets Out of Jail; My Friend* is a 16mm black-and-white short that features a man bending over a roadway and discussing his incarceration and his rep as a failed cocksman.

1991: *Thanksgiving Prayer*, a poem that trashes the Norman Rockwell image of the United States, is a collaboration with William S. Burroughs.

It is a two-minute, 30-second 35mm black-and-white film. Archival footage utilized in *Thanksgiving Prayer* includes shots of people lined up on the street for food, buildings on fire, the Lincoln Memorial, a space flight, and the American flag. This short was screened at Sundance in January 1992 and was broadcast on PBS as part of the *Alive* series (July 11, 1992).

1996: *Ballad of the Skeletons; Color of a Brisk and Leaping Day* is a video short of Allen Ginsberg reading "Ballad of The Skeletons," with music by Paul McCartney, Lenny Kay, and Philip Glass. It lasts for four minutes and was shot by Eric Allan Edwards. Shown at the Seattle International Film festival, it won the Golden Space Needle award.

2000: *Easter* is based on a Harmony Korine short story and was shot in Kentucky, where Van Sant was born. It centers on an albino couple in an African American community. The husband is gay. His wife burns herself alive. The film was shot on digital beta by Anthony Dod Mantle, director of photography on Korine's *Julien Donkey Boy* (1999).

2001: *Smoking Man* was trashed by writer Bill Smith of the *Willamette Week* as a poor attempt at a comment on the environment that looks like a public service announcement via Disney's nature film series.

2007: In *First Kiss,* a teenage projectionist enters the film on the screen and makes out with a blonde who is in the movie.

2008: In *8,* eight directors share their opinions via short films on the progress, setbacks, and challenges facing the world today. Van Sant's film has no title. The others are Jane Campion, *The Water Diary;* Gael Garcia Bernal, *The Letter;* Jan Kounen, *The Story of Pashin Beka;* Mira Nair—no title; Gaspar Noé, *SIDA;* Abderrhamane, *Tiya's Dream;* and Wim Wenders, *Person to Person.*

2008: *Postcards from the Battleground States, Gus Van Sant in Ohio—Battleground States* is a video that Van Sant made about the 2008 election. The project consists mainly of talking-head interviews with a range of young voters who discuss campaign issues. One man discusses his disappointment over the outcome of the Bush/Kerry election but his hope for the future. The male and female subjects are identified by a black card with white letters, as they were in *Elephant* (2003). We see their names and then go to their interview. The reason for the focus on Ohio is that it was a key state in the election process. The film has hood interview, shooting, and editing style. There are no credits except Van San's.

WORK AS A PRODUCER

1995: *Kids*

Gus Van Sant was one of the executive producers on this controversial film directed by Larry Clark and written by Harmony Korine. This harrowing picture explores with brutal honesty and graphic detail the lives of teenagers in the 1990s. Van Sant has always been interested and committed to films about youth culture, and he felt he would have much to offer Clark and Korine in addition to his name.

Larry Clark is a photographer and filmmaker whose major themes are young people's lifestyles and behaviors, including the infamous trio of sex, drugs, and rock 'n' roll. He has been called a pornographer, a pervert, and a man without values. His books of photography include *Tulsa* (1971), *Teenage Lust: An Autobiography* (1983), and *The Perfect Childhood* (1995). His films include *Bully* (2001), *Ken Park* (2002), and *Wassup Rockers* (2005).

Harmony Korine is a writer and filmmaker who has a friendship with Van Sant and who appeared in *Gus Van Sant's Last Days* (2005) as a "Guy in Club," the character who is questioned about the missing Blake, the fictionalized representation of Kurt Cobain. Earlier he appeared uncredited in *Good Will Hunting* (1997) as Jerve and was a consultant on the subject of jails. Korine's writing credits include *Gummo* (1997), *The Diary of Anne Frank Part II* (1998), and *Julien Donkey Boy* (1999); he was also the director of these projects.

Kids includes a skateboarder. Van Sant would pursue skateboarding as a cultural aspect of youth culture in *Paranoid Park* (2007). The cast was made up of nonprofessionals and nonactors. Three would go on to careers from this incendiary launching pad: Rosario Dawson (*Josie and the Pussycats* [2001], *25th Hour* [2002], *Sin City* [2005]), Chloe Sevigny (*Boys Don't Cry* [1999], *American Psycho* [2000], *The Brown Bunny* [2003]), and Leo Fitzpatrick (*Storytelling* [2001], *Justice* [2003], *El Camino* [2008]).

The story centers on a young man who wants to deflower as many very young virgins as he can. One of these girls has AIDS and is convinced she received the disease from him. She tries to find him and warn him and others. As the group of "Kids" goes through their day, they encounter and participate in sex and violence. *Kids* demonstrates an outsider's view of society. These outcasts despise and exhibit extreme hatred for nine-to-five world that is all around them.

Kids was nominated for the Golden Palm at the 1995 Cannes Film Festival. At the 1996 Independent Spirit Awards, Justin Pierce (*Wild Horses* [1998], *Next Friday* [2000], *Looking for Leonard* [2002]), who played Casper, won for best debut performance. Larry Clark and producer Cary Woods (*Swingers* [1996], *Cop Land* [1997], *Julien Donkey-Boy* [1999]) were nominated for the award for the best first feature. Korine was nominated for the prize for best first screenplay, and Chloe Sevigny was nominated for an award for best supporting female.

Van Sant supports projects that involve his interests and themes. *Kids* was a perfect project for him to support although it may be more brutal and explicit than his own films (with the exception of *Mala Noche* [1985]); it is an uncompromising look at the deep end of the pool of youth culture. As a gay man, Van Sant likely found the introduction of the AIDS theme as a screen topic for public awareness significant.

1998: *Speedway Junky*

This film is an investigation into the gay Las Vegas subculture. In it, a young man falls in love with a male hustler. It features Jesse Bradford and Jordan Brower and was directed by Nickolas Perry.

2003: *Tarnation*

Gus Van Sant was one of the executive producers on *Tarnation*, a documentary directed and created by Jonathan Caouette. Caoutte's first film, he wrote, directed, shot, edited, did the sound, and appeared as himself. Since then, he has gone on to act in *Fat Girls* (2006), *Shortbus* (2006), *The Moon and He* (2008), and *Portland* (2010). He also was the director and editor of *Making of the 15th Raindance Film Festival,* the cinematographer and editor on the 2009 documentary *All Tomorrow's Parties,* and director of *Forrest Grove.*

Tarnation is the true life story of Jonathan Caouette, a gay man, and his schizophrenic mother and her equally disturbed parents. The film uses interviews, home movies, snapshots, Super 8mm footage, answering phone messages, video diaries, early short films, bits of 1980s pop culture, and re-creations to sculpt a cinematic portrait of the American family and the American dream gone haywire.

Van Sant championed this film for several reasons: the gay theme, its portrayal of the youth and film cultures, and the theme of "family." The film is brilliantly edited by Caouette with a polish by editor Brian Kates (*The Laramie Project* [2003], *The Woodsman* [2004], *The Savages* [2007]). To the eye, *Tarnation* looks like one big montage moving through different pacing patterns, depending on the subject matter or the story being told at the moment. It received many nominations and awards, including wins from the Boston Society of Film Critics, the British Film Institute, and the Chlodtrudis Awards, which honored Jonathan Caouette as a filmmaker. It also received nominations for best documentary from GLADD Media, the Gijón International Film Festival, the Gotham Awards, and the Independent Spirit Awards. It won awards for best documentary at the Glitter Awards, the Los Angeles IFP/West Film Festival, and the Milan International Lesbian and Gay Film Festival and from the National Society of Film Critics and the San Diego Film Critics

2006: *Wild Tigers I Have Known*

This films tells the story of a 13-year-old-boy who thinks he may be gay and who becomes friends with an older boy who has girlfriends. When the boys are seen together, their schoolmates make fun of them. It stars Malcolm Stumpf, Max Paradise, and Faruka Balk and was directed by Cam Archer.

2006: *Lightfield's Home Video*
Directed by Lightfield Lewis and with a cast that includes James Caan, Giovanni Ribisi, and Brooke Shields, this film is a compilation of videos of celebrities shot by Lightfield over a 20-year period as he searches to make a real movie.

2006: *Queen of Heart Community Therapists in Drag*
Directed by Jan Haaken, this 48-minute documentary is about a drag queen club where bridegrooms go to see a wild, sexually oriented show before they return to their everyday lives.

2010: *What's Wrong with Virginia*
Van Sant was one of the executive producers of *What's Wrong with Virginia*, directed by Dustin Lance Black, the screenwriter of *Milk* (2008). The film stars Jennifer Connelly and Liam Neeson. The story concerns a sheriff who wants to run for his state's Senate seat but is thwarted because his daughter dates the son of a psychologically disturbed woman with whom the sheriff had a 20-year affair.

2010: *Howl*
Van Sant was one of the Executive Producers of *Howl*, a drama concerning the obscenity trial of Allen Ginsberg, played by James Franco of *Milk* (2008) and written and directed by Rob Epstein (*The Times of Harvey Milk* [1984]).

SELECTED MUSIC VIDEOS

1990: *Thanksgiving Prayer*—William Burroughs

1990: *Tarbelly and Featherfoot*—Victoria Williams

1990: *Fame '90*—David Bowie

1991: *I'm Seventeen*—Tommy Conwell and the Young Rumblers

1991: *Under the Bridge*—Red Hot Chili Peppers

1992: *Bang Bang Bang Bang*—Tracy Chapman

1992: *Anal Torture*—That Kid Art

1992: *The Last Song*—Elton John

1993: *Just Keep Me Moving*—k.d. lang

1993: *Runaway*—Deee-Lite

1993: *Creep* (alternate version)—Stone Temple Pilots

1993: *The Ballad of Skeletons*—Allen Ginsberg, Paul McCartney, Philip Glass, Lenny Kaye

1993: *Solitary Man*—Chris Isaak

1997: *Understanding*—Candlebox

1997: *Miss Misery*—Elliot Smith

1998: *Weird*—Hanson

2005: *Who Did You Think I Was* (turntable version)—John Mayer Trio

2007: *Desecration Smile*—Red Hot Chili Peppers

FEATURE FILM SEGMENTS

2006: *Cinema 16* is a compilation of short films, including Van Sant's *The Discipline of D.E.* (1982). Other films in the package include *Vincent* (1982), Tim Burton; *Freiheit* (1966), George Lucas; *Carmen* (1985), Alexander Payne; *Paperboys* (2001), Mike Mills; *Daybreak Express* (1953), D. A. Pennebaker; *Feelings* (1984), Todd Solondz; *The Lunch Date* (1989), Adam Davidson; *Terminal Bar* (2002), Stefan Nadelman; *George Lucas in Love* (1999), Joe Nussbaum; *The Wrath of Cobble Hill* (2005), Adam Parrish King.

FUTURE PROJECTS

Slated for 2011: Director of *The Golden Suicides,* based on an article by Bret Easton Ellis. The film is stated to be a chronicle of the double suicide of artists Theresa Duncan and Jeremey Blake.

Slated for 2011: Director of *The Electric Kool-Aid Acid Test,* based on the book by Tom Wolfe, adapted by Dustin Lance Black. The film is based on the New Journalism classic that follows Ken Kesey and his Merry Pranksters as they take acid and drive around the country in their bus.

Slated for 2012: Director of *How Starbucks Saved My Life,* based on the book by Michael Gates Gill, screen adaptation by John Orloff, starring Tom Hanks. This film concerns a recently unemployed business man who stops in his local Starbucks and has his life changed.

Conclusions

Gus Van Sant has embraced myriad cinematic styles that he learned from films and filmmakers he admires and then made his own. One of the most notable instances of this is Van Sant's admiration for Orson Welles and his resultant tribute to *Chimes at Midnight* (1965) in *My Own Private Idaho* (1991). On the surface, it might seem as if Van Sant has nothing in common with Welles, but both men demonstrate a fine understanding and handling of actors and performances. And there are other similarities. Welles scholar Peter Tonguette observes:

> Welles, particularly in the films that follow *Chimes at Midnight*, began experimenting dramatically. About *F Is for Fake* (1974), he told film scholar Bill Krohn in *Cahiers du Cinema* that "there isn't a Wellesian shot in it." Van Sant is seemingly making every kind of film not just in every genre but different styles, different scales—he's really stretching himself and this author sees that more and more as Van Sant matures as a filmmaker. It is his willingness to try different things. Some filmmakers became more staid as they get older, but both Welles and Van Sant were willing to try new things and made films that you never would have thought they would have made. If you had seen *Drugstore Cowboy* (1989) or *My Own Private Idaho* (1991) who could have ever anticipated that Van Sant would make a film as radical as *Gerry* (2002) or as conventional, in a good way, as *Good Will Hunting* (1997). To follow *Psycho* (1998) with *Finding Forrester* (2000) says it all about Van Sant's versatility.[1]

Where will Gus Van Sant be positioned in film history in the future? He will be in the company of great filmmakers such as Griffith, Welles, Kubrick, Bergman, Fellini, and Kurosawa, and perhaps, like those masters, he will be considered to be a great artist. As film moves along in its second century, it is still largely perceived as an entertainment form, but a growing awareness of the cinematic process leads many to understand the art of film, any film. There is a select group of filmmakers, a pantheon, in the words of film critic Andrew Sarris, whose members rise above all others. As the decades pass, film will be accepted as an art and the great practitioners will stand side-by-side with the Beethovens and Picassos of the past.

"Van Sant is making all these different kinds of films and stretching himself and doing things he maybe thought he would never do and in that way he is like Hal Ashby [*Harold and Maude* (1971), *Coming Home* (1978), *Being There* (1979)] and Welles," Peter Tonguette states. "His work will absolutely live on and endure as one of the strongest bodies of work of any filmmaker of his generation."

Motion picture editor Pietro Scalia adds:

> Gus is a very special filmmaker. He is someone in whom you can see his artistic touch and poetry in everything that he does. I think he will be considered one of the great auteurs and one that successfully worked with very personal films. Working with Gus is one of the highlights of the directors I've worked with. The other directors I worked with for many years are Ridley Scott and Oliver Stone. In terms of film artists, he will be remembered as a film artist just like Bernardo Bertolucci. In terms of poetry Gus comes closest to Jean Vigo. That and possibly the other one is Kenji Mizoguchi. Vigo, Mizoguchi, and Bertolucci—Gus Van Sant is really up there with them in terms of poetic cinema. He's a very sensitive and delicate film artist.[2]

Valdis Óskardóttir contends, "Gus is as unpredictable as the weather in Iceland. You never know how it's going to be and the same goes for Gus. You never know what he will do next and that's what makes him what he is. A great talented filmmaker and a daring, fearless director that makes his own path and is not afraid of doing what he wants to do. I think he will go where his passion and his drive will take him."[3]

Finally, a list:

- Gus Van Sant is one of the most critically lauded openly gay filmmakers in film history as well as a great filmmaker who happens to be gay.
- There are many audiences who follow Van Sant. Some were there for *To Die For* (1995) and for *Good Will Hunting* (1997) to see a commercial film. The more adventurous managed to see *Mala Noche* (1985), either at a screening or on DVD. *Drugstore Cowboy* (1989) is a drug film and had a limited audience. *Milk* (2008) was a general release and, although gay-themed, was widely seen, enjoyed, and respected by general audiences. *My Own Private Idaho* (1991) was a landmark independent film seen by those intrigued by cutting-edge narrative cinema. *Gerry* (2002), *Elephant* (2003), *Gus Van Sant's Last Days* (2005), and *Paranoid Park* (2007) are experimental films meant for those not cinematically squeamish when it comes to exploring the nature of the medium and off-beat topics. Few went to see *Finding Forrester* (2000) when word went out (erroneously) that it was a flop. Those who have seen it find it appealing and life affirming. *Psycho* (1998) will remain an oddity. At first the audience was out to get Van Sant for tarnishing a classic. Now his take on Hitchcock's masterwork is studied for its contributions

to the cinema of curiosity and as an educational tool for the medium—still the youngest of all the arts. The short films (the ones that are out there are watched on the Internet) demonstrate the growth of a filmmaker. Finally, there must be a cult out there that likes and repeatedly watches *Even Cowgirls Get the Blues* (1993).

- Van Sant is respected by critics, film historians, audiences, film students, and filmmakers because he can't be pinned down and because he constantly surprises, delights, and sometimes irritates (the latter a sign of a vital artist).
- Everyone who has worked with Gus Van Sant has nothing but good things to say about him.
- Gus Van Sant is a maverick filmmaker.
- Gus Van Sant loves Portland, Oregon.
- Thanks to the cinema gods for giving us Gus Van Sant. If he didn't exist, we would have had to invent him.

Filmography

SELECTED SHORT FILMS

1967: *Fun with a Blood Root*

1971: *The Happy Organ*

1972: *Little Johnny*

1973: *1/2 of a Telephone Conversation*

1975: *Late Morning Start*

1976: *The Discipline of D.E.*

1982: *My Friend; Fly Flame*

1983: *Where Did She Go?*

1984: *Nightmare Typhoon* (aka *Hello It's Me*); *Switzerland*

1986: *Five Ways to Kill Yourself*

1987: *Ken Death Gets Out of Jail; My Friend*

1988: *Five Naked Boys and a Gun*

1991: *Thanksgiving Prayer*

1996: *Ballad of the Skeletons; Color of a Brisk and Leaping Day*

2000: *Easter*

2001: *Smoking Man*

FEATURE FILMS
As Executive Producer

1995: *Kids*

2001: *Speedway Junky*

2003: *Tarnation*

2010: *What's Wrong with Virginia*

Howl

Key: D: director; EP: executive producer; AP: associate producer; COP: co-producer; P: producer; PA: production associates; LP: Line producer; SP: Screenplay; DP: Director of Photography; AC: Additional Camera; SC: Special Camera; PD: Production Designer; AD: Art Director; SD: Set Decorator; C: Costumes; S: Sound; SSE: Supervising Sound Editor; E: Editor; AE: Assistant Editor; M: Music.

> 1979: *Alice in Hollywood* (See chapter 2 for production and postproduction history. The film was never released and was cut down from feature length to short film.)
> Round Productions, color, 29 minutes.

EP: Marion Marzynski; P: Gus Van Sant; AP: Peter Scrant, Sherri Lubov, and Melanie Travel; D/SP: Gus Van Sant; S: Tom Yore; DP: Jean Desegonzac; E: Gus Van Sant.

Cast: Alice (Anita Skinner), Roy Brown (Mark Pixler), Policeman (John Berwick), Director's Assistant (Frank Birney), Herb Gold (Nigel Bullard), Tourist (Donna Bruce), Motel Manager (Theo Cleaver), Man in Elevator (Jon Collins), Vietnam Veteran (Sam Diego), Harry Lewelyn (director), Mom (Rae Maguire), Dad (Tom Maguire), the Major (Robert Martin), Cop (Tom O'hara), Dan Patterson (John Dramma), Autograph Hounds (Elaine Parker, Alexa Power), Stanley Dubrick (Wiley Pender), Bag Ladies (Alexa Power, Rae Maguire), Chauffeur (Peter Scranton), Tourist (Tom Sherohman), Big Jim Jones (T. J. Skimmer), Naked Lady (Nancy Smith), Talent Agent (Melanie Traveler), Timmy (David Worden), Bit Parts (David Bynum, Beth Aroya, Berina Berostent, Joan Leizman, Brian Ann Zoccala, Cici Holman, Debby Dugan, Steve Ecclesine, Dianne McKinstry, Greg Conser, Herb Winsted, Michael Fleck).

> 1985: *Mala Noche*
> Northern Film Co., black and white/color, 78 minutes. Not rated.

P: Gus Van Sant; PA: Jack Yost, Chris Monlux; D: Gus Van Sant, based on a story by Walt Curtis; SP: Gus Van Sant; M: Creighton Lindsay; S: Pat Baum; DP: John Campbell; AC: Eric Alan Edwards; E: Gus Van Sant.

Cast: Walt (Tim Streeter), Johnny (Doug Cooyate), Roberto Pepper (Ray Monge), Sarah (Nyla McCarthy), Hotel Clerk (Sam Downey), Drunk Man (Robert Lee Pitchlynn), Policeman (Eric Pedersen), Bar Friend (Marty Christiansen), Wino (George Connor), Don Chambers (himself), George

(Walt Curtis), Street Hustler (Kenny Presler), Arcade Amigo (Conde Benavides), Greek Singer (Cirsto Stoyos), Boxcar Amigo (Matt Cooeyate), Lady with Knife (Maruya Muñoz), Voice of Johnny (Arturu Torres), Bits (Marselus Allen, Anne Buffen, Dieter Reshhe, Frank Euward, John Benneth, Pat Switzler, Steve Young, Preta Porta. G. H. Machie. Judy Anne Leache, Katherine Serlo, Pablo Telles, Chris Monlux, Steve Foster, Havier Valle, Steven Hulse, Denny Chericone); Building Tenant (Gus Van Sant).

1989: *Drugstore Cowboy*
Avenue Pictures Productions, color, 102 minutes. Rated R.

P: Karen Murphy, Nick Weschler; D: Gus Van Sant; S: Gus Van Sant, based on the novel *Drugstore Cowboy,* by James Fogel; M: Eliot Goldenthal; PD: David Brisbin; DP: Robert Yeoman; E: Mary Bauer, Curtiss Clayton; C: Beatix Aruna Pasztor; SSE: Dane A. Davis; S: Mark "Frito" Long.
    Cast: Bob (Matt Dillon), Dianne (Kelly Lynch), Rick (James LeGros), Nadine (Heather Graham), Druggist (Eric Hull), David (Max Perlich), Gentry (James Remar), Cop (John Kelly), Bob's Mother (Grace Zabriskie), Trousinski (George Catalano), Neighbor Lady (Janet Baumhover), Neighborhood Man (Ted D'Arms), Halamer (Neal Thomas), Motel Manager (Stephen Rutledge), Drug Counselor (Beah Richards), Hotel Clerk (Robert Lee Pitchlynn), Machinist (Roger Handcock), Accomplice (Ray Monge), Panda the Dog (Woody).

1991: *My Own Private Idaho*
Fine Line Features, color, 104 minutes. Rated R.

EP: Gus Van Sant; COP: Allan Mindel; P: Laurie Parker; LP: Tony Brand; D/ SP: Gus Van Sant; PD: David Briskin; AD: Ken Hardy; SD: Melissa Stewart; C: Beatrix Aruna Pasztor; M: Bill Stafford; S: Reinhard Stergar, Roger Marts, Jan Cyr, Jon Huck; SSE: Kelley Barker. DP: Eric Alan Edwards, John Campbell; SC: Bruce Weber; E: Curtiss Clayton; AE: Amy E. Duddleston.
    Cast: Mike Waters (River Phoenix), Scott Favor (Keanu Reeves), Richard Waters (James Russo), Bob Pigeon (William Richert), Gary (Rodney Harvey), Carmella (Chiara Caselli), Digger (Michael Parker), Denise (Jessie Thomas), Budd (Flea), Alena (Grace Zabriskie), Jack Favor (Tom Troupe), Hans (Udo Kier), Jane Lightwork (Sally Curtice), Walt (Robert Lee Pitchlynn), Daddy Carroll (Mickey Cottrell), Wade (Wade Evans), Porno Magazine Cover Boys (Matt Ebert, Scott Patrick Green, Tom Cramer), Sharon Waters (Vana O'Brien), Café Kids (Scott Patrick Green, Shaun Jordan, Shawn Jones), Bad George (George Comer), Native American Cop (Oliver Kirk), Dirtman (Stanley Hainesworth), Baby Mike (Joshua Halladay), Little Richard (Douglas Tollenen), Family Tree Hotel Manager (Clark Pachosa), Disco Manager (Lannie Swerdlow), Rock Promoters (Wally Gaarsland, Bryan Wilson,

Mark Weaver, Conrad "Bud" Montgomery), Cops (Pat Patterson, Steve Vernelson, Mike Cascadden), Mayor's Aide (Eric Hull), Minister (James A. Arling), Airline Clerk (James Caviezel), Stewardness (Ana Cavinato), Lounge Hostess (Melanie Mosely), Carl (Greg Murphy), Yuppie at Jake's (David Reppinhagen), Tiger Warren (himself), Italian Street Boys (Massimo De Cataldo, Pao Pei Andreoli, Robert Egon, Paolo Baiocco), Mike's Italian Client (Mario Stracciarolo), Family Tree Bellboy (Gus Van Sant).

1993: *Even Cowgirls Get the Blues*
Fine Line Features, color, 95 minutes Rated R.

P: Mary Ann Marino; D: Gus Van Sant, based on the novel *Even Cowgirls Get the Blues*, by Tom Robbins; S: Gus Van Sant; PD: Missy Stewart; AD: Dan Self; SD: Nina Bradford; CD: Beatrix Aruna Pasztor; M: K. D. Lang, Ben Mink; SSE: Kelley Baker; S: Jon Huck; DP: John Campbell, Eric Alan Edwards; E: Curtiss Clayton.

Cast: Sissy Hankshaw (Uma Thurman), the Countess (John Hurt), Bonanza Jellybean (Rain Phoenix), the Chink (Noriyuki "Pat" Morita), Jullian Gitche (Keanu Reeves), Delores Del Ruby (Lorraine Bracco), Miss Adriana (Angie Dickinson), Rupert (Ed Begley Jr.), Carla (Carol Kane), Marie Barth (Sean Young), Howard Barth (Crispin Glover), Madame Zoe (Roseanne Arnold), Dr. Dreyfus (Buck Henry), Mrs. Hankshaw (Grace Zabriskie), Young Sissy (Treva Jeffryes), Sissy's Daddy (Ken Kesey), Sissy's Uncle (Ken Babbs), Lionel (Allen Arnold) Cowgirl Debbie (Victoria Williams), Cowgirl Heather (Heather Graham), Cowgirl Gloria (Judy Robinson), Cowgirl Mary (Betsy Roth), Big Red (Arlene Wewa), Cowgirl Donna (Heather Hershey), Cowgirl Kim (Dee Fowler), Commercial Director (Udo Kier), Cameraman (Wade Evans), Crewman (Tom Peterson), Rubber Rose Bird Expert (Alexa D'Avalon), White House Undersecretary (Eric Hull), Sheriff (Oliver Kirk), FBI Director (Joe Ivy), FBI Agent (Greg McMickle), Rubber Rose Maid (Lin Shaye), Brain Surgeon (Chel White), Salsa Singer (Molly Little), Pilgrim Man (Scott Patrick Green), Pilgrim Woman (Suzane Solgot), Pilgrim Driver (Michael Parker), William Burroughs (himself), Cowgirls (Sherry Alps, Eliza Butterfly, Boo Connolly, Christie Flenniken, Stacey Hyder, Tina Knaggs), Narrator (Tom Robbins).

1995: *To Die For*
Columbia Pictures Corporation, color 106 minutes. Rated R.

P: Laura Ziskin; D: Gus Van Sant, based on the novel *To Die For,* by Joyce Maynard; S: Buck Henry; PD: Missy Stewart; AD: Vlasta Svoboda; SD: Carol A. Lavoie; CD: Beatrix Aruna Pasztor; M: Danny Elfman; SSE: Kelley Baker; S: Robert Fernandez; DP: Eric Alan Edwards; E: Curtiss Clayton.

Cast: Suzzane Stone Maretto (Nicole Kidman), Larry Maretto (Matt Dillon), Jimmy Emmett (Joaquin Phoenix), Russel Hines (Casey Affleck),

Janice Marretto (Illeana Douglas), Lydia Mertz (Alson Folland), Joe Maretto (Dan Hedaya), Ed Grant (Wayne Knight), Earl Stone (Kurtwood Smith), Carol Stone (Holland Taylor), Faye Stone (Susan Traylor), Angela Maretto (Maria Tucci), Mike Warden (Tim Hopper), Ben DeLuca (Michael Rispoli), Mr. H. Finlaysson (Buck Henry), George (Gerry Quigley), Fishermen (Tom Forrester, Alan Edward Lewis), Sexy Woman (Nadine Mackinnon), Weaselly Guy (Conrad Coates), Sal (Ron Gabriel), Students (Ian Heath, Graeme Millington, Sean Ryan), Detective (Nicholas Pasco), Lawyer (Joyce Maynard), Reporters (David Collins, Eve Crawford, Janet Lo), Man at Lake (David Cronenberg), Skating Promoter (Tom Quinn), Priest (Peter Glenn), Suzanne Age 5 (Amber-Lee Campbell), Valerie Mertz (Colleen Williams), Chester (Simon Richards), Babe Hines (Philip Williams), June Hines (Susan Backs), Mary Emmett (Kyra Harper), Band Members (Adam Roth, Andrew Scott), Chick #2 at Bar (Tamara Gorski), Girls at Bar (Katie Griffin, Carla Renee).

1997: *Good Will Hunting*
Miramax Films, color, 126 minutes. Rated R.

P: Lawrence Bender; D: Gus Van Sant; S: Matt Damon, Ben Affleck; PD: Melissa Stewart; AD: James McAteer; SD: Kelley Baker; CD: Beatrix Aruna Pasztor; M: Danny Elfman; SSE: Kelley Baker; S: Steve Kohler; DP: Jean Yves Escoffier; E: Pietro Scalia.

Cast: Sean Maguire (Robin Williams), Will Hunting (Matt Damon), Chuckie Sullivan (Ben Affleck), Prof. Gerald Lambeau (Stellan Skarsgård), Skylar (Minnie Driver), Morgan O'Mally (Casey Affleck), Billy McBride (Cole Hauser), Tom, Lambeau's Teaching Assistant (John Mighton), Krystn (Rachel Majorowski), Cathy (Colleen McCauley), Barbershop Quartet (Matt Mercier, Ralph St. George, Rob Lynds, Dan Washington), M.I.T. Students (Alison Folland, Derrick Bridgeman, Vic Sahay), Girl on Street (Shannon Egleson), Carmine Scarpaglia (Rob Lyons), Carmine Friend #1 (Steven Kozlowski), Lydia (Jennifer Deathe), Clark (Scott William Winters), Terry, Head Custodian (Phillip Williams), Marty, Assistant Custodian (Patrick O'Donnell), Courtroom Guard (Kevin Rushton), Judge George H. Malone (Jimmy Flynn), Prosecutor (Joe Cannon), Court Officer (Ann Matacunas), Henry Lipkin, Psychologist (George Plimpton), Rich Hypnotherapist (Francesco Clemente), Maurine-Bunker Hill College Students (Jessica Morton, Barna Moricz), Toy Store Cashier (Libby Geller), M.I.T Professor (Chas Lawther), Timmy (Richard Fitzpatrick), Executives (Chris Britton, David Eisner, Frank Nakashima), NSA Agents (Bruce Hunter, Robert Talvano), Security Guard, (James Allodi).

1998: *Psycho*
Universal Pictures, color, 105 minutes. Rated R.

P: Brian Grazer; D: Gus Van Sant; S: Joseph Stefano, based on the novel *Psycho*, by Robert Bloch; PD: Tom Foden; AD: Carlos Barbosa; C: Beatrix Aruna Pasztor; M: Danny Elfman, adaptor of the original score by Bernard Herrmann; SD: Kelley Baker; S: Ron Judkins; DP: Christopher Doyle; E: Amy E Duddleston.

Cast: Norman Bates (Vince Vaughn), Marion Crane (Anne Heche), Lila Crane (Julianne Moore), Samuel "Sam" Loomis (Viggo Mortensen), Milton Arbogast (William H. Macy), Dr. Fred Simon (Robert Forster), Sheriff Al Chambers (Philip Baker Hall), Mrs. Eliza Chambers (Anne Haney), Tom Cassidy (Chad Everett), Mr. Howard (Rance Howard), Caroline (Rita Wilson), Patrolman (James Remar), Charlie the Car Dealer (James LeGros), Police Guard (Steven Clark Pachosa), Mechanic (O. B. Babbs), Bob Summerfield (Flea), Woman Customer (Marjorie Lovett), Chief of Police (Ryan Cutrona), District Attorney (Ken Jenkins).

2000: *Finding Forrester*
Columbia Pictures Corporation, color, 136 minutes. Rated PG-13.

P: Sean Connery; D: Gus Van Sant; S: Mike Rich; PD: Jane Musky; AD: Robert Guerra, Darrell K. Keister; C: Ann Roth; M: Bill Frisell; SSD: Kelley Baker; S: Frank Rinella; DP: Harris Savides; E: Valdis Óskardóttir.

Cast: William Forrester (Sean Connery), Jamal Wallace (Rob Brown), Prof. Robert Crawford (F. Murray Abraham), Claire Spence (Anna Paquin), Terrell Wallace (Busta Rhymes), Ms. Joyce (April Grace), John Coleridge (Michael Pitt), Dr. Spence (Michael Nouri), Prof. Matthews (Richard Easton), Massie, Forrester's Delivery Man (Glenn Fitzgerald), Damon (Zane Copeland Jr.), Janice Wallace (Stephanie Berry), Fly (Fly Williams III), Kenzo (Damany Mathis), Clay (Damion Lee), Coach Garrick (Tom Kearns), John Hartwell (Matthew Noah Word), Dr. Simon (Charles Bernstein), David Bradley (Matt Malloy), Steven Sanderson (Matt Damon), Rapper (Jimmy Bobbitt), Student (James T. Williams II), Clair's Friend (Cassandra Kubinski), Librarian (Sophia Wu), Student Speaker (Gerry Rosenthal), Student Manager (Tim Hall), Old Money Man (Tom Mullica), Kid in the Hall (David Madison), Night Man (Joey Buttafuoco), Referees (Jamie McCraig, William Modeste), Hallway Boy (Daniel Rodriguez), Creston Player (Samuel Tyson), Big Band Leader (Vince Giordano), Violinist (Gregory Singer), Trumpet Player (Kerry Mackillop), Trombone Player (Harvey Tibbs), Sax Players (Jack Stuckey, Mark Lopeman, Marc Phaneup, Larry Wade), Piano Player (Conal Fowkes), Guitarist (Matt Munisteri), Drummer (John Meyers), Mailor Priest (Ron Morgan), Jeopardy Contestant (Alison Folland), Alex Trebeck (himself).

2002: *Gerry*
Miramax, color, 103 minutes. Rated R.

P: Dany Wolf; D: Gus Van Sant; S: Gus Van Sant, Matt Damon, Casey Affleck; SD: Leslie Shatz; S: Felix Andrew; DP: Harris Savides; E: Gus Van Sant, Matt Damon, Casey Affleck.

Cast: Gerry (Casey Affleck), Gerry (Matt Damon).

2003: *Elephant*
HBO Films, Fine Line Features, Meno Films, Blue Relief Productions, color, 81 minutes. Rated R.

P: Dany Wolf; D: Gus Van Sant; S: Gus Van Sant; AD: Benjamin Hayden; S: Felix Andrew; DP: Harris Savides; E: Gus Van Sant.

Cast: Alex (Alex Frost), Eric (Eric Deulen), John McFarland (John Robinson), Elias (Elias McConnell), Jordan (Jordon Taylor), Carrie (Carrie Finklea), Nicole (Nicole George), Brittany (Brittany Mountain), Acadia (Alicia Miles), Michelle (Kristen Hicks), Benny (Benny Dixon), Nathan (Nathan Tyson), Mr. McFarland (Timothy Bottoms), Mr. Luce (Matt Malloy), GSA Teacher (Elis E. Williams), Noelle (Chantelle Chriestenson), Assistant Principal's Secretary (Kim Kenny), Assistant Secretary (Marci Buntrock), Red-Haired Kid (Roman Ostrovsky), P.E. Instructor (Vana O'Brien), Bully (Michael Paulsen), Mr. Fong (Alfred Ono), Alex's Mom (Marychris Mass), Alex's Dad (Jim Steinpreis), Delivery Man (Jeremy Simpson), Teachers (Sherilyn Lawson, Sarah Lucht, Larry Laverty, Dave Stippich), Kid on Bike (Jimmy Gomez), Science Teacher (Joe Cronin), Punk Guy (Wolfgang Williams), Punk Girl (Caroline Donovan Boyd), Science Student (Travis Ferguson), GSA Teacher (Ernest Truly), GSA Students (Mary Muldrew, Sarah Bing, Kether Heydenm Natascha Snellman, Ruben Bansie, Joe Sackett), GSA Victim (Jason Seitz), Student in Darkroom (Shanti Cho), Eli's Friend (Theara Sao), Eli's Classmate (Tiana Woods), Football Players (Griffin Goins, Max Horner, Thomas Trulinger, Ty Schwoeffermann), Janitor (Ray Monge).

2005: *Gus Van Sant's Last Days*
HBO Films, Meno Film Company, Picturehouse Entertainment, Pie Films, color, 97 minutes. Rated R.

P: Dany Wolf; D: Gus Van Sant; S: Gus Van Sant; DP: Harris Savides; AD: Tim Grimes; E: Gus Van Sant; M: Rodrigo Lopresti; SD: Leslie Schatz; S: Felix Andrews.

Cast: Blake (Michael Pitt), Luke (Lukas Haas), Asia (Asia Argento), Scott (Scott Green), Nicole (Nicole Vicius), Detective (Ricky Jay), Donovan (Ryan Orion), Guy in Club (Harmony Korine), Band in Club (The Hermitt), Elder Fribergs (Adam Friberg, Andy Friberg), Yellow Book Salesman (Thadeus A. Thomas), Tree Trimmer (Chip Marks), TV Voice-overs (Kurt Loder, Michael Azerrad), Phone Voices (Chris Monlux, Jack Gibson, Gus Van Sant, Dawnn Pavlonnis).

2007: *Paranoid Park*
MK2 Productions, Meno Films, color, 85 minutes. Rated R.

P: David Cress, Charles Gillibert, Nathanaël Karmitz, Neil Kopp; D: Gus Van Sant; S: Gus Van Sant, adapted from the novel *Paranoid Park*, by Blake Nelson; DP: Christopher Doyle; AD: John Pearson-Denning; E: Gus Van Sant; SD: Leslie Shatz; S: Felix Andrew.

Cast: Alex (Gabe Nevins), Detective Richard Liu (Dan Liu), Jared (Jake Miller), Jennifer (Taylor Momsen), Macy (Lauren McKinney), Scratch (Scott Green), Security Guard (John "Mike" Burrowes), Alex's Mom (Grace Carter), Alex's Dad (Jay "Smay" Williamson), Uncle Tommy (Christopher Doyle), Henry (Dillon Hines), Paisley (Emma Nevins), Jolt (Brad Peterson), Christian (Winfield Henry Jackson), Paul (Joe Schweitzer), Cal (Oliver Garnier), Ryan (Mubarak Ra'oof), Other Kids (Eric Anderson, Jeremy Anderson), Another Kid (Addison Owen), Detective #2 (Richard Miller), Rachel (Emily Galash), Elizabeth Goulet (Esther Vaca), Elizabeth's Friend (Jordy Weimer), Police Officer (Andrés Alcalá), Police Officer #2 (Paul Dolbey), Ms. Adams (Susan Ploetz), Math Teacher (M Blash), Science Teacher (John Pearson-Denning), Skate Shop Employee (Chester Stallings), Cafeteria Kid (Nick Culbertson), News Anchor (Ken Boddie), Café Girl (Amanda Winkler), Waiter (Ben Burrowes), Phone Operator (Chrissy Conant), Skateboarders (Sage Bolyard, Chuck Willis, Danny Minnick, Francisco Kico Pedrasa, Tanner Kewley, Adam Kiedrowski, Bodhi Briggs, Tristan Brillanceau-Lewis, Kyle Davis, Michael Davis, Spencer Crimin, LeShaun Williams, Spencer Brillanceau-Lewis, Diya Ra'oof, Elbert Garner, Kevin Nickoloff, Rick Charnoski).

2008: *Milk*
Focus Features, color/ black-and-white, 128 minutes. Rated R.

P: Bruce Coen, Dan Jinks; D: Gus Van Sant; S: Dustin Lance Black; PD: Bill Groom; AD: Charley Beal; SSE: Robert Jackson; S: Felix Andes; CD: Danny Glick; M: Danny Elfman; DP: Harris Savides; E: Elliot Graham.

Cast: Harvey Milk (Sean Penn), Cleve Jones (Emile Hirsch), Dan White (Josh Brolin), Jack Lira (Diego Luna), Scott Smith (James Franco), Anne Kronenberg (Alison Pill), Mayor George Moscone (Victor Garber), State Senator John Briggs (Denis O'Hare), Dick Pabick (Joseph Cross), Rick Stokes (Stephen Spinella), Danny Nicoletta (Lucas Grabeel), David Goodstein (Howard Rosenman), Michael Wong (Kelvin Yu), Art Agnos (Jeff Koons), Dennis Peron (Ted Jan Roberts), Denton Smith (Boyd Holbrook), Frank Robinson, Allan Baird, Tom Ammiano (themselves), Thelma (Carol Ruth Silver), Mary Anne White (Hope Goblirsch), McConnely (Steve Wig), Dianne Feinstein (Ashlee Temple), Carol Ruth Silver (Wendy Tremont-King), Gordon Lau (Kelvin Han Yee), Phil Burton (Robert Chimento), Lily (Ginabel Machado), Young Teen (Daniel Landroche), Boy with Flyer (Trace

Webb), Morning Show Host (Vlina Brown), House Boy (Scott Patrick Green), Channel 5 Reporter (Mary Dilts), City Hall Engineer (Roman Alcides), San Francisco Cops (Robert George Nelson, Brian Danker), Riot Cop (Richard Gross), Senator Brigg's Driver (Borzin Mottaghian), Gay Man (Brian Yates Sharber), Medora Paine (Camron Palmer), Assistant Sheriff (Cully Fredicksen), Sylvester (Mark Martinez), Customer (Danny Glicker), Opera Performer, Tosca (Catherine Cook), Opera Performer, Spoletta (Joe Myers), Another Protester (Dominic Sahagun), Barber (William McElroy), Union Man (Joey Hoeber), Priest (Mark E. Stanger), Chamber Clerk (Jesse Caldwell), Supervisors (Paul Arnold, Jack Dunston, Ron Gruetter, Awele Makeba, Tony Vella, William M, Verducci), Telephone Trees (Gilbert Baker, Shavi Blake, Brent Corrigan, Draco Dewar, Dave Franco, Alex Gonzalez, Olen Holm, Elias McConnell, Tom Ramdol), Moscone's Secretary (Lynn McRee), Don Amador (Cleve Jones), Castro Man (John Parson), Speaker (Jay Kerzner), Anne's Friend (Kristen Marie Holly), Relative (Sandi Lppolito), Reporter (Roger Groh), Girl on Motorcycle (Maggie Weiland), Castro Clone (Dustin Lance Black), Pizza Delivery Man (Drew Kuhse), Robert Hillborough (Eric Cook).

Notes

CHAPTER 1

1. Regular 8mm cameras were used by families and others to document the story of their lives. These cameras used 16mm film that, after being exposed on both sides, was slit down the middle by the lab and placed on a plastic reel for home projection. Super 8mm was invented to give a wider picture area; it could also be stripped for sound recording. Super 8mm was intended for home use, but professionals also embraced the gauge for their use.
2. 16mm is a gauge developed for home use (by those who could afford it). 35mm film (and other gauges) are projected in movie theaters and has been the gauge of choice for Hollywood studios in both the past and the present. Film students embraced 16mm because it was affordable and accessible to them.
3. His grandmother's advice to "buy IBM" is reminiscent of the classic line "Plastics," career advice given to Benjamin Braddock by an older family friend in *The Graduate* (1967).

CHAPTER 2

1. Created by novelist and playwright J. M. Barrie, Peter Pan is a boy who refuses to grow up. Both Michael Jackson and Steven Spielberg were long fascinated with putting the story on film, but neither never did. Spielberg did, however, direct *Hook* (1991), which was a variation on the story. Van Sant is also obsessed with Peter Pan because of the endless childhood theme. Van Sant is an adult who remains attracted to youth and youth culture.
2. Lewis Carroll's *Alice in Wonderland* is the story of a girl who falls through a rabbit hole into a fantastical world of strange creatures. Her adventures and interactions have allegorical connections and political references.
3. The Beat Generation was a group of writers and poets who established themselves in the 1950s. Sometimes called Beatniks, these men (there were few exceptions) were nonconformists and set out to live their lives and promote everything America wasn't. They freely associated themselves with sexual freedom and drug use, and their religion embraced Far Eastern spirituality, especially Zen

philosophy. William S. Burroughs was a major figure in the movement, which was led by Jack Kerouac, author of the beat bible *On the Road*, and Allen Ginsberg, the poet who created "Howl," a seminal work expressing the Beat philosophy. The Beat Generation lasted into the early 1960s and eventually merged into the hippie movement. Ironically, Kerouac hated hippies and died bitter and isolated in 1969 at age 47.

4. There is a variation in the literature as to the exact date of this film's release.
5. Zen is a spiritual mode of expression that emphasizes meditation and a compassion for all living things. Developed in China in the seventh century, it became a major tenet of Buddhism. As well, Zen represents the coming together of all knowledge in order to allow people to excel at almost any task.
6. The Rolling Stones released their album "Sticky Fingers" in 1971. The cover was created by Van Sant idol Andy Warhol and featured a black-and-white photograph of a man in jeans with a real, working zipper that, when unzipped, revealed a man in cotton briefs. The picture was photographed by Billy Name, the man responsible for making The Factory (Warhol's studio) silver, and the cover was designed by John Pache, who also created covers for Jimi Hendrix, David Bowie (another Van Sant idol), and Jethro Tull. The man was Warhol superstar Joe Dallesandro, it was believed that the photo was of the Stones' front man, Mick Jagger.
7. A time cut is an edit that eliminates or shortenss or compresses the time line of a story.
8. A cut to black occurs when an edit goes from an image to a black screen. Over time, the colors white and red have become fashionable. Often a cut to black is used to end a scene or a movie. Both *Bonnie and Clyde* (1967) and *Fame* (1980) make very effective use of a cut to black to end a film.
9. A fade to black (or any color) occurs when the image gradually gets darker until it is pure color. It is used to end a scene or a film.
10. A dissolve is an editorial transition in which one image fades out while another image fades in. It is used as a link between scenes or to indicate a passage of time,
11. In a fade from black, the screen is full color, and an image steadily comes up to full strength. Usually this is used in conjunction with a fade to black of one scene and a fade from black to the next scene.
12. Shot/reverse shot is an old Hollywood invention. In a two-person dialog scene, shot one shows one character; then the camera cuts to the other or reverse side, shooting at the other character. This device makes movies cinematic and demonstrates an action that can not be done in live theater.
13. Guerrilla filmmaking is moviemaking on the cheap, with little equipment or crew. It rarely utilizes sets but instead uses actual locations.
14. Pole Position is a video game that was first released in 1982. It features a race car driving one lap as other cars and other intrusions force the player/driver to manipulate the steering well and pedals to avoid a crash.
15. Intercuts occur when one shot is intercut or intertwined with another, causing a back-and-forth relationship that links two shots or scenes.
16. Walla is the background sound of a crowd at a bar, a stadium, a party, or any scene that has a large group of people. In old Hollywood, filmmakers had a group of voices saying the word "Walla" in a recording studio to simulate the background sound. Currently, highly trained specialists do the voices and tailor the accent to fit the location and purpose of a scene.

17. During the Hollywood studio era, B movies were made to round out a double feature, the A movie being a major production with stars, a popular genre, and high production values, directed by an A-list director. B movies were low budget and utilized second-tier actors and directors. The genres were from the standard fare, but the stories were offbeat, sometimes controversial, and often the content flew under the radar of studio chiefs.

18. Film noir is French for "black film." The genre that grew out of the disillusionment experienced by veterans and others in the United States after World War II. Largely crime films, noirs feature an omnipresent sense of overwhelming doom. The films feature a femme fatale, a woman who brings down the protagonist. Stylistically, film noir features deep-shadowed photography, streaks of light, seedy rooms, and endless alleyways.

19. A choker close-up is a television term referring to an extreme tight close-up where the face fills the entire screen.

20. Structural film is a school of experimental film founded by P. Adams Sitney. After a move away from more poetic and free-form films, artists such as Peter Kubelka, Hollis Frampton, Paul Sharits, Joyce Weilland, Michael Snow, and Ernie Gehr began creating works that emphasized physical structure, eschewed content, and were often predetermined in form and execution. Some structural films are *Wavelength* (1966–1967), *Zorn's Lemma* (1970), and *Serene Velocity* (1970).

21. The road movie is a motion picture that takes place largely in a vehicle with the character traveling on a personal or psychological journey. Often, great physical distances are involved.

22. Voice-over, also considered narration, is the use of the voice of an actor who may or may not be in the film to talk about the story. The voice may be the younger or older voice of a character or that of someone whose function is to narrate, as in *Barry Lyndon* (1975), in which the unseen narrator is voiced by Michael Hordern.

23. *Streetwise* (1984), directed by Martin Bell, is a documentary on teenagers in Seattle. *Streetwise* (1988), directed by Bruce Brown, is a film concerning young crack dealers in Washington, D.C.

24. Experimental filmmaking is a mode of creating a motion picture that goes against the rules for style, storytelling, character development, and structure used in conventional Hollywood or mainstream films.

25. Dziga Vertov (1896–1954) was a Russian filmmaker and theorist. His most famous film, *Man with a Movie* Camera (1929), is an experimental documentary in which the city of St. Petersburg is explored in detail.

26. James Joyce (1882–1941) was an Irish writer whose legendary novel *Ulysses* (1922) explored the many facets of the city of Dublin in sociological, personal, narrative, and character detail.

27. Jean-Pierre Léaud is a French film actor most famous for his participation in a series of films directed by François Truffaut in which he portrayed Antoine Doinel, an autobiography figure used by Truffaut to tell his life story. Léaud has worked with many directors, French and otherwise, including Jean-Luc Godard, Jacques Rivette, and Bernardo Bertolucci.

28. American film actor who has been in many Martin Scorsese pictures. In *Who's That Knocking on My Door* (1969) and *Mean Streets* (1973), he is a stand-in for his director, his on-screen persona. He has also played one of Jesus' apostles, a

pimp, and an out-of-control suitor. Keitel has worked with many directors, including Robert Altman, Ridley Scott, Jane Campion, and Wayne Wang.

29. The avant-garde are artists and others who reject the status quo and establish their own, often radical culture. There is an avant-garde movement in most of the arts: film, literature, painting, and music. The poster child for the avant-garde is the late painter and filmmaker Salvador Dali.

30. *Hondling* is a Yiddish expression for trying to make a deal to get a price reduced.

31. While in office, President Bill Clinton had a sexual relationship with an intern, Monica Lewinsky. Impeachment proceedings were brought but in the end the president finished out his term. Lewinsky later wrote a book and tried to make a living designing and selling ladies handbags.

32. Criterion is a company that manufactures foreign and domestic DVDs. It takes great pains in restoring its titles (films that have been previously released). Its discs come with director's commentaries and unique documentary and other specials that are most often created by the company for a specific title.

33. Creighton Lindsay was an American roots music specialist who was popular in the 1970s for his spirited recordings.

34. Sammy Davis, Jr. (1925–1990) was the consummate African American entertainer. He could sing, dance, act, and do impressions, and in his nightclub act he was able to handle a gun like any decent cowboy. He was a member of Frank Sinatra's legendary Rat Pack.

35. Cesar Romero (1907–1994) was an actor of stage and screen, noted for his portrayal of The Joker on the *Batman* television series (1966–1968). Although Romero was gay, he never officially came out of the closet.

36. Ed McMahon (1923–2009) was the legendary announcer for *The Tonight Show with Johnny Carson* and the Jerry Lewis Labor Day telethon. He was also a pitchman for many products, most notably Budweiser Beer.

37. Samuel Beckett's (1906–1989) existential play *Waiting for Godot* features two characters, Vladimir and Estragon, who are waiting for someone who never arrives. This work is vastly overinterpreted but is essentially about man waiting for God, who never appears. Written during 1948 and 1949, it premiered on January 5, 1953, at the Theátre de Babylone, in Paris.

38. Legendary music producer famous for creating "the Wall of Sound," a torrent of instruments and singing voice run through massive echo chambers. Currently, Phil Spector is serving a sentence of 19 years to life for the murder of actress Lana Clarkson. In 1969, he appeared as a cocaine dealer in the opening of *Easy Rider,* a film highly regarded by Van Sant.

39. Robert Rauschenberg (1925–2008) was a gay American painter who followed the genres of Abstract Expressionism and Pop Art.

40. Jasper Johns is an American painter most famous for his paintings of the American flags, maps, and numbers.

CHAPTER 3

1. Grunge rock is a musical movement started in Seattle, Washington, by Nirvana, fronted by the late Kurt Cobain (February 20, 1967–April 5, 1994). *Gus Van*

Sant's Last Days (2005) is loosely and creatively based on the final times of Cobain, who in the film is a character named Blake. The other forerunners of grunge are Pearl Jam, whose singer Eddie Vedder had an obsession with Jim Morrison (the Doors). Grunge was forged out of several rock forms, including alternative rock, indie rock, heavy metal, and punk. Lyrics speak to the tortured minds of adolescent males, and the music features very distorted electric guitars.

2. Fellatio, known on the street as a blow job, is an act in which either a male or a female puts a penis in his or her mouth and "sucks" or moves up and down on the member until the receiver has an orgasm, discharging semen. This oral sexual act is most notoriously featured in the Andy Warhol short film *Blow-Job* (1963), in which the receiver is shown on camera but the giver is off-screen.

3. Abbey Lincoln (1930–), born Anna Marie Wooldridge, is a jazz vocalist and actress. Her haunting vocalization of "For All We Know" is featured in *Drugstore Cowboy* (1989). Other songs sung by Abbey Lincoln include "In the Red," "Lost in the Stars," and "Thursday's Child." Her screen performances include *Nothing but a Man* (1964), *For the Love of Ivy* (1968), and *Mo' Better Blues* (1990).

4. Fred Carlin (1936–2004) is an Oscar-winning American composer for his song "For All We Know." He also wrote "Come Saturday Morning" for *The Sterile Cuckoo* (1969), and "Can It Be True" for *Marriage of a Young Stockbroker* (1971), and "And So it Begins" for *Loving Couples*.

5. Desmond Dekker (1941–2006) was the first Jamaican musician to have a hit record in the United States while retaining his island roots.

6. Leslie Kong (1933–1971), a Chinese Jamaican reggae producer who co-wrote "The Israelites" with Desmond Dekker. His bizarre death at 38 of a heart attack is blamed by some on a curse put on him by Bunny Livingston of the Wailers, the group headed by Bob Marley, who many feel was murdered by political enemies who put a poisonous substance in his cannabis.

7. Motion picture film has grain, but digital imagery has pixels, which are small particles that combine to form a picture on a television monitor or computer screen.

8. Illusion Arts is a visual effects company, founded in 1985 by owners Syd Dutton and Bill Taylor, that serves the motion picture industry. In addition to its relationship to the films of Gus Van Sant, it has been involved with many filmmakers and films, including *Cat People* (1982), Paul Schrader, *Spaceballs* (1987), Mel Brooks, and *Cape Fear* (1981), directed by Martin Scorsese.

9. The term "psychedelic" pertains to a mind-expanding experience in which the senses are heightened, reality is enhanced, and hallucinations, both aural and in the mind's eye, are experienced. The psychedelic state is most often achieved through the ingestion of LSD, Ecstasy, or psilocybin mushrooms or the smoking of hashish. Rock bands whose music is intended as re-creation of the psychedelic experience include Iron Butterfly, Blues Magoos, 13 Floor Elevators, Hawkwind, Pink Floyd, Vanilla Fudge, King Crimson, the Stooges, MC5, Velvet Underground, and the Dandy Warhols. Motion pictures that intentionally use picture and sound to induce a psychedelic experience in the viewer's mind include *Chappaqua* (1966), *The Trip* (1967), *Head* (1968), *Psych-Out* (1968), *The Holy Mountain* (1973), *Steppenwolf* (1974), and *Fear and Loathing in Las Vegas* (1998).

10. Vincent LoBrutto, "Three Moods Prevail in *Dead Presidents*," *American Cinematographer* 76, no. 9 (1995): 62–63.

11. Marilyn Quayle (1949–), wife of former Vice President Dan Quayle, at the 1992 Republican Convention said, "Not everyone demonstrated, dropped out, took drugs, joined in the sexual revolution, or dodged the draft." Her belief that not every American was part of the counterculture ignored the fact that the so-called counterculture became (for better or worse) an integral aspect of American culture.

12. Queer cinema is a term and concept introduced at the Toronto Festival of Festivals in 1991 to codify films of the late 1980s that reexamined the images of gays. Derek Jarman's *Edward II* (1991), Tom Kalin's *Swoon* (1992), and the early films of Gus Van Sant, Todd Haynes, Jenny Livingston, and Gregg Araki are examples of this political and social gay movement. Rose Troche's 1994 debut film *Go Fish* eschewed gay film conventions by focusing on everyday lives, rather than sexuality. In 1999's *Bedrooms and Hallways,* Troche focused more attention on sexual identities and followed a more conventional style but maintained her affinity for gender and queer identities. Queer theory began to be applied to Hollywood films from Nicholas Ray's *Johnny Guitar* (1954) to George Roy Hill's *Butch Cassidy and the Sundance Kid* (1969) to define and identify gay behavior and to make it better understood as a positive, acceptable social lifestyle.

13. See NHS Direct, www.nhsdirect.wales.nhs.uk/encyclopaedia/n/.../narcolepsy/.

14. Fine Line Pictures was the specialty films department of New Line Cinema. Some of the films released by Fine Line include *My Own Private Idaho* (1991), *The Player* (1992), *Short Cuts* (1993), *Spanking the Monkey* (1994), *Crash* (1996), *Dancer in the Dark* (2000), *Hedwig and the Angry Inch* (2001), *A Dirty Shame* (2004), and *The Holy Girl* (2004).

15. *The Wizard of Oz* is a 1939 color motion picture directed by Victor Fleming, released by MGM, and based on the novel by Frank L. Baum. It has long been speculated that Mervyn LeRoy, Richard Thorpe, and King Vidor directed parts of the film, which starred a young Judy Garland as Dorothy and featured her vocal performance of "Somewhere over the Rainbow." This perennial motion picture fav has special importance for gay, lesbian, and transgender people, and Judy Garland would grow up to be a gay icon. The film is seen by the community as camp (when something bad is considered to be good). It also identifies with the heroes and villains of the film, who are perceived as misfits and embody the concept of living a double or hidden life. The lion is identified by the community as a sissy, the tin man is an artificial creature who can't stop crying, and the witches are seen as butch/femmes.

16. A bisexual is a male or female who is comfortable having sexual relations with persons of either sex.

17. Buddy Holly (1936–1959), born Charles Hardin Holly, was an American singer-songwriter of tunes, including "That'll Be the Day" (1956), "Words of Love" (1956), and "Maybe Baby" (1957). Holly, along with Ritchie Valens and the Big Bopper, was killed in a plane crash on February 3, 1959, referred to as "the day the music died" in the song "American Pie," written by Don McLean.

18. Ritchie Valens (1941–1959) was a Chicano musician singer and composer of songs such as "Donna," "La Bamba," and Come on Let's Go."

19. The Big Bopper (1930–1959), born Jiles Perry Richardson Jr., was famous for the songs "Chantilly Lace," "White Lightning," and "Running Bear."

20. "Fish," *Dream Dictionary,* http://www.unclesirbobby.org.uk/dreamessayfish.php.
21. The *Vertigo* shot was created and first employed by Alfred Hitchcock in his masterwork *Vertigo* in 1958. In a *Vertigo* shot, the camera, most often mounted on a dolly, moves forward as a zoom lens on the camera zooms back, creating a pit-of-the-stomach nauseated feeling in the viewer, who is artificially experiencing vertigo—the fear of heights. Other films that use this technique include *Jaws* (1974), and *GoodFellas* (1990).
22. A hippie is a man or woman who wears long hair and psychedelic clothing, takes psychotropic drugs, listens to hard rock, and is anti-establishment. Although the hippie movement began in the mid-1960s, many baby boomers and their children, friends, colleagues, and acquaintances continue to dress and live the lifestyle of the hippie movement.
23. William Shakespeare (1564–1616) was a poet and playwright who is universally considered the greatest dramatist who ever lived. His plays include *As You Like It, Henry V,* and *Hamlet.* Throughout the centuries, there have been those who believe it was Sir Francis Bacon (1561–1626), an English philosopher, statesman, scientist, lawyer, jurist, and author, who actually wrote the plays attributed to William Shakespeare. Bacon's writings include *Essays* (1597), *Elements of the Common Law of England* (1597), and *A Declaration of the Practises & Treasons Attempted and Committed by Robert, Late of Earl of Essex and His Complices* (1601). In his landmark book *Author Unknown: Tales of a Literary Detective,* also known as "*Author Unknown: On the Trail of Anonymous,* author Don Foster claims to have proved that Shakespeare wrote the plays attributed to him, but he later had to recant his findings when it was pointed out that there were several mistakes in his scholarship.
24. This and subsequent comments by Peter Tonguette are from an interview with the author on February 27, 2009.
25. Keith Baxter (1933–) is a Welsh theater, television, and film actor who played Prince Hal in the stage and was in the film production of *Chimes at Midnight,* directed by Orson Welles.
26. Margaret Rutherford (1892–1972) was an English actress who played Mistress Quickly in the Orson Welles motion picture production of *Chimes at Midnight* in 1966.
27. The Western motion picture film genre is set in the second half of the 19th century, a time when cowboys roamed the streets. Indians (Native Americans) are depicted as the fierce enemies of the white man and his holdings. In the classic American Western, good guys and bad guys are clearly defined. Revisionist Westerns revise the poetic and documentary facts put forth by the classic Western. Old-school Westerns include *Stagecoach* (1939), *Red River* (1948), and *The Big Trail* (1930). Revisionist Westerns include *The Wild Bunch* (1969), *Little Big Man* (1970), and *McCabe and Mrs. Miller* (1971).
28. Strobe lights are high-intensity white lights, installed in a box, that go on and off in a rapid succession. When used in the dark, strobe lights cause an animation-like effect on anyone or anything in front of the lighting instrument. They were very popular in the 1960s in clubs and other venues to create a psychedelic environment.

29. Op art, also known as optical art, creates illusions in the mind and eyes of the viewer. Op art can be produced in black-and-white or in color, usually using geometric shapes. Op artists include Bridget Riley, Richard Allen, and Josef Albers.

30. Skateboarding was invented in the late 1940s or early 1950s so that water surfers would have a way to practice in the down season. First popular in California, the craze swept the country all the way to the East Coast. A skateboard is about two feet long and about six inches wide and is made of smooth wood with roller-skating wheels on the underside. The skater kicks his right or left foot onto the ground, moving the skateboard forward. The faster this action is, the faster the board and rider go. At first, skateboarders used their boards to get around until they realized they could perform death-defying tricks (and some more mundane ones) on them. Into the 1970s, boarders would perform in public places like New York's Central Park to large and cheering crowds. As time wore on, the skaters began to skate on public property and were charged by law enforcement with defacing public property, even thought they went back and repaired the damage in most cases. Skate parks were built legally and illegally so that the players could ply their sport. As of 2009, skateboarding was broadcast on television, and boarding in the park is not the nefarious activity it once was. Motion pictures that feature skateboarding include *Thrashin'* (1986), starring Josh Brolin and directed by David Winters, *Gleaming the Cube* (1989), starring Christian Slater and directed by Graeme Clifford, and the made-for-television movie *Dishdogz* (2005), starring Luke Perry and directed by Mikey Hilb.

31. A top shot is a camera angle in which the camera is mounted on a ceiling or crane and shoots straight down on the action or scene below. Also known as God's point of view, it has been employed by many great film directors, including Busby Berkeley (*42nd Street* [1930], *Gold Diggers of 1933* [1933], *Dames* [1944]), as well as Martin Scorsese (*Taxi Driver* [1976], *GoodFellas* [1990], *Casino* [1995]).

32. Ryan Seacrest (1974–) is an American best known for his radio show and his hosting of the widely popular television show *American Idol*. Rumors have persisted since the beginning of his reign on the reality talent show that Seacrest is gay, but no substantial proof has been presented

33. Tom Cruise (1962–) is an American motion picture superstar who has appeared in many movies, including *Risky Business* (1983), *Rain Man* (1998), and *Valkyrie* (2008). Rumors that Tom Cruise is gay continue to hound the actor. Although he has been married several times, many have come forth to say that they have been his male lover. Cruise has successfully sued and won cases against these individuals.

34. The Jonas Brothers are an American rock/pop band consisting of Joe, Nick, and Kevin Jonas. Rumors continue to swirl around the question "Which of the Jonas Brothers is gay?" Investigation on the Internet has not revealed a name or evidence that any of the Jonas Brothers is gay.

35. Kenny Chesney (1968–) is a highly successful country and western performer. When his very short-lived marriage to actress Renee Zellweger broke up for undisclosed reasons, rumors started that Chesney is gay. Again, no proof has been found.

36. Lou Reed (1942–) is an American rock musician known for his work with the Velvet Underground and for his long and successful solo career. Reed has been

gay at times but is currently married to fellow musical experimentalist Laurie Anderson. Reed's music ranges from hard rock to avant-garde ventures to concept albums and poetry readings. His voice is featured in *Gus Van Sant's Last Days* (2005) as inspiration for the band and Blake, a singer modeled on the late Kurt Cobain.

37. A montage is a series of shots that establishes the passage of time or compresses an action or event. There are four versions of montage, which is the French word for "editing" and translates to something more like "collage." Other versions include the Russian School, pioneered by Sergei Eisenstein; the American School as practiced by Slavko Vorkapich on Hollywood features, most notably in the films of Frank Capra; and montage-style. Directors such as Sam Peckinpah, Oliver Stone, Martin Scorsese, and John Woo create scenes with short pieces of film primarily but not exclusively. Montage techniques are also used during postproduction.

CHAPTER 4

1. In a match cut, an action is matched from one shot to the next. In *All That Jazz* (1979), there are two shots in which film editor Alan Heim matches a shot of actor Ben Vereen starting to put on his sunglass with a second shot that completes the action.

2. Intercutting is an editing technique in which shots or scenes are cut together in alternate sequence to create a dramatic relationship.

3. John Huston (1906–1987) was a film director, actor, and screenwriter whose most respected works include *The Treasure of the Sierra Madre* (1948), *The Misfits* (1961), and *Prizzi's Honor* (1985). He was the son of Walter Huston and the father of Anjelica and Tony Huston.

4. *Moby Dick* was written by Herman Melville (1819–1891) and published in 1851. It weighs in at around 640 pages (there are many editions available). It was influenced by big books that came before before it going back many centuries, such as *One Thousand and One Nights, Canterbury Tales,* and *Don Quixote.* Since the first appearance of *Moby Dick,* it has inspired many long books such as *Gravity's Rainbow, The Recognitions, Women and Men, Underworld, You Bright and Risen Angels, Infinite Jest,* and *The Corrections.*

5. *Ulysses,* considered by many to be among the best novels of the 20th century, was written by James Joyce (1882–1941). It was published in 1922 at 736 pages. It is the story of Stephen Dedalus and Leopold Bloom and their exploits in Dublin on June 16, 1904. The book is one of the more difficult metafictional reads because of its complex and vexing use of language, the narrative structure, and the sheer length of many of its sentences. *Ulysses* has also been censored, banned, and defiled as a dirty and unreadable mess.

6. Jack Kerouac (1922–1969) was, along with Allen Ginsberg (1926–1997) and William S. Burroughs (1914–1997), the leader of the Beat Generation movement, which rejected mainstream American values, experimented with drugs, explored alternate modes of sexuality, and explored Eastern forms of spirituality such as Zen Buddhism. As a novelist, Kerouac was best known for *On the Road,* which inspired the road movie genre. Although not documented, it appears

that the novel had a significant influence on Dennis Hopper and Peter Fonda's own canonical work, *Easy Rider* (1969). Kerouac's literary outputs includes *The Dharma Bums, The Subterraneans,* and *Visions of Cody.* Ironically, the man who invented the beatnik (along with others) and died at the tender age of 47 hated hippies for some of the same reasons people disliked beatniks.

7. Neal Cassady (1926–1968), like Kerouac, Burroughs, and Ginsberg, was one of the founding members of the Beat Generation. Movie-star handsome and athletic, Cassady, like his fellow Beats, was a writer and poet. All his accomplishments were overshadowed by his uncanny skills as a driver, especially long distance. Kerouac, a man with whom he may have had a homosexual relationship, wrote him into his canonical *On the Road* as Dean Moriarty, the master driver who takes Sal Paradise, based on Kerouac, cross-country as they discover America. Cassady did have an on-again-off-again sexual relationship with Ginsberg that lasted 20 years. Later, Cassady drove cross-country in the day-glo painted bus "Further," filled with hippies and led by Ken Kesey. They were loaded on drugs, especially LSD, as immortalized in Tom Wolfe's fact-based novel *The Electric Kool-Acid Test.*

8. Gonzo journalism was founded by the late Hunter S. Thompson, who wrote dispatches and articles for *Rolling Stone* magazine, the most famous of which, "Fear and Loathing in Las Vegas," was adapted into a motion picture by Terry Gilliam in 1998. Gonzo journalism is a reporting style in which the author puts himself or herself into the heart of the story and focuses on style more than the accuracy of the account. Exaggeration and bawdy if not pornographic humor mark such Thompson works as *Fear and Loathing on the Campaign Trail '72, The Great Shark Hunt,* and, *Better Than Sex.*

9. Alfred, Lord Tennyson (1809–1892) was poet laureate of the United Kingdom during much of the reign of Queen Victoria and is best remembered for "The Charge of the Light Brigade."

10. Dante Gabriel Rossetti (1828–1882) was an English poet, painter, and founder of the pre-Raphaelite Brotherhood, a precursor of the Aesthetic Movement.

11. Joyce Maynard (1953–) is best known as a writer who lived with the legendary J. D. Salinger (1919–2010), author of the great American novel *The Catcher in the Rye.* Maynard wrote about her experiences with Salinger in the 1973 memoir *Looking Back.* Other nonfiction includes *Domestic Affairs, At Home in the World,* and *Internal Combustion.* Novels include *To Die For,* which was adapted into a motion picture by Gus Van Sant. In the film, she had a cameo of Suzanne Stone's lawyer.

12. Stan Laurel (1890–1965) and Oliver Hardy (1892–1957) were a legendary and beloved comedy team in silent and talking pictures. Stan, also known as Skinny, and Hardy, as Fatty, played friends who got themselves into comical and daunting situations in short and feature films. Their most renowned long-form films include *Sons of the Desert, A Chump at Oxford,* and *Saps at Sea.*

13. Joaquin Phoenix (1974–) is the brother of the late River Phoenix (1970–1993) and Rain Phoenix (1972–). All three have appeared in Van Sant movies. Joaquin has also been in *Inventing the Abbotts* (1997), *Gladiator* (2000), and *Walk the Line* (2005). During an interview with David Letterman on February 11, 2009, looking disheveled and confused, he made a public announcement that he was retiring from acting to concentrate on a career as a rapper.

14. Casey Affleck (1975–) is the brother of Ben Affleck (1972–) and has appeared in Van Sant's *Good Will Hunting* (1997), *To Die For* (1995), and *Gerry* (2002). Casey's other roles include *Hamlet* (2000), *The Assassination of Jesse James by the Coward Robert Ford* (2007), and *Gone Baby Gone* (2007), directed by his brother, Ben.

15. Alison Folland (1978–) is an actress who appeared in Van Sant's *To Die For* (1995), *Good Will Hunting* (1997), and *Finding Forrester* (2000), in which she plays a *Jeopardy* contestant seen on a television in Forrester's apartment. She has also worked as a performer in *Boys Don't Cry* (1999), *I'm Not There* (2007), and *The Happening* (2008).

16. Aaron Copland (1900–1990) was an American composer who worked in the concert and recording fields, as well as in motion pictures. His compositions include *Billy the Kid* (1938), *Appalachian Spring* (1944), and *Three Latin American Sketches* (1971). His film work includes the scores for *Of Mice and Men* (1939), *The Heiress* (1949), and the documentary *The City* (1939).

17. "Self-referential" is a term for films that, either in whole or in part, refer to themselves. For example, an actor may address the camera directly, the film may show on screen the making of the movie the audience is watching, or the movie can employ any trope that makes the viewer aware of and a participant in the cinematographic process.

18. A flashback is a scene in which the screenwriter or editor and director write or cut in a scene that takes place before the time frame already established by the film.

19. A cheat is an act by the director and film crew during the production process and later by the director and editor that alters time and space. A production cheat can involve moving actors closer or further away from the camera to give the appearance that they are either near or far from each other. Moving an object on a table during a dialogue sequence so that it doesn't block the face of one of the performers is another form of cheat. In postproduction, a cheat is any cut to picture or sound that is made to correct continuity errors or to move the film narrative forward.

20. The backstory is information about the narrative or the characters that refers to events that took place before a scene or the movie begin.

21. Jane Pauley (1950–) is an American journalist who was once host of NBC's *The Today Show* and *Dateline NBC*.

22. The television series *Leave It to Beaver* ran on the CBS network from 1957 to 1963. In *Leave It to Beaver,* American society was devoid of financial hardship, violence, crime, and almost any negative issue that in reality was plaguing the country. The Cleaver family was composed of two sons, Theodore, nicknamed Beaver, acted by Jerry Mathers (1948–) and Wally, played by Tony Dow (1945–), and their parents, June (Barbara Billingsley [1915–]) and Ward (Hugh Beaumont [1909–1982]). Two urban legends followed the program. The first concerns Wally's friend Eddie Haskell (Ken Osmond [1943–]). The rumors had the obnoxious young man growing up to be either shock rocker Alice Cooper (1948–) or porn star John Holmes (1944–1988). Mather, it was claimed, was killed during the Vietnam War, even though he is (as of this writing) alive and well.

23. Edward R. Murrow (1908–1965) was a pioneer media journalist who covered world events on radio and then television. Murrow is best known for his "take no prisoners" interview technique and as the man who brought down the

red-baiting Communist hunter fanatic Senator Joseph McCarthy. Murrow's coverage of World War II and his work as a news anchor set the standard for television news.

24. Walter Cronkite (1916–2009) was one of "Murrow's Boys." Cronkite covered World War II and is best known as the anchor of *The CBS Evening News,* a job he held for 19 years until the company forced him to retire at age 65. Once considered the most trusted man in America, Cronkite covered the great news events of his time and was noted for his live broadcast from the CBS television studio when President John F. Kennedy was assassinated in November 1963. Cronkite kept his composure, fighting off emotion by wiping his eyes and repeatedly putting his eyeglasses on and off while breaking news poured into his earpiece.

25. Black comedy is storytelling that makes light of serious themes, such as nuclear annihilation, serial murders, rape, and incest, that the public rarely if at all finds humorous. The most infamous example is the Stanley Kubrick film *Dr. Strangelove, or How I Learned to Stop Worrying and Love the Bomb,* in which the maniacal Brigadier General Jack Ripper (Sterling Hayden) is responsible for launching aircraft loaded with nuclear warheads, forcing the U.S. president (Peter Sellers) to phone the Russian premier where he learns that the Russians have triggered their Doomsday Machine, which if activated would eliminate all life on earth.

26. Rain Phoenix (1972–) is an American actress who has appeared in Van Sant films. Other performances by Rain Phoenix can be found in *O* (2001), *Hitch* (2005), and *Kids in America* (2005).

27. John Boorman (1933–) is a British film director who has worked in the United Kingdom and in Hollywood. He is noted for using potentially treacherous locations simply to help him make a good movie. For *Deliverance* (1972), he took his cast and crew into the backwoods and worked on a river that was so high it had to be drained during shooting periods; the water was returned to full when the shot was done. *The Emerald Forest* (1985) featured the director's son Charley, who played Tome. The movie was shot in a densely foliaged rain forest, and the cast and crew had to act and shoot under nearly impossible conditions. *Beyond Rangoon* (1995) was shot in Burma. The story concerns a young woman who leaves for vacation in Burma to get away from the horror of the murder of her husband and son. Once there, she joins a student group and is harassed and hunted by the soldiers of a vicious dictator. Again, the cast and crew worked on location under difficult conditions and were constantly on the move as they told this true story. Boorman is also the author of an autobiography and a journal of the making of *The Emerald Forest,* which one hopes will one day inspire Van Sant to do the same.

28. *Velvet Goldmine* (1998), directed by Todd Haynes (1961–), like *Citizen Kane* (1941), has complex characters and uses a reporter, kept largely in the background, to interview those who knew and either loved or hated or were indifferent to the main character as he tracks down the story. The Welles film is largely based on the life of William Randolph Hearst. Many feel *Velvet Goldmine* is based on the life of the rock legend David Bowie (1947–), one of the many performers for whom Van Sant has directed music videos.

29. A double flashback occurs when a film is in its present time and then cuts to the past, signaling flashback 1. During that scene, characters are talking, and one tells another story about the past, and the viewer now sees that second scene,

flashback 2. Double flashbacks are rare. A notable example occurs in *Killer's Kiss* (1955), directed by Stanley Kubrick. Other double flashbacks occur in *The Man Who Shot Liberty Valance* (1962, directed by John Ford), *Six Degrees of Separation* (1993, directed by Fred Schepisi), and *Passage to Marseille* (1944, directed by Michael Curtiz).

30. Eric Carmen (1949–) is a former member of the Raspberries. The singer, songwriter, musician, and heartthrob has been associated with many songs, both on albums and in the movies. His motion picture soundtrack work includes *Footloose* (1984), *Dirty Dancing* (1987), *Almost Famous* (2000), and *Bridget Jones' Diary* (2004).

31. *The Stepford Wives* is a satirical horror novel published in 1972 by Ira Levin (1929–2007) in which a young woman who has moved into a suburban neighborhood in Connecticut with her husband begins to think that all the local women are robots created by their husbands. The woman all look and act perfect and are totally subservient to their mates. There were two films that adapted this chilling, sardonic book in which suburban wives are turned into submissive Barbie Doll-like creatures by their diabolical husbands, *The Stepford Wives,* released in 1975, was directed by Bryan Forbes, with a screenplay by William Goldman, and started Katherine Ross, Paula Prentiss, Peter Masterson, Nanette Newman, and Tina Louise. *The Stepford Wives,* released in 2004, was directed by Frank Oz, with a screenplay by Paul Rudnick, and starred Nicole Kidman, Matthew Broderick, Bette Midler, Glenn Close, Christopher Walken, and Roger Bart.

32. *Desperate Housewives* is a television series (2004–) that stars Teri Hatcher, Felicity Huffman, Marcia Cross, Eva Longoria Parker, Ricardo Chavira, Brenda Strong, Nicollette Sheridan, and Doug Savant. This megahit dramedy investigates secrets and truths as seen through the eyes of beautiful and glamorous suburban woman after the mysterious suicide of a neighbor. The funny, sad, sexy, and always provocative goings-on take place on Wisteria Lane, the fictional street devised by the creators.

33. McLuhanism is a media philosophy developed by Marshall McLuhan (1911–1980) that examines the narrative and stylistic elements of motion pictures, television, and digital technology. Although McLuhan didn't have a theory about the Internet, one of his followers was inspired to do so. As a lecturer, teacher, and writer, McLuhan spread the word on the impact of the media on humanity. His books include *Understanding Media: The Extensions of Man* (1964), *The Medium Is the Massage: An Inventory of Effects* (1967), and *War and Peace in the Global Village* (1968). He made a legendary motion picture appearance in Woody Allen's *Annie Hall* (1977) in which he hides behind a movie poster panel and is pulled out by Alvy Singer (Woody Allen) to answer back to a wiseacre professor who has been carrying on about McLuhan's philosophy in full voice while waiting on the ticket line. He is best remembered for the slogan "The medium is the message" and for the phrase "the global village."

34. Pink is a color value associated with lipstick. It was used by the Nazis during World War II to identify homosexuals and was also used in a novel written by Gus Van Sant and published in 1998. The books plot concerns a director of infomercials and his friends and hangers-on. Critics have accused Van Sant as attempting to write like William S. Burroughs or Tom Robbins, with Andy Warhol and Kurt

Vonnegut thrown in for good measure. They also expressed their dissatisfaction with the autobiographical strands, including the death of River Phoenix, the male-to-male relationships, and the Kurt Cobain story.

35. Kelly McGillis (1957–) is an actress who appeared in *Witness* (1985), *Top Gun* (1986), *The Accused* (1988), and *North* (1994). McGillis came out as a lesbian in 2009 during an interview on SheWired.com, an LGBT Web site.

36. DeVeren Bookwalter (1939–1987) was the actor receiving fellatio from an off-screen Williard Maas, a legendary experimental filmmaker. Bookwalter appeared on stage and in films, including *Twelfth Night, Hamlet,* and *Othello* on the boards and on videotape, as well as in *The Omega Man* (1971) and *The Enforcer* (1976) in movies.

37. Pietro Scalia interview with the author.

38. Ibid.

39. Robin Williams (1951–) is an American actor who got his big break on the television series *Mork and Mindy* (1978–1982), in which he played an alien whose mission was to study earthlings. Williams, who won the Oscar for Best Supporting Actor for Van Sant's *Good Will Hunting* (1997), is famous for his manic standup routines. Just some of the movies he has appeared in include *Popeye* (1980), *Dead Poets Society* (1989), and *One Hour Photo* (2002).

40. Pietro Scalia interview with the author.

41. Minnie Driver (1970–) is a London-born actress who, in addition to playing Skylar in Van Sant's *Good Will Hunting* (1997), has appeared in many films, including *Big Night* (1996), *Hope Springs* (2003), and *Delirious* (2006).

42. Pietro Scalia interview with the author.

43. Michael Kahn (1935–) is an Academy Award–winning film editor who works most frequently with director Steven Spielberg. He edited *Schindler's List* (1993), the Indiana Jones chronicles, *Saving Private Ryan* (1998), and countless other Hollywood films.

44. Vincent LoBrutto, *Selected Takes: Film Editors On Editing* (New York: Praeger, 1991), 172–173.

45. Pietro Scalia interview with the author.

46. Ibid.

47. Elaine May (1932–) is a film director, actress, screenwriter, and part of the landmark comedy duo Nichols and May, which paired her with Mike Nichols. She is notorious for directing *Istar* (1987), widely considered by critics and audiences to be among the worst motion pictures ever made. The film starred Warren Beatty and Dustin Hoffman as a singing duo who sang worst than badly and found themselves involved with a woman, played by Isabelle Adjani, and a plot involving the CIA and the Emir of Ishtar and rebel forces. As a screenwriter, May is the author of *Such Good Friends* (1972), *Reds* (1981), and *Tootsie* (1982). Her credits as director include *A New Leaf* (1971), *The Heartbreak Kid* (1972), and *Mikey and Nicky* (1976).

CHAPTER 5

1. "We blew it" is a prophetic line spoken by Peter Fonda, playing Wyatt, to Dennis Hopper, portraying Billy, in *Easy Rider* (1969). Wyatt is referring to the money they made selling cocaine and their plans to continue traveling cross-country. Wyatt keeps repeating "We blew it." Billy tells him they have enough money

to retire in Florida. Wyatt lies down to sleep, the American flag stitched to his black leather Captain America jacket facing camera. By the end of the 1970s and into the early 1980s. the line "We blew it" referred to whether the American New Wave filmmakers, minus Lucas and Spielberg, who invented the blockbuster and were instant millionaires, were in any way successful. Scorsese, Coppola, De Palma, Bogdanovich, and many, many others lived and worked in what could only be called an American Renaissance of filmmaking. But few of the movies made real money. The players lived to see another day and decades, but the great majority of the 1970s filmmakers were driven out of the business. Time had passed them by. Audiences by and large didn't want to see message films; they wanted to be entertained. Did the baby-boom generation of filmmakers change the cinematic world? Many say yes, it's a legacy that is still with us. Those in the know, however, understand that, with their excesses in style and budget, the American New Wave did "blow it": they had a chance to really change the world, the way movies were made and the daring content that they investigate, but—they blew it.

2. Anthony Perkins (1932–1992) died of AIDS at age 60. A bisexual man, he was married to Berry Berenson, Marisa Berenson's (*Barry Lyndon*) sister. He played many roles on stage and screen. His films include *Fear Strikes Out* (1957), *The Trial* (1962, directed by Orson Welles), and *Winter Kills* (1979, directed by William Richert, who played Bob in Van Sant's *My Own Private Idaho* [1991]). For all his accomplishments, Anthony Perkins will always be remembered as the actor who helped create and who played Norman Bates in Alfred Hitchcock's masterwork *Psycho* (1960). He became typecast as the homicidal transvestite mother murder, but he took it in stride and in fact played Bates again in *Psycho II* (1983), directed by Richard Franklin, and reprised the role again as well as directed *Psycho III* (1986). Perkins had movie star good looks, but under that veneer was a conflicted and neurotic man. He played a troubled young man in *Fear Strikes Out,* the true story of baseball player Jimmy Piersol; a mentally disturbed man in *Pretty Poison* (1968); and a Jekyll and Hyde character in *The Edge of Sanity* (1989). It has long been said that nobody could play Norman Bates like Anthony Perkins; although Vince Vaughn did a fine job in the Van Sant update, he pales in comparison to the man who *was* Norman Bates.

3. Drew Barrymore (1975–) is a member of the elite theater and film family that includes Lionel, Ethel, and John Barrymore. Drew Barrymore made her film debut in *Altered States* (1982), but it was her role as Gertie in Spielberg's *E.T.* that most consider her first significant part. She has gone on to act and produce many motion pictures and has had starring or featured roles in *Firestarter* (1984), *Guncrazy* (1992), and *Charlie's Angels* (1982), which she also produced. In 1996 she played Casey Becker in Wes Craven's *Scream,* in which, like Janet Leigh in Hitchcock's *Psycho* (1960) and Anne Heche in Van Sant's *Psycho* (1998), she was a major movie star murdered near the opening of the movie.

4. The Steadicam was invented by Garrett Brown (1943–) and was first used in Hal Ashby's *Bound for Glory* (1976). The Steadicam is a camera device that allows the operator to perform absolutely even movements without any camera shake. The rig is mounted onto the body of the operator, who, while watching what he is shooting on a monitor attached to the Steadicam, can move in any director, quickly or slowly, without the jostling that plagued handheld cameramen from the beginning of the motion picture industry.

5. Stephen Rebello, *Alfred Hitchcock and the Making of Psycho* (New York: Dembner Books), 112.
6. Janet Leigh, with Christopher Nickens, *Psycho: Behind the Scenes of the Classic Thriller* (New York: Harmony Books, 1995), 75.
7. Ibid.
8. Philip J. Skerry, *Psycho in the Shower: The History of Cinema's Most Famous Scene* (New York: Continuum, 2009), 269.
9. Miles Davis (1926–1991) was a jazz trumpet player who is widely considered to be the most influential and greatest musician of the 20th century. Davis was either part of or created many movements in jazz and popular youth music, including bop, the cool school, freeform jazz, and fusion. Davis is best known as a musician who experienced, participated in, and created many artistic periods, as Pablo Picasso did in painting and Gus Van Sant has done in film.
10. *Jeopardy!* is a long-running television quiz show that first aired on NBC from March 20, 1964, to September 5, 1975, followed by a weekly syndicated form from September 9, 1974, to September 5, 1975, as well as a revival from October 2, 1978, to March 2, 1979, all hosted by Art Fleming with Don Pardo as his announcer. On September 10, 1984, *Jeopardy!* was syndicated and hosted by Alex Trebek with Johnny Gilbert as his announcer, and this version of the show continues to run and is enjoyed by a wide viewership. The show was created by Merv Griffin. Three contestants play against each other for prize money. They choose a topic and dollar amount and are given the answer to a question such as "The current president of the United States" or "Bank of America." The contestant must then come up with the question (e.g., "Who is Barack Obama?" or "What is the largest bank in the United States?"). In Van Sant's *Finding Forrester* (2000), William Forrester and Jamal Wallace watch *Jeopardy!* every night to test their intelligence. On one such night, one of the contestants is Alison Folland, who played Lydia Mertz in *To Die For* (1995), in a clever cameo planned by Van Sant.
11. Homer Lusk Collyer (1881–1947) and Langley Collyer (1885–1947), commonly known as the Collyer Brothers, were compulsive horders who collected everything from newspapers to magazines, furniture, and most anything else they could get their hands on.
12. Philip G. Epstein (1909–1952) and Julius J. Epstein (1909–2000) were twin brothers who at times collaborated on screenplays, including the film many people feel is the greatest of all time, *Casablanca* (1942), which was the winner of an Academy Award for Best Screenplay.
13. Mark Robson (1913–1978) was a film editor whose postproduction credits include *Citizen Kane* (1941, with Robert Wise), *Cat People* (1942), and *I Walked with a Zombie* (1942). As a director, Robson worked on *Champion* (1949), *The Harder They Fall* (1956), and *Earthquake* (1974). Milton Arbogast is the name of the private investigator played by Martin Balsam (1919–1996) in Hitchcock's *Psycho* (1960) and by William H. Macy in the 1998 production of *Psycho* directed by Gus Van Sant.
14. "Just do it" is a slogan created for the Nike shoe company in 1998. *Advertising Age* magazine crowned it as one of the top 10 ad slogans of the 20th century.
15. This and subsequent comments by Valdis Óskardóttir are from e-mail correspondence with the author.

16. AVID is the company that created the AVID digital motion picture editing system and displayed it for the first time at the National Association of Broadcasters (NAB) show in April 1989. Computer or nonlinear editing allows the creator and operator to quickly cut, move, or add transitions to film or video images loaded into the system and gives them the luxury of doing so in any which way that appeals to them.

CHAPTER 6

1. Jeffrey Sward, "Notable Use of the Long Take in Motion Picture Films," http://www.jeffreysward.com/editorials/longtake.htm.
2. Andrei Tarkovsky (1934–1986) was a Soviet filmmaker. In 1982, he traveled to Italy for the second time and directed *Nostalgia*. In 1981, Tarkovsky traveled to the United Kingdom and Sweden. It was at this time that he strongly considered defecting because of the injustices, censorship, and alterations he had endured from officials in the Soviet Union, but he changed his mind and returned to his wife and son, who were still living in the Soviet Union. At the Cannes Film Festival, *Nostalgia* won the Grand Prix Spécial du Jury, but Soviet authorities saw to it that Tarkovsky didn't win the honor of the Palme d'Or. At that time, the master filmmaker, known for his long, often choreographed camera movements and significant and controversial content, resolved never to make another film in the country of his birth. On July 10, 1984, Tarkovsky announced he would live in the West and never return to the Soviet Union. His last film before dying of cancer at 54 was *The Sacrifice,* shot in 1985. and the film won the Grand Prix Spécial du Jury at the Cannes Film Festival, but, unfortunately, Tarkovsky was too ill to pick up the prize, which was received by his son Andrei Jr. Inscribed on his tombstone are the words "To the man who saw the Angel."
3. Rob Blackwelder, "Gus Van Sant Returns to His Off-the-Wall Indie Roots with Experimental, Existential, 'Gerry,'" *SPLICEDwire.* http://splicedwire.com/03features/gvansant.html.
4. Harvey Weinstein (1952–) and Bob Weinstein (1954–) founded Miramax Films in 1979. It was a leading independent film production and distribution company that was sold to the Walt Disney Company in 1993. Of the two, it was Harvey who aggressively pursued the Miramax (a name with is the combination of their parents first names) product in terms of acquisitions and readying films for distribution, which most often involved severe re-editing by Harvey, who enjoyed a great track record for success. The filmmakers were livid, but he made the audiences happy. In 2005, the brothers formed the Weinstein Company and released many films, including *Transamerica* (2005), *Clerks II* (2006), and *The Reader* (2008). Some of the films released by Miramax include *Pulp Fiction* (1994), *The English Patient* (1996), and *Gangs of New York* (2002).
5. Marguerite Duras (1914–1996) was a member of the French Resistance during World War II and a devout Communist. A respected writer, screenwriter, and motion picture director, Duras, a leading intellectual in her time, has credits that include the novels *The Square* (1955), *Ten-Thirty on a Summer Night* (1960), and *The Lover* (1998). Her screenplays include *Hiroshima Mon Amour* (1959), directed by Alain Renais; *Moderato Cantabile* (1960), directed by Peter Brook;

and *The Sailor from Gibraltar* (1967), directed by Tony Richardson. Duras's credits as a film director include *La Musica* (1967), *Jaune le Soleil* (1972), and *Nathalie Granger* (1972). Her notorious experimental film *The Truck* (1977) played the New York Film Festival, where the majority of the audience walked out, exasperated and confused as well as angry. In *The Truck,* Duras investigated, like Gus Van Sant in *Gerry* (2002), the use of long takes and dialogue.

6. Alexander Ballinger, *New Cinematographers* (New York: Collins Design, 2004), 179.
7. Robert F. Kennedy (1925–1968), member of America's foremost political family of the 20th century, was brother to John F. Kennedy (1917–1963) and Edward M. Kennedy (1932–2009). Robert, U.S. attorney general in the administrations of his brother and of President Lyndon B. Johnson and later a U.S. senator from New York, decided in 1968 to run for president of the United States. He was the front-runner for the Democratic Party nomination over Senator Eugene McCarthy when, after giving his victory speech at L.A.'s Ambassador Hotel after winning the California primary, he was assassinated by Sirhan Sirhan.
8. Dogme 95 is a radical moviemaking philosophy espoused by Lars von Trier and Thomas Vinterberg, which in its manifesto lists rules about creating motion pictures. Just some of the 10 rules include these:

   1. Shooting must be done on location. Props and sets must not be brought in. If a particular prop is necessary for the story, a location must be chosen where this prop can be found.
   3. The camera must be a hand-held camera. Any movement or immobility attainable in the hand is permitted. The film must not take place where the camera is standing; filming must take place where the action takes place.
   10. The director must not be credited.

   See Richard Kelly, *The Name of This Book is Dogme95* (London: Faber and Faber, 2000), 8, 10.
9. P. Adams Sitney (1944–) is a historian of experimental or avant-garde cinema and the founder (with others) of Anthology Film Archives. At this writing, he is Professor of the Council of the Humanities and Visual Arts at Princeton University in New Jersey. Sitney was long associated with *Film Culture* magazine. After an argument with Jonas Mekas, a co-founder of Anthology Film Archives and *Film Culture* magazine, he stopped talking to him; the feud continues to this day. Sitney is the author of many books on the cinema, including *Modernist Montage: The Obscurity of Vision in Cinema and Literature* (1992), *Film Culture Reader* (1970), and the seminal *Visionary Film: The American Avant-Garde 1943–1974,* updated in 1979 and 2002, in which he created the genre of structural filmmaking, in which the artist searches for a simpler form, style, and content of moviemaking than is usual in Hollywood and in which the shape of the project is crucial. Van Sant's experimental period was an investigation into the elements of structural filmmaking, among other aesthetic and narrative or nonnarrative tropes.
10. Ballinger, *New Cinematographers*, p. 185.
11. A flash forward occurs after the real time of a film has been established and the director and editor cut to a scene that takes place in the future and then, when ready, cut back to the real time of the movie. The most famous flash forward in film history takes place in the New Orleans brothel scene in *Easy Rider* (1969). Wyatt, played by Peter Fonda, looks upward at a statue. When his eyeline reaches the top,

he see a piece of the statue that has a phrase written on it. At this precise moment there is a cut to a future scene during which Wyatt and Billy (Dennis Hopper) lay dead on the asphalt of the two-lane road.

12. Sean Axmaker, "Gus Van Sant: 'A cinema that might have existed,'" https://www.greencine.com/central/node/416.

13. Courtney Love (1964–) is a rock singer and actress who was married to Nirvana front man and composer Kurt Cobain (1967–1994), who shot himself in the head with a shotgun, killing himself instantly. Courtney Love is the mother of Francis Bean Cobain, the daughter of the late singer and musician. As an actress, Love appeared in *Beat* (2000), *Sid and Nancy* (1986), and *The People vs. Larry Flint* (1996). Love's musical career includes work as a singer in the rock band Faith No More; she is the founder of the all-girl group Babes in Toyland, and lead vocalist of the bands Hole and Bastid (2001). Courtney Love is a controversial figure known for her excessive drug use; for her antics in art (e.g., being on the cover of the book *Heaven to Hell,* which depicts Love and a dying Kurt Cobain posed similar to Michelangelo's *Pieta*); for her outrageous hair, make-up, and clothing style; and for her rumored legal challenges to stop the filming and/or distribution of the Van Sant film *Gus Van Sant's Last Days.*

14. Yasujiro Ozu (1903–1963) was a Japanese film director known for placing his camera in a low position as if he were photographing Kabuki theater. Other signatures of Ozu's cinematic style are long, lock-off camera takes and blocking of actors that calls for little movement on their part. His films identified by screenwriter, theorist, and film director Paul Schrader as transcendental include *Tokyo Story* (1953), *Floating Weeds* (1959), and *An Autumn Afternoon* (1962).

15. Ben Kingsley (1943–) is a British actor best known for his performance as Mohandas Gandhi in the motion picture *Gandhi* (1982), directed by Richard Attenborough, which won eight Academy Awards, including Best Actor in a Leading Role for Kingsley and Best Director and Best Picture for Attenborough. Few actors in the history of the American cinema have successfully achieved the feat of inhabiting (taking on the physical and psychological aspects of a character) a biopic subject. Others include Lou Diamond Phillips as ill-fated rocker Richie Valens in *La Bamba* (1987), directed by Luis Valdez; Philip Seymour Hoffman as writer Truman Capote in *Capote* (2005), directed by Bennett Miller; Henry Fonda as Abraham Lincoln in *Young Mr. Lincoln* (1939), directed by John Ford; and, of course, Sean Penn as Harvey Milk in *Milk* (2008), directed by Gus Van Sant.

16. A slow backtracking shot is one in which a motion picture camera, either handheld or mounted on metal rails, travels backward photographing what is in front of the lens. The slow speed of the camera movement is intended to create for the viewer a dramatic presence.

17. Existentialism is a philosophy most associated with Jean-Paul Sartre. It deals with the confusion and disorientation of an individual who faces an absurd and meaningless world. Noted existentialists include Albert Camus, Friedrich Nietzsche, Franz Kafka, Fyodor Dostoyevsky, Simone de Beauvoir, Søren Kierkegaard, and Norman Mailer.

18. Nino Rota (1911–1979) was a film composer. He is best known for creating the theme to *The Godfather* (1972) and for his work with director Federico Fellini. His work with the Italian master of cinematic interpretive reality and the world of dreams includes scores for *The White Sheik* (1952), *I Vitelloni* (1953), *La Strada* (1954), *Nights of Cabiria* (1957), *La Dolce Vita* (1960),

Federico Fellini's 8 1/2 (1963), *Juliet of the Spirits* (1965), *Fellini Satyricon* (1969), *Fellini's Roma* (1972), *Amarcord* (1973), *Fellini's Casanova* (1976), and *Orchestra Rehearsal* (1978). Rota's music for Fellini at times reminds people of the circus or a carnival, which is the feeling Van Sant wanted to create in *Paranoid Park* (2007). A little-known and bizarre fact is that, when in post-production on *Barry Lyndon* (1975), the film's director, Stanley Kubrick, asked the composer, Leonard Rosenman (who incidentally scored the James Dean film *Rebel Without a Cause* [1955], directed by Nicholas Ray) to purchase the rights to the theme from *The Godfather*. The flabbergasted Rosenman told Kubrick in so many words that the Coppola film was about the Mafia in the 20th century, whereas *Barry Lyndon* took place in the 18th century and was largely about aristocrats. Kubrick just shrugged his shoulders, saying he liked *The Godfather* tune. Of course, Rota's legendary theme is not in Kubrick's film; it's in others, but not *Barry Lyndon*.

19. Paul Schrader, *Transcendental Style in Film: Ozu, Bresson, Dreyer* (New York: Da Capo Press, 1988), 11.

20. Vincent LoBrutto, *Sound-On-Film: Interviews with Creators of Film Sound* (Westport, CT: Praeger, 1994), 84.

21. Charlie Chan is a fictitious Asian detective created by Earl Derr Biggers in 1923. Charlie Chan has appeared in novels, on radio programs, and in movies. Throughout the years, many protest groups, Asian and non-Asian, have cried out for the banishment of Charlie Chan from the bookshelves, the radio air-waves, and the motion picture theaters. This protest movement became so serious that any television station or network planning on airing a Charlie Chan movie had to show it in segments that were accompanied by a panel discussion involving leading Asian actors, politicians, and celebrities, who lectured the view-ing public on the evils of stereotyping. In *Paranoid Park* (2007), Gus Van Sant was trying to subvert this image of the all-knowing and subservient Oriental detective by casting an Asian actor but turning the personality established by Hollywood upside down. What really angered the protesters was the fact that Caucasian and European actors played Chan, rather than an Asian actor. Over the decades, Chan has been played by the Swedish actor Sidney Toler, American ac-tors Roland Winters and Ross Martin, and British actor Peter Ustinov. Just some of the Charlie Chan motion pictures include *Charlie Chan at the Opera* (1936), *Charlie Chan at the Circus* (1936), and *Charlie Chan in Honolulu* (1938). In 1961, the *Dick Tracy* cartoon show featured an Asian detective named Jo Jitsu who also had audiences up in arms, demanding that he be taken off the air and banished to the tape or film vault for eternity.

22. Mr. Moto is a fictional Japanese secret agent created by the writer John P. Marquand. Mr. Moto, like Charlie Chan, appeared in novels, on radio, and in the movies. Moto was played in the movies principally by the Hungarian-born actor Peter Lorre, of *M* (1931) and *The Maltese Falcon* (1941); one time, he was played by American actor Henry Silva. Mr. Moto was created to keep the studio coffers filled after Earl Derr Biggers died. Some of Lorre's performances as Mr. Moto include *Thank You Mr. Moto* (1937), *Mysterious Mr. Moto* (1938), and *Mr. Moto Takes a Vacation* (1939). It is assumed that Gus Van Sant was familiar with both Charlie Chan and Mr. Moto and took the opportunity in *Paranoid Park* (2007) to have Richard Lu played by an Asian, Daniel Lu.

23. A Perry Mason moment is the point in each episode of the *Perry Mason* television series in which Mason, a successful and dynamic lawyer played by actor Raymond Burr, another gay actor, pulls a "gotcha" on someone he is questioning in court, forcing the man or women to break down and admit his or her guilt in the murder case being tried in court.

24. Henry Rollins (1961–) is a singer/songwriter, DJ, activist, comedian, and publisher. Rollins is best known as the front man for the California hardcore punk band Black Flag, for the book *See a Grown Man Cry, Now Watch Him Die,* and for his appearance in the 1995 film *Johnny Mnemonic,* directed by American painter and sculptor Robert Longo and featuring Keanu Reeves. Rollins thus links Van Sant and Longo, in their separate but distinct ways.

25. Cinéma vérité is a documentary film style begun in France, largely by Jean Rouch. For *Chronicle of a Summer* (1960), Rouch follows Parisians around with a lightweight camera. Instead of having to depend on narration, he told his story through the real actions and talk of real people doing what they do. The American version of cinéma vérité, called direct cinema, was inspired by Rouch and others and had its own pioneers, including D. A. Pennebaker (*Don't Look Back*), Richard Leacock, cameraman on Robert Flaherty's *Louisiana Story* (1948), and Albert and David Maysles (*Salesman,* 1968).

CHAPTER 7

1. Brian Singer (1965–) is a gay but not openly gay film director who was forced out via a lawsuit concerning his crew's behavior on *Apt Pupil* (1998). He attended the School of Visual Arts in New York City, in the college's film department, until he was caught drinking a beer on the school's premises and was asked to leave. His most popular motion picture is *The Usual Suspects* (1995). Other credits include *X-Men* (2003), *Superman Returns* (2006), and *Valkyrie* (2008).

2. Daniel Day Lewis (1957–) is a heterosexual British actor who played gay man in *My Beautiful Laundrette* (1985). James Woods (1947–) is a heterosexual American actor who played the gay/bisexual lawyer Roy Cohn who joined Senator Joseph McCarthy in witch hunt for Communists where they didn't exist in the TV movie *Citizen Cohn* (1992).

3. A docudrama is a motion picture or television movie that is based on a true story. The most famous motion picture docudrama is Oliver Stone's *JFK* (1991), which was based on the assassination of President John F. Kennedy but speculated about those involved in the plot, created characters who were not part of the real story, and optically/digitally manipulated the Zapruder film, an 8mm record of the shooting (see note 6). Another docudrama, the British Television movie *The Beckoning Silence,* tells the true story of German mountain climber Toni Kurtz, who died during a treacherous climb. The action was re-created, and, as always, some manipulation of the story and characters took place.

4. Anita Bryant is a U.S. singer who hit the top 10 four times during the 1950s. In the 1970s she became an outspoken opponent of gay rights; she believed that proponents of the lifestyle should not receive any protection under the law and believed that homosexuals were condemned by God.

5. Miklós Rózsa is a film composer best known for the score for *Ben-Hur* (1959).

6. The Zapruder film was a home movie shot by Abraham Zapruder (1905–1970) during President Kennedy's visit to Dallas, Texas. The camera was rolling when the killer's bullets struck the president in the head and in other parts of his body. The 8mm film was originally bought by *Life* magazine and then was donated to the Sixth Floor Museum in the Texas Book Depository building at Dealey Plaza, in Dallas.

7. Stop-motion photography is a type of animation technique in which a motion picture or video camera is set to expose a set number of frames in a set amount of time I order to capture in a short compressed format an event that would take a long time. This technique is famously used in *Koyaanisqatsi* (1982), which was directed by Godfrey Reggio and photographed by Ron Frickie. George Lucas and his team of moviemakers have applied stop motion in *Raiders of the Lost Ark* (1981) and *The Empire Strikes Back* (1980), among other films.

8. Known as the Briggs Initiative or Proposition 6, this was an issue voted on by Californians on November 7, 1978. The sponsor, State Senator John Briggs, a conservative behind the proposed bill failed, but he had attempted to pass a law that would make it impossible for anyone in the larger gay community to work in a public school.

9. Malcolm X was born Malcolm Little on May 19, 1925, and was assassinated on February 21, 1965, in the Audubon Ballroom in New York City by a team of gunman who many believe were operating on orders given by Louis Farrakhan (1933–), a Muslim leader best known for organizing The Million Man March in Washington, D.C., on October 16, 1995, an event held to preach to black males about the need to take responsibility for the way they treat their girlfriends, wives, and children and for supporting themselves and their families. Spike Lee dramatized the journey to this spiritual and life-changing event in his motion picture *Get on the Bus* (1996). After a fiery war of words with Norman Jewison and other Caucasian members of the film industry, Lee finally got to direct *Malcolm X* (1992), an epic film about the slain leader, which, at 202 minutes, is not just one of his longest pictures but also clearly a labor of love and which became his master work. In the title role, Denzel Washington (1954–) gave another one of those inhabitation performances in which he became Malcolm X on the screen. Washington, who won an Oscar for best actor in 2002 for *Training Day* (2001), was nominated in 1992 for best actor in a leading role for *Malcolm X* but, surprisingly, he lost to Anthony Hopkins for his portrayal of Hannibal Lecter in *The Silence of the Lambs*, directed by Jonathan Demme.

10. Magical realism is a form of literature in which spiritual or magical happenings occur at realistic times or at times when mundane actions would be expected to occur. Latin American writers are best known for writing in this style. They include Jorge Amado (*Donna Flor and Her Two Husbands* [1966]), Gabriel Garcia Marquez (*One Hundred Years of Solitude* [1967]), and Carlos Fuentes (*Terra Nostra* [1975]).

CONCLUSIONS

1. Peter Tonguette, interview with the author.
2. Pietro Scalia, interview with the author.
3. Valdis Óskardóttir, interview with the author.

Bibliography

ABC Television Network Technical Training and Development Department. *The Language of Television: A Glossary of Television Network Terms.* New York: ABC Television Technical Publications, 1983.

Antonioni, Michelangelo, Ellio Bartolini, and Tonino Guerra. *L'Avventura.* New York: Grove Press, 1969.

Aronson, Marc. *Art Attack: A Short Cultural History of the Avant-Garde.* New York: Clarion Books, 1998.

Baal-Teshuva, ed., with contributions by David Bourdon, Pierre Restany, Jacob Baal-Teshuva, Gene R. Swendon, and Paul Taylor. *Andy Warhol: 1928–1987: Works from the Collections of José Mugrabi and an Isle of Man Company.* Munich: Prestel, 1993.

Ball, Phillip. *Bright Earth: Art and the Invention of Color.* New York: Farrar, Straus and Giroux, 2001.

Ballinger, Alexander. *New Cinematographyers.* New York: HarperCollins, 2004.

Bangs, Lester, and John Morthland, eds. *Mainlines, Blood Feasts, and Bad Taste: A Lester Bangs Reader.* New York: Anchor Books, 2003.

Benke, Britta. *Georgia O'Keeffe 1887–1986, Flowers in the Desert.* Köln: Taschen, 2005.

Bergan, Michael. *Eisenstein: A Life in Conflict.* Woodstock, NY: Overlook Press, 1999.

Bordwell, David. *The Way Hollywood Tells It.* Berkeley: University of California Press, 2006.

Bowser, Eileen. *The Transformation of Cinema, Vol. 2: 1907–1915: History of the American Cinema.* Berkeley: University of California Press, 1990.

Brakhage, Stan. *The Brakhage Lectures: Georges Méliès, David Wark Griffith, Carl Theodore Dreyer, Sergei Eisenstein.* Chicago, IL: Good Lion, 1972.

Brakhage, Stan. *Essential Brakhage: Selected Writings on Filmmaking by Stan Brakhage,* edited by Bruce R. McPherson. New York: McPherson, 2001.

Brakhage, Stan. *Telling Time: Essays of a Visionary Filmmaker.* New York: McPherson, 2003.

Breslin, James E. B. *Mark Rothko: A Biography.* Chicago: University of Chicago Press, 1993.

Brandt, Bill. *Shadow of Light.* New York: Viking Press, 1966.

Brown, Alison. *The Renaissance,* 2nd ed. Harlow, England: Pearson Education, 1999.

Burgess, Anthony. *Shakespeare.* New York: Knopf, 1970.

Burroughs, William S. *Exterminator! A Novel.* New York: Viking Press, 1973.

Butler, Adam, Claire Van Cleave, and Susan Stiriling. *The Art Book.* London: Phaidon, 1994.

Chandler, Charlotte. *It's Only a Movie: Alfred Hitchcock: A Personal Biography.* New York: Applause Theater and Cinema Books, 2005.

Chandler, Gael. *Cut by Cut: Editing Your Film or Video.* Studio City, CA: Michael Wise Productions, 2004.

Clark, Larry. *Tulsa.* New York: Grove Press, 1971.

Cubitt, Sean. *The Cinema Effect.* Cambridge, MA: MIT Press, 2004.

Curtis, James. *James Whale: A New World of Gods and Monsters.* Minneapolis: University of Minnesota Press, 1998.

Curtis, Walt. *Mala Noche & Other "Illegal" Adventures.* Portland, OR: Bridge City Books, 1977.

Dalton David. *James Dean: The Mutant King.* New York: St. Martin's Press, 1974.

Dalton, David, and Ron Cayen. *James Dead: American Idol.* New York: St. Martin's Press, 1984.

Damon, Matt, and Ben Affleck. *Good Will Hunting: A Screenplay.* New York: Miramax Books/Hyperion, 1997.

Danto, Arthur C. *Unnatural Wonders: Essays from the Gap between Art and Life.* New York: Farrar, Straus and Giroux, 2005.

Davidson, Abraham A. *The Story of American Painting.* New York: Abrams.

DeGroot, Gerard J. *The Sixties Unplugged: A Kaleidoscopic History of a Disorderly Decade.* Cambridge, MA: Harvard University Press, 2008.

Descharnes, Robert, and Gilles Néret. *Salvador Dalí, 1904–1989.* Köln: Taschen, 1998.

Dunton-Downer, Leslie, and Alan Riding. *Essential Shakespeare Handbook.* London: DK Publishing, 2004,

Elder, Bruce R. *The Films of Stan Brakhage in the American Tradition of Ezra Pound, Gertrude Stein, and Charles Olson.* Waterloo, Ontario, Canada: Wilfred Laurier University Press, 1998.

Elkins, James. *What Painting Is: How to Think about Oil Painting, Using the Language of Alchemy.* New York: Routledge, 2000.

Flint, David. *Babylon Blue: An Illustrated History of Adult Cinema.* London: Creation Books International, 1999.

Fogel, James. *Drugstore Cowboy.* New York: Dell, 1990.

Franc, Helen M. *An Invitation to See: 100 Works from the Museum Modern Art.* New York: Museum of Modern Art, 1992.

Fry, Stephen. *Moab Is My Washpot: An Autobiography.* New York: Random House, 1997.

Fujiwara, Chris, gen. ed. *Defining Moments in Movies: The Greatest Films, Stars, Scenes, and Events That Made Movie Magic.* New York: Sterling, 2008.

Gage, John. *Color and Culture: Practice and Meaning from Antiquity to Abstraction.* Boston: Little, Brown, 1993.

Gerstner, David. *Manly Arts: Masculinity and Nation in Early American Cinema.* Durham, NC: Duke University Press, 2006.

Gibbs, John. *Mise-en-Scène: Film Style and Interpretation.* London: Wallflower, 2002.

Gitlin, Todd. *The Sixties: Years of Hope, Days of Rage.* New York: Bantam, 1987.

Goodman. Cynthia. *Hans Hofman.* New York: Abbeville Press, 1986.

Greenberg, Clement, and John O'Brian. *The Collected Essays and Criticism. Vol. I: Perceptions and Judgments, 1939–1944.* Chicago: University of Chicago Press, 1986.

Greenberg, Clement, and John O'Brian. *The Collected Essays and Criticism. Vol. 2: Arrogant Purpose, 1945–1949.* Chicago: University of Chicago Press, 1988.

Greenberg, Clement, and John O'Brian. *The Collected Essays and Criticism. Vol. 3: Affirmations and Refusals, 1950–1956.* Chicago: University of Chicago Press, 1993.

Greenberg, Clement, and John O'Brian. *The Collected Essays and Criticism. Vol. 4: Modernism with a Vengeance, 1957–1969.* Chicago: University of Chicago Press, 1995.

Hackett, Pat, ed. *The Andy Warhol Diaries.* New York: Warner Books, 1989.

Herlihy, James Leo. *Midnight Cowboy.* New York: Dell, 1965.

Hoberman, J., and Jonathan Rosenbaum. *Midnight Movies.* New York: Da Capo, 1983.

Hockney, David. *Secret Knowledge: Rediscovering the Lost Techniques of the Old Masters.* New York: Viking Studio, 2001.

Jacobs, Diane. *Hollywood Resaissance.* New York: Delta, 1977.

James, David E. *Allegories of Cinema: American Film in the Sixties.* Princeton: Princeton University Press, 1989.

Janus, Sam, Barbara Bess, and Carol Saltus. *A Sexual Profile of Men in Power.* Englewood Cliffs, NJ: Prentice Hall, 1977.

Johnson, Cathy. *Creating Textures in Watercolor: A Guide to Painting 83 Textures from Grass to Glass to Tree Bark to Fur.* Cincinnati, OH: North Light Books, 1992.

Josephson, Matthew. *Life among the Surrealists: A Memoir.* New York: Holt, Rinehart and Winston, 1962.

Kaiser, Charles. *The Gay Metropolis: The Landmark History of Gay Life in America.* New York: Grove Press, 1997.

Kerouac, Jack. *On the Road.* New York: Viking Press, 1957.

Kerouac, Jack. *Visions of Cody.* New York: McGraw-Hill, 1972.

Kesey, Ken. *One Flew over the Cuckoo's Nest: Text and Criticism.* Edited by John C. Pratt. New York: Viking Press, 1973.

Kesey, Ken. *Demon Box.* New York: Viking Press, 1986.

Leigh, Janet, and Christopher Nickens. *Psycho: Behind the Scenes of the Classic Thriller.* New York: Harmony Books, 1995.

Levy, Emanuel. *Cinema of Outsiders: The Rise of American Independent Film.* New York: New York University Press, 1999.

LoBrutto, Vincent. *The Encyclopedia of American Independent Filmmaking.* Westport, CT: Greenwood Press, 2000.

LoBrutto, Vincent. *Sound-on-Film: Interviews with Creators of Film Sound.* Westport, CT: Praeger, 1994.

MacCabe, Colin, ed., with Mark Francis and Peter Wollen. *Who is Andy Warhol?* London: British Film Institute, 1997.

MacDonald, Scott. *Screen Writings: Scripts and Texts by Independent Filmmakers.* Berkeley: University of California Press, 1995.

MacDonald, Scott. *The Garden in the Machine: A Field Guide to Independent Films a about Place.* Berkeley: University of California Press, 2001.

MacDonald, Scott. *A Critical Cinema 5: Interviews with Independent Filmmakers.* Berkeley: University of California Press, 2006.

MacDonald, Scott. *Canyon Cinema: The Life and Times of an Independent Film Distributor.* Berkeley: University of California Press, 2008.

MacGowan, Kenneth. *Behind the Screen: The History and Techniques of the Motion Picture.* New York: Delacorte, 1965.

Maltin, Leonard. *Behind the Camera: The Cinematographer's Art.* New York: Signet, 1971.

Manso, Peter. *Brando: The Biography.* New York: Hyperion, 1994.

Marcus, Greil. *Lipstick Traces: A Secret History of the Twentieth Century.* Cambridge, MA: Harvard University Press, 1990.

Maynard, Joyce. *To Die For.* New York: Dutton, 2003.

McNieil, Legs, and Gillian McCain. *Please Kill Me: The Uncensored Oral History of Punk.* New York: Grove Press, 1996.

McShine, Kynaston, ed. *Andy Warhol A Retrospective.* New York: Museum of Modern Art, 1989.

Meltzer, Richard. *The Aesthetics of Rock.* New York: Something Else Press, 1970.

Miller, James, *Flowers in the Dustbin: The Rise of Rock and Roll 1947–1977.* New York: Simon and Schuster, 1999.

Morgan, Ted. *The Life and Times of William S. Burroughs.* New York: Avon Books, 1988.

Murch, Walter. *In the Blink of an Eye: A Perspective on Film Editing,* 2nd ed. Los Angeles, CA: Silman-James Press, 2001.

Nelson, Blake. *Paranoid Park.* New York: Viking, 2006.

Oakey, Virginia. *Dictionary of Film and Televison Terms.* New York: Barnes and Noble Books, 1983.

Oldham, Gabriella. *First Cut: Conversations with Film Editors.* Berkeley: University of California Press, 1992.

Olson, Charles. *The Maximus Poems.* Edited by George F. Butterick. Berkeley: University of California Press, 1983.

O'Neil, Tom. *Movie Awards: The Ultimate, Unofficial Guide to the Oscars, Golden Globes, Critics, Guilds and Indie Honors.* New York: Berkley, 2001.

Parini, Jay, ed., and Brett C. Miller, assoc. ed. *The Columbia History of American Poetry.* New York: Columbia University Press, 1993.

Parish, James Robert. *Gus Van Sant: An Unauthorized Biography.* New York: Thunder's Mouth Press, 2001.

Peake, Tony. *Derek Jarman: A Biography.* Woodstock and New York: Overlook Press, 1999.

Perl, Jed. *New Art City: Manhattan at Mid-Century.* New York: Knopf, 2005.

Perone, James E. *The Words and Music of David Bowie.* Westport, CT: Praeger, 2007.

Picasso, Pablo. *347 Engravings 16/3/68–5/10/68*. London: Institute of Contemporary Arts, 1968.

Pierson, John, with Kevin Smith. *Spike, Mikes, Slackers, and Dykes: A Guided Tour across a Decade of American Independent Cinema*. New York: Hyperion, 1995.

Porter, Darwin, and Danforth Prince. *Blood Moon's Guide to Gay and Lesbian Film*, 2nd ed. New York: Blood Moon Productions, 2007.

Pound, Ezra. *Poems and Translations*. New York: Library of America, 2003.

Pye, Michael, and Lynda Myles. *The Movie Brats: How the Film Generation Took over Hollywood*. New York: Holt, Rinehart and Winston, 1979.

Quiller, Stephen. *Acrylic Painting Techniques*. New York: Watson-Guptill, 1994.

Ray, Man. *Man Ray 1966*. Los Angeles, CA: Los Angeles County Museum of Art, 1966.

Rebello, Stephen. *Alfred Hitchcock and the Making of Psycho*. New York: Dembner Books, 1990.

Richardson, John, with Marilyn McCully. *A Life of Picasso: The Triumphant Years 1917–1932*. New York: Knopf, 2007.

Rosenbaum, Jonathan. *Film: The Front Line 1983*. Denver, CO: Arden Press, 1983.

Rotolo, Suze. *A Freewheelin' Time: A Memoir of Greenwich Village in the Sixties*. New York: Broadway Books, 2008.

Rowse, A. L. *Homosexuals in History: Ambivalence in Society, Literature and the Arts*. New York: MacMillan, 1977.

Ruskin, John. *Modern Painters: By a Graduate of Oxford: Part I.–II. Vol. I*. New York: Wiley, 1882.

Ruskin, John. *Of the Imaginative and Theoretic Faculties. Vol. II, Containing Part II, Sections I. and II*. New York: Wiley, 1882.

Ruskin, John. *Of Many Things. Vol. III, Containing Part IV*. New York: Wiley, 1882

Ruskin, John. *Of Mountain Beauty. Vol. IV, Containing Part V*. New York: Wiley, 1882.

Ruskin, John. *VI. Of Leaf Beauty—VII. Of Cloud Beauty. VIII. Of Ideas of Relation. 1. Of Invention Formal. IX. Of Ideas of Relation. 2. Of Invention Spiritual*. New York: Wiley, 1882.

Schulman, Bruce J. *The Seventies: The Great Shift in American Culture, Society, and Politics*. New York: Free Press, 2002.

Schumach, Murray. *The Face on the Cutting Room Floor: The Story of Movie and Television Censorship*. New York: Morrow, 1964.

Siciliano, Enzo. *Pasolini: A Biography*. New York: Random House, 1982.

Sidaway, Ian. *Color Mixing Bible: All You'll Ever Need to Know about Mixing Pigments in Oil, Acrylic, Watercolor, Gouache, Soft Pastel, Pencil, and Ink*. New York: Watson-Guptill, 2002.

Solomon, Deborah. *Utopia Parkway: The Life and Work of Joseph Cornell*. New York: Farrar, Straus and Giroux, 1997.

Stella, Frank. *Working Space*. Cambridge, MA: Harvard University Press, 1986.

Stevens, Mark, and Annalyn Swan. *De Kooning: An American Master*. New York: Knopf, 2004.

Summers, Claude J., ed. *The Queer Encyclopedia of Film and Television*. San Francisco, CA: Cleis Press, 2005.

Thomas, Deborah. *Reading Hollywood: Spaces and Meanings in American Film.* London: Wallflower Press, 2001.

Tobias, Michael, ed. *The Search for Reality: The Art of Documentary Filmmaking.* Studio City, CA; Michael Wiese Productions, 1998.

Tuchman, Maurice, with Judi Freeman. *The Spiritual in Art: Abstract Painting 1890–1985.* New York: Abbeville Press, 1986.

Tupitsyn, Margarita. *Malevich and Film.* New Haven, CT: Yale University Press, 2002.

Turner, Adrian. *Hollywood 1950s.* New York: Gallery Books, 1986

Tyler, Parker. *A Pictorial History of Sex in Films.* Secaucus, NJ: Citadel Press, 1974

Vacche, Angela Dalle. *Cinema and Painting: How Art Is Used in Film.* Austin: University of Texas Press, 1996.

Vanity Fair. "The Hollywood Issue." March 2008.

Van Sant, Gus. *Even Cowgirls Get the Blues, My Own Private Idaho—Screenplays.* London: Faber and Faber, 1993.

Van Sant, Gus. *Pink: A Novel.* New York: Doubleday, 1997.

Ward, Ed, Geoffrey Stokes, and Ken Tucker. *Rock of Ages: The Rolling Stone History of Rock and Roll.* New York: Rolling Stone Press/Summit Books, 1986.

Watson, Steven. *Factory Made: Warhol and the Sixties.* New York: Pantheon, 2003.

Webb, Peter. *Portrait of David Hockney.* Toronto and Montreal: McGraw-Hill Ryerson, 1988.

Wenner, Jann S., and Corey Seymour. *Gonzo: The Life of Hunter S. Thompson. An Oral Biography.* New York: Little, Brown, 2007.

White, Glenn D. *The Audio Dictionary,* 2nd ed., rev. and expanded. Seattle: University of Washington Press, 1991.

Williams, Linda. *Hard Core: Power, Pleasure, and the Frenzy of the Visible.* Berkeley: University of California Press, 1989.

Winecoff, Charles. *Split Image: The Life of Anthony Perkins.* New York: Penguin Books, 1996.

Winston Dixon, Wheeler. *The Exploding Eye: A Re-Visionary History of the 1960s.* New York: State University of New York Press, 1997.

Index

Idaho, 45; cameo appearance in
Psycho (1998), 78; cameo appear-
ance in *To Die For* (audio), 45; ex-
perimental period, 17, 67, 98, 105,
112, 125
Van Sant, Gus Green (father), 1, 2
Van Sant, Malinda "sissy" Anne (sis-
ter), 1, 50
Velvet Goldmine, 35, 59, 138
Velvet Underground (rock group),
112
"Venus in Furs" (song), 112
Vertigo shot, 40
Vietnam War, 76, 98
Violence, 60, 73, 77, 78, 81, 98, 134,
139, 143
Viper Room Club, 14
Voice-over (VO): *Mala Noche,* 20;
Milk, 129; *Paranoid Park,* 117,
120, 121, 122, 123; *To Die For,*
55
Voyeurism, 19, 20, 104

Wallace, David Foster, 84
Warhol, Andy, 2, 19, 30, 34, 58, 112
Warner Bros., 24, 50, 127
Water, waterfalls, 23
Wavelength, 84, 105
Weekend, 19, 102
Weiland, Joyce, 105
Weinstein, Bob, 70, 96
Weinstein, Harvey, 70, 89, 96

Welles, Orson, 38, 41, 42, 44, 47, 94,
102, 124, 138, 147, 148
Wertmüller, Lina, 5
Westerns, 13, 14, 22–23, 43, 117
Whiskey A Go Go, 9
White, Dan, 127, 131, 134, 135, 136,
137, 138, 139
"White Rabbit" (song), 9
Who's That Knocking at My Door
(movie), 14, 45
Wide angle lens, 104
Wild Bunch, The (slow motion
photography), 22, 60, 87, 95, 121
Wilder, Billy, 76, 89
Williams, Robin, 68–69, 71, 127
Wilson, Rita, 78
The Wizard of Oz (movie), 27, 39, 45,
90
Wolf, Dany, 83, 91, 99
Wolfe, Tom, 37, 54
Woman's movement, 133; women, 28,
29, 43, 49, 51, 53, 56, 59, 66, 79,
83, 122

Yankee Stadium, 85, 89
Youth culture, 35, 64, 67, 83, 86, 98,
100, 101, 103, 110, 112
Yuppies, 107

Zabriskie, Grace, 43
Zen, 50, 53, 112, 118, 12; *Zen and
the Art of Archery* (book), 12

About the Author

VINCENT LOBRUTTO is instructor of motion picture editing and cinema studies at the School of Visual Arts in the Department of Film, Video, and Animation in New York City. He is also a thesis advisor and member of the thesis committee. He is the author of many books on film, including *Stanley Kubrick: A Biography*, and the Praeger titles *Martin Scorsese: A Biography* and *Becoming Film Literate: The Art and Craft of Motion Pictures*.